Examples illustrating
AACR 2 1988 REVISION

Eric J. Hunter MA FLA AMIET MIInfSc
Reader School of Information Science
and Technology, Liverpool Polytechnic

THE LIBRARY ASSOCIATION

LONDON

© 1989 Eric J. Hunter

Published by
Library Association Publishing Ltd
7 Ridgmount Street
London WC1E 7AE

First published 1989

Examples illustrating AACR
by Eric J. Hunter published 1973
Examples illustrating AACR 2
by Eric J. Hunter and Nicholas J. Fox published 1980

British Library Cataloguing-in-Publication Data

Hunter, Eric J. (Eric Joseph)
    Examples illustrating AACR2, 1988 revision : second edition
    1. Documents. Author & descriptive cataloguing
    rules : Anglo-American cataloguing rules. 2nd ed.
    I. Title
    025.3'2

ISBN 0-85365-649-5

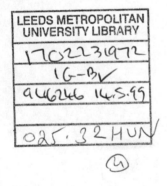
Typeset in 11pt Baskerville and 9pt Univers by Library Association Publishing Ltd.
Printed and made in Great Britain by Dotesios Printers Ltd, Trowbridge, Wiltshire

Examples illustrating

AACR 2 1988 REVISION

A revision and enlargement of
Examples illustrating AACR 2
by E. J. Hunter and N. J. Fox

CONTENTS

ACKNOWLEDGMENTS

The assistance given by the staff of various libraries and other organizations and institutions, in particular Liverpool City Libraries and Liverpool Polytechnic Libraries (especially Jim Ainsworth, Rob Caley and Carol Raper), is gratefully acknowledged. Sincere thanks are also due to Ken Bakewell, Keith Trickey, Ben Tucker and Paul Winkler for the help and/or advice willingly given and a special thank you must go to my wife, Enid, for her continual support and practical help.

In addition, mention should be made again of those people who helped when the previous edition of this sampler was being prepared, viz: R. M. Andrews, Joan M. Bibby, R. M. Brunt, I. C. Butchart, Joyce E. Butcher, R. A. Christophers, J. C. Downing, J. Faughey, D. J. Ferris, M. J. Gorman, Ellen J. Gredley, G. E. Hamilton, Frances Hendrix, A. E. Jeffreys, H. L. de Mink, Liz Phelan, V. de P. Roper, E. H. Seagroatt, M. R. Shifrin and R. A. Wall.

Facsimiles of title pages and illustrations of other media are reproduced by kind permission of the publishers concerned. In most instances the names of these publishers are apparent from the related entries but copyright has changed hands in two instances and the co-operation of Drake Educational Productions (example no. 1) and Oxford University Press (example no. 425) is very much appreciated.

EJH
March 1989

INTRODUCTION

Firstly, it is stressed that there is no intention in this work of presenting an official view of how particular rules in AACR 2 1988 Revision are to be interpreted. Some rules deliberately provide for more than one interpretation. Indeed, section 0.7 of AACR 2 explains that there are a number of rules which are designated as *alternative rules*, or as *optional additions*, and some other rules or parts of rules are introduced by the word *optionally*. Further, it will always be possible to produce convincing arguments for favouring at least two *different* rules for deciding the same point when cataloguing certain items. In fact, if this collection provokes discussion of alternative solutions to a problem, one of its objectives will be achieved.

The work may be used in several ways:

i   To find an example illustrating a particular cataloguing problem.

ii To find an example illustrating a particular and previously identified AACR 2 rule.

iii As a medium to browse through to discover how AACR 2 approaches various cataloguing difficulties.

In previous editions of this work the examples were arranged in one alphabetical sequence of main entries and, indeed, AACR 2 is designed to facilitate the integration of entries for various media. However, as the number of examples relating to media other than printed monographs now makes up a sizeable proportion of the total and because of the nature and purpose of this work, a new arrangement has been adopted with the entries in separate alphabetical sections according to the type of material illustrated. The sections are presented in the same order as the chapters in Part I of AACR 2. It is hoped that this arrangement will be more helpful to the user. The entries in each

sequence are filed in accordance with the *ALA filing rules* (American Library Association, 1980) and the complete set of examples is numbered consecutively for indexing purposes.

AACR 2 recognizes that many libraries no longer find it necessary to distinguish between the main entry and other entries but Part II of the rules is still based upon the proposition that one main entry is made for each item described and that this is supplemented by added entries.

Each main entry in this sampler is followed by a tracing showing the headings for any necessary added entries. These tracings do not relate to any standard method of presentation but are simply given in a form which is considered to be the most suitable for this work. Selected examples of added entries, illustrating the various circumstances in which they should be made, are included in Appendix 1.

After the tracing, a brief indication is given of the problems involved in the cataloguing of the item concerned, together with the numbers of the relevant rules which are illustrated. Detailed indexes of these problems and rules precede the main entry sections. As well as these general indexes, brief, separate alphabetical indexes to descriptive problems are provided at the beginning of each sequence of examples relating to a particular type of material.

It will be clear that certain rules must have been used repeatedly in formulating the examples, e.g. rule 1.1B1 (transcription of the title proper). To note, and index, a rule every time that it has been used would be both unnecessary and uneconomic. Rules are therefore noted, and indexed, selectively according to the illustrative purpose of each example.

However, the first example in each sequence illustrates the basic layout for the particular medium and includes a reasonably comprehensive statement of the rules used in its production. In example no. 8, the first printed monograph entry, a complete statement of every rule which has been consulted in producing the entry is given.

To help reveal the nature of some items and to make clear why the entries for particular items take the form that they do, illustrations — mostly reproductions of the chief sources of information — are provided. These may prove useful when, for example, the entry for a printed monograph is conditioned by the typography of the title page or the entry for a sound recording by the information that appears (or does not appear) on the label. These reproductions (title page facsimiles, etc.) appear with the entries that they illustrate. The first example in each section is accompanied by such a visual.

Entry layout
The layout of each main entry follows a standard pattern and the areas into which the description of an item may be divided are given in the order laid down in AACR 2, i.e.

> HEADING
>   Title and statement of responsibility. — Edition. — Material (or type of publication) specific details. — Publication, distribution, etc.
>   Physical description. — (Series).
>   Note(s).
>   Standard number.

A general material designation may be included, following the title proper. As this is *optional*, such designations are not included in these examples. However, a short explanation of general material designations will be found preceding the main entry sections.

Each area, other than the first area, must be preceded by a full stop, space, dash, space (. —) unless the area begins a new paragraph. Whether paragraphing is adopted, and to what extent it is adopted, will depend upon the in-house style of the individual cataloguing agency. The 'in-house' style of this sampler agrees with that of its predecessor (see below) in that paragraphing is used for the physical description area, the note(s) area and the standard number area. The paragraphing of the physical description area has the advantage of making the specific material designation more prominent. Selected examples showing the appearance of entries when paragraphing is not employed will be found in Appendix 3.

The amount of information given in each example is a maximum set, i.e. a third level of description. For those cataloguing agencies not requiring this amount, AACR 2 indicates (in rule 1.0D) the elements that are to be included in less detailed second and first levels.

It is appreciated that the word processor is now a common tool and typefaces such as bold, italic, etc. can easily be produced, but, for continuity and comparative purposes, the entries, as in previous editions, continue to be shown as they would appear if a standard typewriter (with the addition of a dash (—) and square brackets) were used to produce them. However, as AACR 2 states (0.14), examples must not be *prescriptive* and it should be stressed that AACR 2 does not link description to a typed or printed 'card' format. The rules acknowledge the fact that the computer has enabled cataloguing agencies to produce variously formatted records from one machine-readable database.

The heading for each entry is capitalized to bring it into prominence although AACR 2 does not prohibit the use of lower case if preferred. No designations of function are required in main entry headings. (Some designations *may* be added to headings for added entries as indicated in Appendix 1).

Usually, the references that would be required from variant forms of an entry heading will be reasonably obvious. Where this is not so, a note concerning them is given. As with added entries, selected examples of references are provided (Appendix 2).

Scope of the work
The previous edition of this sampler, published in 1980, contained 383 examples. Most of these are still relevant and, after careful checking and revision where necessary, they have been retained. A few examples have been discarded for various reasons and some 100 new examples have been added. Computer

files are now more adequately covered; entries for new media such as optical laser discs are included; and important new rules (e.g. 5.3 – Musical presentation statement) are illustrated.

Despite the fact that a vast number of rules are illustrated, no claim is made for exhaustivity, nor anything approaching it. Some sections of AACR 2 have been represented very selectively, for instance 22.21–22.28 (Special rules for names in certain languages) and 25.18B–25.18M (Sacred scriptures for religions other than Christianity). Nevertheless, the cataloguer will find included here suggested solutions to a high percentage of the everyday difficulties which he or she is likely to encounter.

PROBLEM AND GENERAL INDEX

All references are to numbers in the main entry sequence of this sampler except where page numbers are quoted.

This general index covers both description and headings but, where description is concerned, individual alphabetic indexes are also provided at the beginning of each sequence of examples relating to a particular type of material. Because of this, the number of subheadings under entries for specific media in this general index is minimal.

Although broadly compatible with Bakewell's excellent index to AACR 2 itself, the approach adopted in this sampler must, by its very nature, be somewhat different, as will be seen if entries such as: accompanying materials; capitalization; churches; illustrative matter; pagination; and entries under specific types of material, e.g. computer files, are examined and compared in the two works.

Inevitably, indexing is not exhaustive in that a particular problem cannot be linked to every example that includes a solution. The date of publication, distribution, etc., for instance, *must* appear in some form in every example. More specifically, there are a number of examples where an approximate date has been supplied but only a representative selection of these will be found in the index.

AACR 2 deals with *conditions* of authorship and *not* individual cases (e.g. particular institutions) or types of publication (e.g. books of quotations or encyclopedias). Cases and types of publication mentioned here are merely illustrative of how AACR 2 rules are to be interpreted.

dimensions *(continued)*

graphics 351 – 2, 354, 369, 384
  folded 368
  frames 356, 359, 364
inappropriate 405, 410
manuscripts 292, 294
  folded 294
  size of items in collection not uniform 293
microforms 426 – 7
  gauge (width) of microfilms 430
  omission of standard dimensions of microfiche 425, 428
motion pictures and videorecordings
  diameter of discs 342
  gauge (width) of films, etc. 341
  not given for videocassettes 343
multimedia items 2
  optionally dimensions of container given for items of various sizes 1, 5 – 6
music 298
not recorded if standard 88, 331, 336, 340, 425, 430
printed monographs 8
  height 8
    under 10 cm 34, 118
  sheets 80, 123
    folded 116, 123, 208
  width greater than height 118, 165, 212
  width less than half the height 81 – 2
serials 431 – 2
  changes of 434, 450, 456
sound recordings
  diameter of discs 318
  diameter of reels 331
  omission of standard dimensions of cassette or cartridge 336, 340
  omission of standard width of tape 336, 340
three-dimensional artefacts and realia 402, 403
  explanatory words added 402, 406, 409, 411, 413, 422, 424
  not recorded 405, 410
  of base 422
word added to indicate which dimension is being given 374, 402, 406, 409, 411, 413, 424
dioceses 49
dioramas 414
direct or indirect subheading *see under* subordinate bodies

discs/disks
computer files 385, 388, 389, 392, 396, 397
  as accompanying materials 98
  as part of multimedia item 5
sound recordings 319, 322 – 7, 330, 332 – 4, 338, 339
  as accompanying materials 48
  as part of multimedia item 2 – 4
  with accompanying materials 334
videorecordings 342
discussions 29
display units 408
displayed items 411
dissertations 430
distinguishing terms *see under* corporate names; governments; personal names
distribution, places of *see* places of publication, distribution, etc.
distributors 205, 248, 341, 420, 423
  statements of function added 177, 205, 248, 281, 324, 341, 420
  notes on 160
'division'
  word implying administrative subordination 216
Dolby process
  sound recordings 336
drawings, technical 354
duplicating masters 172, 255
duration
  motion pictures and videorecordings 341 – 2, 345, 348
  music 305, 309, 317
  sound recordings 318, 320
    omission 338

early printed monographs 267 – 271
  see also works created before 1501
ecclesiastical officials 180, 263
edition
  see also edition statements
  date of 8, 23, 56
    reissues 165, 196
  notes on 123, 156, 160, 289
edition and history
  notes on 117, 123, 138, 212, 272, 276, 313, 343, 396 – 7, 414
edition statements 8
  see also edition
  abbreviations 16, 170, 267
  edition produced exclusively for specific retail outlet 106
  more than one 33, 56
  reprinting of edition 94

personal names *(continued)*

headings
additions
dates 108 – 12
distinguishing between names which
are the same 99, 108-12,143, 189,
209 – 10, 259
no dates, distinguishing terms, etc.
available 293, 354
fuller form of name 109 – 10, 189,
209 – 10
monarchs and royalty 10, 126, 169
phrases and words associated with
name 125, 138
popes 135
titles of nobility 31, 155, 225
vernacular term of address for
person of religious vocation 188
consisting of initials 71
entry element 8, 201
entry under phrase 176, 194, 268,
270
entry under proper name, if known,
even if characterizing phrase
appears in chief source of
information 176
established English language form
of name not in Roman alphabet
18, 326
form determined by way in which it
appears in author's works 11, 108,
114, 317
form determined by way in which it
appears in reference sources
317
in different language forms 54
name by which person is commonly
known and identified 29, 67, 95,
154, 323, 330
omissions 143, 318
phrase denoting place of origin 125
references *see under* references
Roman 170, 171, 267
romanization 117, 225
well-established English form 18,
267
with prefixes 68, 94, 223, 253, 305,
307, 422
without surname 9, 125
persons, headings for *see* personal names
phonogram (copyright) dates 319, 336
phonorecords *see* sound recordings
photographers as personal authors 10,
93, 375

photographs 10, 375
phrases *see* words or phrases
physical description area 8
see also specific elements, e.g.:
dimensions; illustrations; number of
physical units; pagination; specific
material designations; and particular
types of material, e.g.: music; serials;
sound recordings; etc.
accompanying materials given in *see
under* accompanying materials
multimedia items 1 – 7
notes on 66, 81, 93, 122, 172, 197, 226,
281 – 2, 285, 292 – 3, 341, 356, 359, 379,
386, 399 – 400, 404, 408, 416, 418, 424,
434, 442
pictures 360, 373, 379
see also art originals; motion pictures
and videorecordings; photographs; etc.
inappropriate as specific material
designations 373, 381
'pieces'
use of term to describe items of varying
character assembled together 6, 205,
415 – 6
number of particular pieces recorded
418
place names
see also counties; countries; governments; states; etc.
abbreviations 122, 204
additions to headings
corporate bodies
branch that carries out activities in
particular locality 84
conferences 55, 129
distinguishing between bodies of
same name 148, 347
if body could be confused with other
bodies of the same or similar
names 102, 290
local churches 254
personal names 125
places of publication 204, 349
as headings for corporate bodies 24,
39, 235, 248, 266
changes of name 61, 347
jurisdiction no longer existing 61,
198, 347
places of manufacture 406, 409, 417,
423
places of origin of personal authors,
phrases denoting 125
places of printing
early printed monographs 267, 268

places of publication, distribution, etc.
8, 266, 299, 351
  abbreviations 95
  additions
    address 267
    country, state, province, etc. 122, 204,
      356
  country named as 218, 404
  more than one 14, 43, 56, 88, 126, 222
  name of larger place added 122, 204
  probable place 200, 332
  recorded in form in which it appears
    in item 266, 267 – 8, 299
  unknown 320
  which cannot readily be ascertained 404
  see also publication, distribution, etc. area
places of writing
  manuscripts 295
plans 275, 291
  accompanying materials 226, 293
  illustrative matter 63
plate numbers
  music
    notes on 310
plates
  pagination 60, 186
players, actors see cast; performers
playing cards 418
playing speeds
  sound recordings 318, 336
playing times see duration
plays
  collective uniform titles 196
pockets containing accompanying material
  or illustrative matter
  printed monographs 79, 159
polytechnics 448 – 9, 456
'pop-up' books 15
popes 135
porcelain 406
portfolios 123
portraits
  illustrative matter 31, 60, 134
positive microforms 429
postcards 352, 371, 383
posters 357
  as accompanying materials 219
pottery 409
prayer books 28
prefixes
  surnames 69, 94, 223, 253, 305, 307,
    330, 422
prescribed sources of information see
  chief sources of information and under
  specific types of material, e.g.: graphics;

three-dimensional artefacts and realia; etc.
presidents 250, 460
prime ministers 243
princes 169
principal responsibility
  see under shared responsibility
printed monographs 8 – 266
  see also particular types of work, e.g.:
    encyclopaedias (which are included
    merely as illustrations of how AACR 2
    rules are to be interpreted)
  as accompanying material 47, 205, 334,
    358, 363, 381 – 2, 405, 408
  as part of multimedia item 2, 4
  serials which could be described as
    monographs 213, 458
printers
  early printed monographs 267, 269
printing
  dates see dates of printing
printing processes
  graphics 356
prints, art 356
prints, study see study prints
probable authorship 164
probable date of publication 284, 332
probable place of publication 284, 332
probable publisher 291
probable responsible body 278
proceedings (conferences) see conferences
processes
  art prints 356
producers
  filmstrips 378
  motion pictures and videorecordings
    341, 343, 349
program files 386, 388, 392 – 3
programmed texts 151
programmers 386, 392 – 3
programmes of events 124
programming languages
  computer files
    notes on 393
programs
  computer files 386, 388, 392 – 3
projections
  cartographic materials 289
projection speeds
  motion pictures and videorecordings 341
'prominently stated'
  meaning 193
promulgation, dates of
  single modern laws
    additions
      uniform titles 234

reproductions *(continued)*

    in different material 419
    notes on original 375, 383, 425, 427
responsibility, statements of *see* statements
    of responsibility
restricted access *see* access, restrictions on
restrictions on showing of films or video-
    recordings 346, 348
revisions
    entry under original author 153
    entry under reviser 14, 191
ROM chips 386
Roman Catholic Church *see* Catholic Church
Roman names 170 – 1, 267
Roman numerals
    additions to names of rulers 169
    Arabic substituted for 267, 432
romanization 117, 225
Romans of classical times 171
rulers 10, 126, 169
running times *see* duration
Russian, items printed in 225

S.I., use of 320
sacred scriptures
    uniform titles 34 – 6, 107, 144, 173
saints 138
sand paintings 364
scales
    cartographic materials 272, 278 – 9,
        281, 284 – 6, 290 – 1
    technical drawings 354
schools 102
scope of item
    notes on *see* nature, scope or artistic
        form of item, notes on
scores
    music 298, 301, 304, 306, 309, 315, 317
Scottish ordinary lords of session 155
scriptures *see* sacred scriptures
sculptures 422
secondary entries *see* added entries
sections
    maps, plans, etc. in 279, 291
'see' and 'see also' references *see under*
    references
segments
    maps, plans, etc. in 279, 291
selections 192
    see also extracts; parts of works
    uniform titles
        Bibles 34
        music 300, 301, 307, 309, 315
        printed monographs 74, 196, 360

self-teaching books 122, 151
seminars *see* conferences
serials 431 – 60
    analytical added entries 445
    indexes published separately 75
    special issues 59
    which could also be described as
        printed monographs 213
series statements
    added entries *see under* added entries
    beginning with name of responsible body
        89, 91
    common authorship of series and part
        of series 131, 334
    enclosed in parentheses 21, 221
    from source other than item 223, 426
    given in two forms 286, 384
    including separate letters or initials 89,
        91
    ISSN 130
    issues of a serial part of 434
    more than one 57, 139, 146, 171, 221,
        229, 363
    numbering 21, 57, 131, 171, 205, 229,
        230
        date given as numbering 57, 230
        recorded in terms given in item and
            preceded by semi-colon 4, 13, 21,
            57, 131, 171, 229, 230
    other title information 6, 155, 221
    parallel titles 158, 425
    sources of information 223
    statements of responsibility 2, 89, 101,
        131, 139, 249
    subseries 118, 120, 168, 221, 426
    transcription 2, 4, 6, 21, 89, 91, 101,
        131, 139, 223, 334, 361, 384,
        389, 420, 425 – 7
    variant titles
        in the one item
            notes on 286, 384
shared authorship *see* shared responsibility
shared pseudonyms 175
shared responsibility
    see also mixed responsibility
    between persons and corporate body
        218, 378
    principal responsibility indicated 58,
        297, 332
    principal responsibility not indicated
        more than three responsible persons or
            bodies 21, 79, 178
        two or three responsible persons or
            bodies 2, 7, 51, 59, 89, 95, 103, 148,
            203, 209, 218, 221, 393

shared responsibility *(continued)*

    shared pseudonyms 175

sheets 116, 208

    containing panel designed to appear on
        outside when sheet is folded 291

    in columns 211

    more than one map, plan, etc. on one
        sheet 275, 291

signatories

    treaties

        notes on 229

signatures

    early printed monographs 267 – 8

silverware 417

sine loco, use of 320

singers *see* performers

Sir

    additions to personal names 41, 190,
        304, 323

size *see* dimensions

sleeves *see* containers

slides

    as accompanying materials 88

    as part of multimedia item 3

    microscope slides 407

sobriquets *see* given names, etc.; words
    or phrases

societies and associations 13, 16, 173, 199,
    256, 410

sonatas

    uniform titles 301

songs

    collections 311, 315

soprano

    abbreviations 307

sound cartridges 340

sound cassettes 328 – 9, 336

    as part of multimedia items 2 – 4

sound channels, number of

    sound recordings 318

sound characteristics

    computer files 386

    motion pictures and videorecordings
        341 – 2, 344, 348

sound discs 318 – 27, 330, 332 – 5, 337 – 9

    as accompanying materials 48

    with accompanying materials 334

sound recordings 318 – 40

    as accompanying materials 48

    as part of multimedia items 2 – 4

    collections

        with collective title 324, 327, 333,
            336, 338 – 9, 340, 344

        without collective title 322

    two or more works by the same
        person 326

    literary works

    of one work 320 – 1, 325, 337

    of two or more works 326

    related works 335

    serials 457

    speeches 323

    with accompanying materials 328, 334

sound tape reels 331

source of item

    notes on 422

source of title

    notes on 292, 372

sources of information

    see chief sources of information;
        particular elements of description,
        e.g.: series statements; and under
        specific types of material, e.g.:
        graphic materials

sovereigns 10

special features of copy

    early printed monographs

        notes on 267 – 9, 271

special issues of serials 59

specific material designations

    see also number of physical parts;
        pagination

    cartographic materials 272, 278, 284

    computer files 385 – 6, 389, 394

    graphic materials 351 – 2, 354, 367

    microforms 425

    motion pictures and videorecordings
        341 – 2, 344

    multimedia items 1 – 7

    music 298 – 9, 300, 315

    printed monographs 80, 116

    serials 431 – 2, 448 – 9

    sound recordings 318

    three-dimensional objects and realia
        402 – 3, 405, 411

speeches 323

speeds, playing

    sound recordings 318, 336

speeds, projection

    motion pictures and videorecordings 341

spelled-out numerals 82

spirit masters 172, 255

square brackets, use of

    additions to titles and statements of
        responsibility 292, 322, 325, 356

        not required 275

    et al. 16, 21, 199, 388

    scales 279

    series statements 223, 426

RULE INDEX

All references are to numbers in the main entry sequence of this volume.

As with the Problem and general index, rules are indexed selectively and only when they are specifically mentioned in a particular example.

The rules from Part 1 of AACR 2 are arranged (except for Ch.13) according to the numbers of the rules in Ch.1 so that, for instance, 1.1B and its divisions precede 2.1B, 3.1B, 4.1B, 5.1B, etc. and their divisions which precede 1.1C and its divisions. Rules from chapters other than Ch.1 are indented. If, therefore, the user wishes to find an example illustrating rule 6.1F1, this will be found indexed in the indented sequence following the divisions of 1.1F. This pattern has been adopted because of the close relationship between the rules in Ch.1 and other chapters and because of the mnemonic structure of the rule numbering.

0.8	134, 193	3.1B1	272
0.24	419	4.1B2	292 – 3, 294 – 5, 297
0.28	318	5.1B1	298, 302, 320
1.0A1	334, 345	6.1B1	318, 320 – 1
2.0B1	8, 81, 260, 278, 285	7.1B1	341 – 6
2.0B2	167, 223	8.1B1	351, 354
3.0B1	278, 285	8.1B2	372
3.0B2	272, 281, 286	9.1B1	385, 395 – 6, 398, 401
4.0B1	292, 297	11.1B1	425
5.0B1	298	12.1B1	431 – 2, 452
6.0B1	318, 336, 339	12.1B4	443
7.0B1	341	12.1B5	443
8.0B1	351 – 2	12.1B7	458
9.0A1	386	1.1C3	419
9.0B1	385, 387, 390, 396, 398	1.1D1	130, 158, 280, 305, 320, 407, 411, 451
10.0B1	403, 405, 423		
11.0B1	425	3.1D1	280
12.0B1	431 – 2, 450	5.1D1	305, 320
12.0B2	446, 457	6.1D1	320
1.0C	458	12.1D1	451
1.0C1	165, 276, 291, 434	1.1E1	9, 351, 401, 447, 454
1.0E1	117, 225	1.1E2	45
1.0F1	299, 431	1.1E3	133, 165, 313
1.0H1(a)	151, 318	1.1E4	31
1.0H1(d)	81, 123	1.1E5	75
1.0H2	2 – 4	1.1E6	42, 124, 208, 402
3.0J1	285 – 6	2.1E1	9
1.1A1	8 – 9, 31, 190	5.1E1	298, 321
1.1A2	59	8.1E1	351
2.1A1	9, 308	9.1E1	401
1.1B	33, 271, 298, 385, 425	12.1E1	447, 454
1.1B1	8, 16, 27, 117, 121, 131, 154, 225, 272, 276, 292, 298, 318, 320 – 1, 341 – 3, 345 – 6, 351, 431, 452, 454	1.1F	33, 298, 425
		1.1F1	8, 16, 19, 37, 58 – 9, 63, 70, 103, 163, 215, 283, 318, 332, 336 – 7, 343, 423, 429
1.1B2	89, 167	1.1F2	73, 134, 164, 334, 411
1.1B3	409	1.1F3	267
1.1B4	241	1.1F4	12, 58
1.1B5	275	1.1F5	16, 21, 58, 178, 199, 338
1.1B6	89, 91, 185	1.1F6	9, 38, 41, 142, 168, 190, 219, 336
1.1B7	372, 403, 413, 419		
1.1B8	36	1.1F7	8, 41, 165, 180, 194
1.1B9	144	1.1F8	161, 219, 259
1.1B10	100, 222, 231	1.1F10	130, 451
2.1B1	8, 33, 271	1.1F12	9, 35, 360

32

Chapter 13 Analysis (See also Appendix 1)

PART 2 HEADINGS, UNIFORM TITLES AND REFERENCES

Chapter 21 Choice of access points

21.2A1	434, 437 – 8, 448 – 9	21.25B	29
21.2C1	437 – 8, 448 – 9	21.28A1	59, 75, 308
21.3B1	435, 440 – 1	21.28B1	59 – 60, 75, 133, 147, 156, 308, 335, 339, 346
21.4A1	4, 8, 10, 12, 28, 37, 67, 77, 121, 134, 179, 190, 287 – 8, 298, 318, 323, 325, 330, 360, 380, 385, 392, 425	21.29C	9
		21.30A1	50, 167 (*For examples of added entries – see also Appendix 1*)
21.4B1	42, 45, 52, 181		
21.4C1	268	21.30B1	318, 332, 338, 343
21.4D1	39, 238, 243, 250, 460	21.30C1	42, 161
21.4D2	135	21.30D1	50, 76, 167
21.5A	64, 86, 90, 113, 137, 160, 185 – 6, 257, 330, 351 – 2	21.30E1	1, 12, 59, 79, 91, 199, 206, 220, 243, 434
21.5B	164, 268, 278	21.30F1	16, 126, 178, 237, 292, 294, 341, 343
21.5C	270		
21.6A1	2, 51, 85, 148, 218, 378	21.30G1	22, 75, 212, 396
21.6B1	58, 297, 332	21.30H1	338, 371
21.6C1	2, 7, 21, 51, 59, 85, 89, 95, 103, 148, 203, 209, 218, 221, 378, 386, 393	21.30J1	280, 396, 449
		21.30J1(a)	125, 128, 142, 208, 285, 318, 454
21.6C2	21, 79, 199, 431	21.30J1(b)	292
21.6D1	175	21.30K1	125, 173, 187
21.7A1	41, 60, 78, 100, 130, 262, 299, 355, 371	21.30K1(a)	9, 138
		21.30K1(b)	138
21.7B1	27, 41, 50, 60, 100, 130, 158, 167, 178, 231, 262, 299, 303, 311, 355, 371	21.30K1(c)	65
		21.30K1(e)	173
		21.30K2(c)	29
21.7C1	63, 113	21.30L1	210, 221
21.9A	22	21.30L1(a)	34, 70
21.10A	11, 22, 38, 97, 145, 168, 212, 222	21.31B1	101, 233 – 4, 246
		21.31B2	158
21.11A1	33, 87, 90, 122, 172	21.31B3	241 – 2
21.11B	228	21.31C1	126
21.12A1	66, 153, 184, 238, 334	21.33A	266
21.12B1	14, 191	21.35A1	24, 232
21.13B1	44, 107	21.35A2	229
21.13C1	126	21.35E1	57
21.13D1	92	21.35F3	158
21.14A	65, 113, 171	21.36A1	269
21.14B	113, 231	21.37A	35, 173
21.15A	92	21.39A1	28, 49, 303
21.16B	375, 383, 415	21.39A3	28, 303
21.17A1	358		
21.17B1	120, 161		
21.18B1	300, 307, 317	**Chapter 22 Headings for persons**	
21.18C1	313, 317		
21.19A1	311 – 2, 316, 337	22.1A	8, 67, 95, 154, 169, 268, 330, 332
21.20A	305		
21.22A	303	22.1B	8, 67
21.23A1	320 – 1, 325, 334, 337	22.1C	41, 304
21.23B1	318, 326	22.1D2	47
21.23C1	324, 327, 333, 336, 338 – 40, 342, 344	22.2A1	317, 323
		22.2B1	67, 76
		22.2B2	11, 76
21.24A	93, 172, 195, 228, 353	22.2B3	76, 108, 114 – 5, 149, 163
21.25A	29	22.3B1	54

Chapter 23 Geographic names

Chapter 24 Headings for corporate bodies

GENERAL MATERIAL DESIGNATIONS

An optional inclusion, following the title proper, is a 'general material designation'. This consists of a term chosen from a supplied list enclosed within square brackets. AACR 2 includes (rule 1.1C1) two lists of designations, one for the use of British agencies (List 1) and the other for the use of agencies in Australia, Canada, and the United States (List 2).

List 1	List 2
braille	braille
cartographic material	{ globe
	map
computer file	computer file
	art original
	art reproduction
	chart
	filmstrip
graphic	{ flash card
	picture
	slide
	technical drawing
	transparency
manuscript	manuscript
microform	microform
motion picture	motion picture
multimedia	kit
music	music
	diorama
	game
object	{ microscope slide
	model
	realia
	toy
sound recording	sound recording
text	text
videorecording	videorecording

For materials for the visually impaired, where List 2 only is concerned, (large print) or (tactile) may be added, when appropriate, and (braille) may be added, when appropriate, to any term other than braille or text.

As explained in the introduction to this work, general material designations, being optional, are excluded from the examples presented here.

However, the following selection of headings and title statements from this sampler, together with their appropriate general material designations, illustrate the way in which entries would appear if such designations were desired. '1' indicates British usage and '2' Australian or North American usage.

ABRAHAMS, Gerald
   Trade unions and the law [text]

ACCRINGTON town centre [cartographic material]   1

ACCRINGTON town centre [map]   2

ADAMS, Samuel
   [Letter] 1829 Dec.8, Londonderry
Gaol [manuscript]

ADLER, Samuel
   Canto VII : tuba solo [music]

AGEE, James
   James Agee [sound recording] :
a portrait

AIDS for teaching the mentally retarded
[motion picture]

AIR bearings [graphic] : some
   applications   1

AIR bearings [chart] : some
   applications   2

AIR pollution [multimedia]   1

AIR pollution [kit]   2

[ALARM clock]   [object]   1

[ALARM clock]   [realia]   2

The ALBUM [text]

ARDIZZONE, Edward
    Tim to the lighthouse [microform]

BLOK, Alex
    AMX pagemaker [computer file]

FALLA, Manuel de
    El sombrero de tres picos [music] = Le
tricorne = The three cornered hat : ballet

PTB [sound recording] : personal training
    bulletin

ROSSINI, Gioacchino
    [Il barbiere di Siviglia. Vocal score.
English & Italian]   [music]
    The barber of Seville

STEVENSON, D.E. (Dorothy Emily)
    The house on the cliff [text]   1

STEVENSON, D.E. (Dorothy Emily)
    The house on the cliff [text (large
print)]   2

TURNER, J.M.W.
    The fighting Temeraire [graphic]   1

TURNER, J.M.W.
    The fighting Temeraire [art
reproduction]   2

MAIN ENTRY SEQUENCES

† against a tracing indicates that examples of added entries are included in Appendix 1 (p.221)

* against a tracing or an annotation indicates that a relevant reference is illustrated in Appendix 2 (p.229).

Multimedia

Items made up of more than one material with no predominant component.

Chapter One   Rule 1.10C

Other relevant rules in Chapter One and subsequent chapters are also applicable.

For items with one predominant component, described in terms of that component and with details of the subsidiary component given as accompanying material following the physical description or in a note, refer to the general index under 'accompanying materials'.

For accompanying material recorded in a multilevel description see example no. 20.

1

AIR pollution / The EP Group of Comp-
    panies, Educational Productions
Limited ; produced in collaboration with
British Gas. – Rev. ed. – [Wakefield,
Yorkshire] : EP, 1974.
    6 work cards, 6 study prints, 6 identical
data sheets, 1 teachers' notes ; in folder
22 x 36 cm.
    EP: K2168.

    1.   Educational Productions
    2.   British Gas

Item made up of a number of components.
Extent of each part or group of parts belonging
to each distinct class of material given as the
first element of the physical description –
1.10C2(a). If units are identical, 'identical' is
added – 1.5B1. Optionally, if the parts are in a
container, the container is named and its
dimensions given – 1.10C2(a). Note on
important number borne by item – 1.7B19.

Item emanates from corporate body but does
not fall within any of the categories listed in
21.1B2 and is therefore entered under title –
21.1C1(c). Added entries for prominently named
corporate bodies – 21.30E1. Appropriate
references would be required for Educational
Productions.

2

BESSEL, Richard
   Understanding modern Europe : an introduction. – Milton Keynes : Open University Press, 1984.
   [4] v. (74; 75; 84; 45 p.) : ill., facsims., maps, ports. ; 22 x 30 cm.
   4 sound cassettes : analog, mono.
   In case 32 x 24 x 5 cm.
   (PA 740 ; 1-7 / Open University. Centre for Continuing Education).
   "In cassettes, members of the Course Team discuss ways of working through the exercises and using the material presented in the printed texts".
   Contents: [Vol. 1]. Introduction to the course ; Topic I Political structures in Western Europe ; Topic II Economic development in Western Europe / Richard Bessel – [v. 2]. Topic III Social structures in Western Europe ; Topic IV European trade unions / David Englander – [v. 3]. Topic V Political structures in Eastern Europe ; Topic VI Economic development in Europe / Richard Bessel – [v. 4]. Topic VII The European Economic Community / David Englander.
   Cassettes relate to vols.: cassette 1 is to be used in conjunction with Topics I and II; cassette 2 with Topics III and IV; cassette 3 with Topics V and VI; and cassette 4 with Topic VII;
   ISBN 0-335-10559-9.

1.   Title   2.   Englander, David
3.   Series
4.   Open University. Centre for
       Continuing Education

Item has two major components, neither of which predominates, cassettes are designed to be used in conjunction with the printed texts (and vice versa). If there is no discernible 'first part', the chief source of information becomes the chief source of that part that gives the most information – 1.0H2. In this instance, the fullest information is found on the title pages of the printed volumes. Personal authors are not named in a composite statement of responsibility but only as authors of the individual parts. Their names are not therefore transcribed in a statement of responsibility. Volumes are not numbered as physical units, so numbers are enclosed in square brackets –

2.5B3. Series title requires statement of responsibility for identification – 1.6E1. Contents note – 2.7B18 and 1.7B18. Titles of parts in each volume are separated by semi-colons as they are all by the same person – by analogy with 1.1G3.

Item emanates from a corporate body but does not fall within any of the categories of 21.1B2. It is therefore treated as if no corporate body were involved, as a work of shared responsibility between two persons. Principal responsibility is not attributed to either, so entry is under one named first – 21.6A1 and 21.6C1.

3

BOOKS and libraries / The British
   Council, Audio Visual Unit. –
London : Brit. Counc., 1985.
   1 sound cassette (14 min.) : analog, mono.
   79 slides : col.
   In binder 24 x 21 x 5 cm.
   "Tape/slide"; cassette pulsed for automatic slide change.

1.   British Council. Audio Visual Unit

Item has two major components, neither of which predominates. If there is no discernible 'first part', the chief source of information becomes the chief source of the part that gives the most information – 1.0H2. In this instance, the fullest information is found on the cassette and label and title and statement of responsibility are recorded as they appear there. A separate physical description is made for each class of material and recorded on separate lines – 1.10C2(b). Description of printed monographs – Ch.2. Description of sound cassettes – Ch.6 (playing speed, number of tracks and dimensions are omitted because they are standard). Optionally, if the parts are in a container, the container is named following the last physical description and its dimensions given – 1.10C2(b). Note on nature of item – 1.7B1; if a note is a quotation it is given in quotation marks with no indication of source as this is the chief source – 1.7A3.

Item emanates from corporate body but does not fall within any of the categories listed in 21.1B2 and is therefore entered under title – 21.1C1(c).

FREEMAN, Keith
Computer peripherals / Certified Accountants Educational Trust. – London : CAET, c1979.
22 p. : ill. ; 21 cm.
1 sound cassette : analog, mono.
In container 23 x 17 x 4 cm.
(Data processing and systems design ; no. D13).
"Input, output and storage peripherals, the descriptive features and various applications of each type of equipment" – cassette wrapper.
Material in both workbook and cassette prepared for the Trust by Keith Freeman.

1. Title
2. Certified Accountants Educational Trust
3. Series

Item has two major components, neither of which predominates; the instruction: 'use the workbook and cassette together' is given on the item. If there is no discernible 'first part', the chief source of information becomes the chief source of the part that gives the most information – 1.0H2. In this instance the same amount of information is given and the title and statement of responsibility are recorded as they appear on both the title page of the workbook and the cassette and label. A separate physical description is made for each class of material and recorded on separate lines – 1.10C2(b). Description of printed monographs – Ch.2. Description of sound cassettes – Ch.6 (playing time would have been included if it had been readily ascertainable; playing speed, number of tracks and dimensions are omitted because they are standard). Optionally, if the parts are in a container, the container is named following the last physical description and its dimensions given – 1.10C2(b). Series statement recorded – 1.6B1, with numbering as given in the item – 1.6G1. Note on nature of item – 1.7B1. If note is a quotation it is given in quotation marks and the source indicated, unless that source is the chief source – 1.7A3. Note on statement of responsibility not recorded in the title and statement of responsibility area – 1.7B6.

Entry under person responsible for the intellectual content – 21.1A1, 21.1A2 and 21.4A1.

An INTRODUCTION to building societies : the Halifax project / Halifax Building Society. – [New ed.]. – Halifax : Halifax B.S., [1987].
12 workcards, 5 information cards, 4 wallcharts and posters, 1 book, 1 pamphlet, 10 leaflets, 1 computer disk, 1 teachers' handbook ; in portable container 44 x 46 x 9 cm.
Computer disk contains game: Money-market. System requirement: BBC B or B + .
Designed for use in mixed-ability situations and can be adapted to suit a variety of learning situations with 11–16 year olds.

1. Halifax Building Society

Item is made up of a number of components. Extent of each part or group of parts belonging to each distinct class of material given as the first element of the physical description – 1.10C2(a). Optionally, if parts are in a container, the container is named and its dimensions given – 1.10C2(a). Note on a particular part of the item is given following the physical description – 1.10C3. Note on target audience – 1.7B14.

Item emanates from a corporate body but does not fall within any of the categories listed in 21.1B2 and is therefore entered under title – 21.1C1(c).

See also example no. 395.

6

LIVERPOOL transport through the ages. – Improved and enl. ed. – Liverpool : Scouse Press, [198-].
31 various pieces ; in plastic envelope 25 x 37 cm. – (Liverpool packet : a pictorial history of Liverpool ; no. 3).
Descriptive notes by E.W. Paget-Tomlinson.
Includes photos., postcards, maps, plans, drawings, notices, byelaws, etc., relating to ferries, trams, cabs and buses, 1817-1957.

1. Series
2. Paget-Tomlinson, E.W.

Item is made up of large number of heterogeneous materials. A general term is given as the extent together with the number of pieces if this can be ascertained — 1.10C2(c) (the general term 'pieces', rather than 'various pieces', is used in rule 2.5B18 — see example no.205). Optionally, the name of the container and its dimensions recorded — 1.10C2(c). Other title information of a series included if it provides valuable identifying information — 1.6D1. Statement of responsibility not recorded in statement of responsibility area is given in a note — 1.7B6. Note on content — 1.7B18.

Item does not emanate from a corporate body and authorship is unknown and diffuse. Entry is therefore under title — 21.1C1(a).

7

MACKAY, David
  My sentence maker / David Mackay and Brian Thompson. — London : Longman for the Schools Council, 1970.
  1 folder, 155 cards. — (Breakthrough to literacy. Schools Council programme in linguistics and English teaching).
  Each card contains single word, part of word or punctuation mark, designed to be slotted into folder against same word, part of word or punctuation mark.
  "This sentence maker, together with 26 books and other materials for children and teachers, forms a self-contained scheme of work in initial reading and writing".
  ISBN 0-582-19061-4.

1.   Title   2.   Thompson, Brian
3.   Series

Item has two components. More appropriate, in this instance, to give the extent of each part successively as first element of physical description — 1.10C2(a), rather than making a separate physical description for each as in 1.10C2(b). Optionally, the name of the container and its dimensions could be given after the extent but, in this example, the folder is both a container and an integral part of the item.

Work of shared responsibility produced by the collaboration of two persons with principal responsibility not attributed to either is entered under the heading for the one named first — 21.6C1.

Printed monographs

Chapter One and Chapter Two

For printed monographs as accompanying materials see examples no. 47, 205, 334, 358, 363, 381–2, 405, 408

For printed monographs as part of multimedia items see examples no. 2 and 4.

For printed monographs which could also be described as serials see example no. 458.

See also early printed monographs – examples no. 267–271 and other types of work for which the rules in Ch. 2 may be relevant, e.g. atlases and printed music.

Trade Unions
&
The Law

by

GERALD ABRAHAMS, M.A.

Sometime Scholar of
Wadham College, Oxford:
Of Gray's Inn
and the Northern Circuit,
Barrister-at-law

CASSELL · LONDON

8

ABRAHAMS, Gerald
  Trade unions & the law / by Gerald
Abrahams. – London : Cassell, 1968.
  xix, 254 p. ; 22 cm.
  ISBN 0-304-91599-8.

  1.   Title

Title transcribed from chief source of
information (i.e. the title page – 2.0B1) exactly
as to order, wording and spelling, but not
necessarily as to punctuation – 2.1B1 and
1.1B1. First word only of title capitalized –
A.4A1. Title statement followed by statement of
responsibility – 2.1F1 and 1.1F1, and statement
of responsibility preceded by diagonal slash –
1.1A1. Academic degrees omitted – 1.1F7.
Publication area contains: place of publication –
2.4C1 and 1.4C1; name of publisher – 2.4D1
and 1.4D1; and date of publication which, as

there is no edition statement, is the date of the
first edition – 2.4F1 and 1.4F1. Publisher is
preceded by a colon and date by a comma –
1.4A1. Pagination of each sequence recorded –
2.5B2. Dimensions given – 1.5D1; for books
this is the height in centimetres to the next
whole centimetre up – 2.5D1. Dimensions
preceded by a semi-colon – 1.5A1. ISBN
recorded – 2.8B1 and 1.8B1.

Entry under heading for personal author, i.e. the
writer of the book – 21.1A1, 21.1A2 and
21.4A1. Name by which person is commonly
known chosen as basis for the heading –
22.1A. Determine the name by which person is
commonly known from the chief source of
information of works by that person – 22.1B.
Entry element selected is that part of the name
under which the person would normally be
listed in authoritative alphabetic lists in his or
her language or country – 22.4A. Name
containing surname entered under surname –
22.5A1. If the entry element is not the first
element of the name, it is transposed and the
entry element is followed by a comma –
22.4B3.

9

ALCUIN
  Son well-beloved : six poems / by
Alcuin ; translated by the Benedictines of
Stanbrook. – Worcester : Stanbrook
Abbey Press, 1967.
  viii, 10 p. ; 21 cm.
  Limited ed. of 260 copies.

  1.   Title

Noun phrase occurring in conjunction with
statement of responsibility treated as other title
information if it is indicative of the nature of the
work – 1.1F12. (See also example no. 35).
Other title information preceded by colon –
2.1A1, 1.1A, 2.1E1 and 1.1E1. Subsequent
statement of responsibility preceded by semi-
colon – 1.1A1 and 1.1F6.

Entry for name that does not include surname
– 22.8A1. A case could be made for making an
added entry under the translators since the
translation is in verse – 21.30K1(a). However, it
seems unlikely that users would expect an entry
under this heading, and so it has been omitted
in accordance with general rule for added
entries – 21.29C.

10

ALEXANDRA, <u>Queen, consort of Edward
VII, King of the United Kingdom</u>
Queen Alexandra's Christmas gift book :
photographs from my camera. – London :
Daily Telegraph, 1908.
   [33] leaves : all ill. ; 30 cm.
   "To be sold for charity".

  1. Title

Unnumbered leaves – total ascertained and
given in square brackets – 2.5B7. Work
consisting wholly of illustrations – 2.5C6. Other
physical details, in this case a statement of the
illustration content, preceded by a colon –
1.5A1. Note which is quotation from item given
in quotation marks. Source of quotation is not
included, as it is the chief source of information,
i.e. the title page – 1.7A3.

Entry under heading for person responsible for
the artistic content of the work – 21.1A1 and
21.4A1. Royalty – entry under given name –
22.8A1. Additions to name – 22.16A3.

11

ALICE through the looking glass ... /
  adapted from the story by Lewis
Carroll. – London : L. Miller, [19--].
  20 p. : col. ill. ; 25 cm. – (A jolly
miller production).
  "Alice meets Dum and Dee".

  1. Carroll, Lewis   2. Series

Adaptation by unknown adapter entered under
title – 21.10A. Uniform title could be made
under title proper of original edition (i.e.
'Through the looking glass') if it were
considered that 'Alice through the looking glass'
was not the best-known title – 25.3A and
25.3B. Added entry is for person whose works
have appeared under a real name (Charles
Lutwidge Dodgson) and a pseudonym. Basis of
heading is name used for the particular group of
works – 22.2B2.*

12

ALVES, Colin
  Religion and the secondary school : a
report / undertaken on behalf of the
Education Department of the British
Council of Churches by Colin Alves. –
London : S.C.M. Press, 1968.
  223 p. : ill., forms ; 23 cm.
  Bibliography: p. 220-223.

  1. Title
  2. British Council of Churches.
    <u>Education Department</u> †

Single statement of responsibility recorded as
such whether the two or more persons or
bodies named in it perform the same function
or not – 1.1F4.

Foreword states that Alves is the author and
that this is not an official report of the British
Council of Churches; therefore treated as if no
corporate body were involved, i.e. single
personal authorship – 21.1A1, 21.1A2 and
21.4A1. However, the added entry is needed for
the Council as a prominently-named corporate
body – 21.30E1.

13

AMERICAN LIBRARY ASSOC-
  IATION. <u>Committee on Post-War
  Planning</u>
  Post war standards for public libraries /
prepared by the Committee on Post-War
Planning of the American Library
Association ; Carleton Bruns Joeckel,
Chairman. – Chicago : ALA., 1943.
  92 p. ; 23 cm. – (Planning for
libraries ; no. 1).

  1. Title
  2. Joeckel, Carleton Bruns †
  3. Series

If name of publisher appears in recognizable
form in title or statement of responsibility area,
it is given in shortened form in publication area
– 1.4D4.

Work emanating from corporate body and
recording its collective thought (in this case, the
report of a committee) is entered under heading
for body – 21.1B2(c). Body is entered as a
subheading of the name of the body to which it
is subordinate because its name contains a

word normally implying administrative subordination (i.e. Committee) – 24.13A (Type 2).

14

ANDERSON, James
 Shop theory. – 5th ed. / James Anderson, Earl E. Tatro. – New York ; London : McGraw Hill, 1968.
 522 p. : ill. ; 24 cm.
 Previous ed.: Henry Ford Trade School, Shop Theory Dept. New York : McGraw Hill, 1955.

 1. Title 2. Tatro, Earl E.
 3. Henry Ford Trade School.
   Shop Theory Department.
   Shop Theory

Authors are responsible for edition, not for original work. Their names are therefore transcribed after the edition statement – 1.2C1. When several places of publication are named on the item, the first is always recorded, and if this is not in the home country of the cataloguing agency, it is followed by the first of any subsequent places that are – 1.4C5. 'ill.' is given for an illustrated printed monograph – 2.5C1 and 1.5C1, unless the illustrations are all of one or more of the particular types mentioned in 2.5C2.

If wording of chief source of information indicates that body responsible for original is no longer considered responsible for work, entry is under heading for appropriate reviser – 21.12B1. Name-title added entry is made under heading for original.

15

ANDRIYEVICH, V.
 The fox, the hare and the rooster : a Russian folk tale / designed by V. Andriyevich ; translated by Tom Botting. – Moscow : Malysh Publishing, [197-].
 [16] p. : chiefly col. ill. ; 23 cm.
 Cover title.
 Opens vertically and each double page 'pops up' to form 3-dimensional scene.

 1. Title

No specific rules for 'pop-up' books, so work has been treated as ordinary printed monograph and necessary details have been given as note on physical description – 2.7B10.

16

ANGLO-American cataloguing rules. – 2nd ed., 1988 revision / prepared under the direction of the Joint Steering Committee for Revision of AACR, a committee of The American Library Association ... [et al.] ; edited by Michael Gorman and Paul W. Winkler. – Ottawa : Canadian Library Association, 1988.
 xxv, 677 p. ; 26 cm.
 Published simultaneously: London : Library Association Publishing ; Chicago : American Library Association.
 Issued also in loose-leaf form with binder.
 ISBN 0-88802-242-5 (Canada).
 ISBN 0-85365-509-X (U.K.)
 ISBN 0-8389-3346-7 (U.S.)

 1. Joint Steering Committee for
   Revision of AACR
 2. Gorman, Michael
 3. Winkler, Paul W.

Title transcribed exactly as to wording, order and spelling but not as to capitalization – 1.1B1. Edition statement transcribed as it appears in item but standard abbreviations (Appendix B) used and numerals in place of words – 1.2B1. Statement of responsibility related to a particular edition follows the edition statement (responsibility was not attributed to the Joint Steering Committee in previous editions) – 1.2C1. Statement of responsibility is recorded as it appears in item – 1.1F1. When a single statement of responsibility names more than three bodies with the same degree of responsibility, all but the first of each group of such bodies is omitted – 1.1F5. Omission is indicated by (...) and 'et al.' is added in square brackets – 1.1F5. Note on publication – 2.7B9 and 1.7B9. Note on other formats – 2.7B16 and 1.7B16. Optionally, more than one standard number may be given and a qualification added – 1.8B2 and 1.8E1.

Work emanates from a corporate body but does not fall within any of the categories listed in 21.1B2 and is therefore entered under title – 21.1C1(c). (It might be argued that this work represents the collective thought of the body but the interpretation applied here is that it in fact represents the collective thought not only of the body from which it emanates, i.e. the Joint Steering Committee, but of the cataloguing community as a whole and it therefore does not fall within 21.1B2). In added entry body made up of representatives of two or more other bodies is entered under its own name – 24.15A. If it is considered that the heading for any of the bodies whose representatives make up the Joint Committee provides an important access point, then an added entry could also be made under that heading, e.g. American Library Association – 21.30F1.†

17

[ARABIAN nights. Selections]
Tales from the Arabian nights / illustrated by Brian Wildsmith. – 2nd ed. – London : Oxford University Press, 1961.
281 p. : col. ill. ; 22 cm. – (Oxford illustrated classics).

1. Wildsmith, Brian   2. Series

Shorter form of publisher's name might be used in accordance with 1.4D2, but name is given in full in example at 2.4D1.

Uniform title for work appearing in various manifestations under different titles – 25.1A.* Uniform title for selections – 25.9A. Optionally, a uniform title used as a main entry heading may be recorded without the square brackets – 25.2A.

18

ARISTOTLE
[Ethics. English]
The Nicomachean ethics of Aristotle / translated, with notes, original and selected, an analytical introduction, and questions for the use of students, by R.W. Browne. – London : Bohn, 1850.
lxxxi, 347 p. ; 18 cm. – (Bohn's classical library).

1. Title
2. The Nichomachean ethics of Aristotle
3. Series

Entry under well-established English form of name – 22.3B3. Well-established English title as uniform title for work originally written in classical Greek – 25.4B1. Name of language of item added to uniform title if different from that of original – 25.5C1.

19

ART INSTITUTE OF CHICAGO
Pocketguide to The Art Institute of Chicago / [illustrations selected by James N. Wood and Katharine C. Lee; commentary prepared by Rex Moser; with the assistance of the curatorial staff]. – Chicago : Art Institute, 1983.
64 p. : col. ill. ; 22 x 11 cm.
Accompanied by: Map of the Art Institute of Chicago. 3 plans on 1 sheet : col. ; 43 x 24 cm. folded to 24 x 12 cm. Keyed to Pocketguide.
ISBN 0-086559-054-0.

1. Title   2. Wood, James N.
3. Lee, Katharine C.
4. Moser, Rex

Statement of responsibility taken from a source other than the chief source enclosed in square brackets – 1.1F1. Accompanying material recorded in note area – 1.5E1(c) and 1.7B11.

Work emanating from corporate body describing its resources entered under the heading for the body – 21.1B2(a). Body entered directly under name by which it is commonly identified – 24.1A. Initial article omitted – 24.5A1.

See also next example.

20

ART INSTITUTE OF CHICAGO
Pocketguide to The Art Institute of Chicago / [illustrations selected by James N. Wood and Katharine C. Lee; commentary prepared by Rex Moser; with the assistance of the curatorial staff]. – Chicago : Art Institute, 1983.
64 p. : col. ill. ; 22 x 11 cm.
ISBN 0-086559-054-0.

Map of the Art Institute of Chicago. – Scale indeterminate. – Chicago : Art Institute, [1983?].
3 plans on 1 sheet : col. ; 43 x 24 cm. folded to 24 x 12 cm.
Keyed to Pocketguide.

1. Title   2. Wood, James N.
3. Lee, Katharine C.   4. Moser, Rex
5. Map of the Art Institute of Chicago

Accompanying material recorded in a multilevel description – 1.5E1(b) and 13.6A.

Compare with previous example.

The Communication Research Centre

University College London

Aspects of TRANSLATION

STUDIES IN COMMUNICATION 2

A. D. Booth

Leonard Forster

D. J. Furley

R. Glémet

Joseph Needham

C. Rabin

L. W. Tancock

with a Preface by

A. H. Smith

London
1958 | SECKER AND WARBURG

21

ASPECTS of translation / A.D. Booth ...
[et al.]. – London : Secker and
Warburg, 1958.
  viii, 145 p. ; 22 cm. – (Studies in
communication ; 2).
  At head of title: The Communications
Research Centre. University College
London.

1. Booth, A.D.
2. University College London.
   Communication Research Centre
3. Series

Statement of responsibility refers to more than three persons or bodies; therefore all but the first of these are omitted. Omission is indicated by three dots and 'et al' added in square brackets – 1.1F5. Series statement enclosed in parentheses – 1.6A1. Number of the item within a series recorded in the terms given in the item – 1.6G1. Name appearing in chief source of information but not used in main entry heading and with indeterminate responsibility for work given as 'At head of title' note – 2.7B6.

Work emanates from a corporate body but it does not fall within any of the categories listed in 21.1B2. Personal authorship is also involved but as there are more than three responsible persons, none of whom is indicated as being the principal author, entry is under title – 21.6C2. Heading for added entry under corporate body – 24.13A (Type 5).

22

ATTERBURY, Jasmine
  Heidi / J. Spyri ; adapted by Jasmine
Atterbury ; illustrated by Marianne
Clouzot. – London : Golden Pleasure
Books, 1964.
  60 p. : ill. (some col.) ; 23 cm.

1. Title   2. Spyri, Johanna

Adaptation under the heading for the adapter as it has substantially changed the content of the original work – 21.9A and 21.10A. Added entry for original work would be in the form of a name-title entry if the title of the original work differed from that of the work being catalogued – 21.10A and 21.30G1. Added entry for illustrator not considered necessary under provisions of 21.30K2.

23

AUSTEN, Jane
  Northanger Abbey ; and, Persuasion /
by Jane Austen ; with an introduction by
Austin Dobson ; illustrated by Hugh
Thomson. – London : Macmillan, 1933.
  xvi, 444 p. : 49 ill. ; 18 cm.
  Both works first published: 1818.

1. Title
2. Austen, Jane
   Persuasion
3. Persuasion

Item lacking a collective title and consisting of individually titled works by the same person, in which no one part predominates, described as a unit – 1.1G2. Titles of the individually titled parts transcribed in the order in which they appear in the chief source of information or in the item – 1.1G3. Parts by the same person are separated by semi-colon, even if the titles are linked by a connecting word or phrase – 1.1G3. When there is no edition statement, the date of the first publication of the edition to which the item belongs is given – 1.4F1. The date of the original first edition is given here in a note.

24

AUSTRALIA
   [Treaties, etc. New Zealand, 1965 Aug. 31]
   New Zealand – Australia Free Trade Agreement : with exchange of letters. – Wellington : Govt. Printer, 1965.
      95 p. ; 25 cm. – (A.17).

   1.   Title   2.   New Zealand

Capitalization in title for treaties – A.20A.

Treaties entered under heading for appropriate corporate body – 21.1B2(b). For treaties between two national governments, entry is under first in alphabetical order, with added entry for the other – 21.35A1. Uniform title for single treaties – 25.16B1.

25

AUSTRALIAN WATER RESOURCES
   COUNCIL. Advisory Panel on
   Desalination
   A survey of water desalination methods and their relevance to Australia / prepared by the Advisory Panel on Desalination, Australia Water Resources Council. – Canberra : Dept. of Natural Development, 1966.
      45 p. : ill., maps ; 27 cm. – (Hydro-logical series ; no.1).

   1.   Title   2.   Series

Work emanating from corporate body and recording its collective thought is entered under heading for body – 21.1B2(c). Subordinate body contains term (i.e. 'Panel') implying admin-istrative subordination and so is entered as subheading of higher body – 24.13A (Type 2).

26

AVERY, Karen
   Puss in boots / [illustrated by Karen Avery]. – London : Chatto & Windus, 1975.
      1 v. : col. ill. ; 18 cm. – (A peepshow book).
      Cover title.
      Five apertured scenes which open up and tie together to form one display.
      ISBN 0-7011-2142-6.

   1.   Title   2.   Series

Peepshow books not mentioned specifically in AACR 2, but are here treated as printed monographs. Pagination inappropriate, so '1 v.' used, by analogy with 2.5B9, and further physical details given in a note.

27

The AZ of gardening / edited by Martin
   Parsons. – [New ed.]. – London : Cathay, [198-].
      128 p. : ca.170 col. ill. ; 30 cm.
      Previously published: London : Octopus, 1977.
      ISBN 0-86178-204-6.

   1.   Parsons, Martin

Title transcribed as it appears in chief source of information – 1.1B1. Number of illustrations given if it can be readily ascertained – 2.5C4. In this instance, it is stated on the item that there are 'over 170' coloured illustrations, so this has been recorded as 'ca. 170 col. ill.' Note that the examples in the rules are illustrative and not prescriptive.

Work produced under editorial direction entered under title – 21.7A1(c) and 21.7B1.

28

BAILLIE, John
   A diary of private prayer / by John Baillie. – London : Oxford University Press, 1936.
      135 p. ; 17 cm.

   1.   Title

Although a book of prayers, item is not a liturgical work as defined at 21.39A1, but a book intended for private devotion – 21.39A3(a). Entry is therefore under heading for personal author – 21.4A1.

29

BARRATT, Michael
   Golf with Tony Jacklin : step by step, a great professional shows an enthusiastic amateur how to play every stroke of the game / Michael Barratt ; photographs by Mike Busselle and Behram Kapadia. – London : A. Barker, 1978.
   136 p. : ill. ; 26 cm.
   ISBN 0-213-16684-4.

   1.   Title   2.   Jacklin, Tony
   3.   Busselle, Mike
   4.   Kapadia, Behram

Reports of interviews or exchanges; this work is presented in the form of a conversation. The greater proportion of the words are Jacklin's. However, they are not 'confined' to Jacklin (21.25A), but are 'to a considerable extent' those of Barratt and entry is therefore under the heading for the latter – 21.25B. The added entry for Jacklin is under the form of name by which he is commonly known and a reference would be required. Added entries are necessary for the illustrators because the illustrations are an 'important feature' – 21.30K2(c).

30

BBC
   Talking points, third series : B.B.C. comments on questions that viewers and listeners ask. – London : B.B.C., 1969.
   18 p. ; 22 cm.
   Reprinted from Radio times;
   ISBN 0-563-07444-2.

   1.   Title   2.   Radio times†

Note on bibliographic history of work – 2.7B7.

Work of administrative nature emanating from corporate body and dealing with its internal policies is entered under heading for body – 21.1B2(a).

Variant forms of the name of the body, e.g. BBC, B.B.C. and British Broadcasting Corporation, appear in items issued by the body. The form of name which appears in the chief sources of information should be used (24.2B) but if variant forms of name appear in the chief source of information, as in this case, the name that is presented formally should be used. If no name is presented formally, or if all names are presented formally, again as in this case, the predominant form of name is used. Here, the brief form appears to be the predominant form and, even if no one form predominates, the brief form would still be used – 24.2D.* The brief form used to be presented with full-stops but the predominant current usage omits them – 24.1A.*

See also examples no. 60, 335, and 346.

31

BEDFORD, Mary Russell, Duchess of
   The flying duchess : the diaries and letters of Mary, Duchess of Bedford / edited, with an introduction, by John, Duke of Bedford. – London : Macdonald, 1968.
   216 p., 31 p. of plates : ill., ports. ; 22 cm.

   1.   Title
   2.   Bedford, John Russell, Duke of

Statement of responsibility is integral part of other title information and is transcribed as such – 1.1E4. No further statement relating to this name made – 1.1F13. Subsequent statement of responsibility is normally preceded by semi-colon – 1.1A1. However, if first statement of responsibility is omitted from statement of responsibility area, it can be assumed that the second statement is treated as the first and preceded by diagonal slash.

Entry under proper name in title of nobility if person is commonly known by that title, proper name is followed by the personal name in direct order and the term of rank – 22.4B4 and 22.6A1.*

32

BERGMAN, Ingmar
   Face to face : a film / by Ingmar
Bergman ; translated from the Swedish by
Alan Blair. – London : Marion Boyars,
1976.
   viii, 118 p. : ill. ; 22 cm.
   Originally published as: Ansikte mot
ansikte. Stockholm : Norstedt & Soner,
1976.
   ISBN 0-7145-2584-7.

   1.   Title

Description of a film subsequently published in
book form.

Optionally, the description could have included a
uniform title (see example no. 40).

OSLO and BERGEN

By the staff of Editions Berlitz

33

BERNSTEIN, Ken
   Oslo and Bergen / by the staff of
Editions Berlitz. – Engelsk utg. 1985/1986
ed. – Lausanne, Switzerland : Editions
Berlitz, [1986].
   128 p. : col. ill., maps ; 15 cm. –
(Berlitz travel guides).
   Text: Ken Bernstein; photography:
Walter Imber.
   "Including the Western fjords" – cover.
   ISBN 1-85238-058-6.

   1.   Title   2.   Editions Berlitz
   3.   Series

Title and statement of responsibility recorded as
given in chief source of information, i.e. the title
page – 2.1B1, 1.1B, 2.1F1 and 1.1F. Item has
two edition statements, '1985/1986 edition'
appears on verso of title page and 'Engelsk
utgave' on cover. Both are considered important
so both are recorded although there is no
authority for this. They are recorded as found in
the item – 1.2B1 and 2.2B1, using standard
abbreviations – B.9. Note on responsibility not
recorded in title and statement of responsibility
area – 2.7B6.

Work emanating from a corporate body but not
falling within any of the categories listed in
21.1B2 and therefore treated as if the corporate
body was not involved and entered under
heading appropriate to the text – 21.11A.
Editions Berlitz has now changed its name to
Berlitz Guides and an appropriate reference
would be required.

34

[BIBLE. English. Authorised. Selections.
   1968]
   A little treasury of Christmas / selected
from the words of the Holy Bible by
Kenneth Seeman Giniger. – London :
Collins, 1968.
   62 p. : ill. ; 96 mm. – (Dolphin
booklets).

   1.   A little treasury of Christmas
   2.   Giniger, Kenneth Seeman

Height of volume under 10 centimetres given in
millimetres – 2.5D1.

No added entry under series because items in
series related to each other only by common

physical characteristics – 21.30L1(a). Selections from the Bible under the most specific Bible heading – 25.18A9 (uniform title for the Bible – 25.17A). 'Selections' added (25.18A9) after language (25.18A10), version (25.18A11) and before the year (25.18A13).

35

[BIBLE. N.T. Gospels. English. Rieu. 1952]
The four Gospels / a new translation from the Greek by E.V. Rieu. – Harmondsworth : Penguin, 1952.
xxxiii, 245 p. ; 18 cm. – (Penguin classics ; L32).

1. The four Gospels
2. Rieu, E.V.
3. Series

Noun phrase which occurs in conjunction with statement of responsibility and indicates role of person named rather than nature of work is treated as part of the statement of responsibility – 1.1F12. (See also example no. 9).

Work that is accepted as sacred scripture by a religious group is entered under title – 21.1C1(d) and 21.37A. Group of books consisting of one of groups listed (in this case the Gospels) given as subheading of appropriate testament – 25.18A4, 25.18A1 and 25.18A2. 'Gospels' added to heading – 25.18A4. Language added to heading – 25.18A10. Translator as version – 25.18A11. Year of publication added to heading – 25.18A13.

36

[BIBLE. N.T. Welsh.]
Testament Newydd ein Harglwydd a'n Hiachawdwr Iesu Grist = The New Testament of our Lord and Saviour Jesus Christ. – Denbigh : Clwydian Press, 1824.
548 p. ; 17 cm.
At head of title: Y Testament Newydd dwyieithawg = The duoglott New Testament.
Text printed in parallel columns in Welsh and English.

1. [Bible. N.T. English.]
2. Testament Newydd ein Harglwydd a'n Hiachawdwr Iesu Grist

Title appears in two languages; Welsh is considered to be the main language in this instance and is also the first in order – 1.1B8. Note on variation of title – 1.7B4. Note on language of item and important physical details not included in physical description area – 2.7B2, 1.7B2, 2.7B10 and 1.7B10.

Uniform title for Testament of Bible – 25.17A and 25.18A1.* 'N.T.' added to heading – 25.18A2. Language added to heading – 25.18A10. Version not applicable – 25.18A11 (and see footnote to p. 505). Added entry with name of second language – 25.18A10.

37

BISHOP, Bernard W.
Bishop's concise garden encyclopedia / by Bernard W. Bishop ; drawings by W.E. Davies and Susan Baillie (as initialled). – Kingswood, Surrey : Right Way Books, 1958.
190 p., [16] p. of plates : ill., port. ; 20 cm.

1. Title

Name associated with responsibility transcribed as part of title proper and repeated in statement of responsibility area, because separate statement of responsibility appears in chief source of information – 1.1F13. Statements of responsibility recorded in the form in which they appear in item – 1.1F1.

Single personal authorship – 21.1A1, 21.1A2 and 21.4A1.

38

BLASHFIELD, Jean
The pirates of Penzance / W.S. Gilbert and Arthur Sullivan ; told by Jean Blashfield ; with drawings by Anne and Janet Grahame Johnstone. – [London] : Nelson, [1965].
[28] p. : col. ill. ; 20 x 21 cm. – (Mikado books).
Music and words of Song of Ruth and Song of the major-general on lining papers.

1. Title   2. Gilbert, W.S.
3. Sullivan, Sir Arthur
4. Johnstone, Anne
5. Johnstone, Janet Grahame
6. Series

Statements of responsibility recorded in the order of their sequence on the chief source of information (i.e the title page) – 1.1F6. Name of publisher given in shortest form in which it can be understood internationally – 1.4D2. Therefore, initial has been omitted, as there is no other well-known publisher with this name.

Version in different literary form, i.e. not a libretto but written in story form – also an adaptation for children – entry in either case is under the heading for the adapter – 21.10A.

39

BOOTLE (England). Free Library, Museum and Technical School Committee
Educational work in Bootle, 1884-1900, in connection with the Free Library, Museum and Technical School : a record of municipal enterprise. – Bootle : [Free Library, Museum and Technical School Committee], 1900.
52 p., [19] leaves of plates : ill., plans ; 21 cm.
Prepared by J.J. Ogle, Director of Technical Instruction.
300 copies printed for presentation only.

1.   Title   2.   Ogle, J.J.

Note on publication, distribution, etc. – 2.7B9.

In its preface, this item is stated to be a report prepared by the Director 'by order of the Committee'. It can therefore be said to be an official communication. The question is whether it comes within the context of rule 21.4D1, the wording of which does not make it clear whether such an item is included or not. However, the example 'New York : city at war : a report' seems to indicate that this item is covered by the rule and therefore entry is under the corporate heading for the official, with an added entry under the personal heading. Official is entered under the agency which he/she represents – 24.20E1. Agency with a name which implies subordination and requires the name of the government for identification – 24.18A (Type 2). Name of the geographical entity is used as the name of government – 23.1A. Name of larger place added – 23.4D2.

40

BOREL, Jacques
[L'adoration. English]
The bond / by Jacques Borel ; translated by Norman Denny. – London : Collins, 1968.
479 p. ; 22 cm.
Previously published: Paris : Gallinard, 1965.

1.   Title †   2.   The bond †

Uniform title for translation given as original title, followed by language of translation – 25.3A and 25.5C1. If a work is entered under a personal or corporate heading and a uniform title is used, a name-title reference is made from variants of the title, and an added entry under the title proper – 25.2E2.*

BRITAIN'S GLORIOUS NAVY

Edited by
ADMIRAL SIR REGINALD H. S. BACON
K.C.B., K.C.V.O., D.S.O.

With a Foreword by
ADMIRAL SIR EDWARD R. G. R. EVANS
K.C.B., D.S.O., LL.D.

ODHAMS PRESS LIMITED, LONG ACRE, LONDON. W.C.2

41

BRITAIN's glorious navy / edited by
Sir Reginald H.S. Bacon ; with a
foreword by Sir Edward R.G.R. Evans. –
London : Odhams Press, [1943].
320 p. : ill., ports. ; 23 cm.

1.   Bacon, <u>Sir</u> Reginald H.S.

Omission of decorations and title from
statement of responsibility – 1.1F7. Writer of
foreword recorded in second statement of
responsibility – 1.1F6.

Work produced under editorial direction entered
under title – 21.7A1(c) and 21.7B1. Omission of
'Admiral' from heading for added entry –
22.15C. 'Sir' included but italicized – 22.1C and
22.12B1.

42

BRITISH MUSEUM
Handlist of Persian manuscripts :
[acquired by the British Museum] 1895-
1966 / by G.M. Meredith-Owens. –
London : The Museum, 1968.
x, 126 p. ; 26 cm.
ISBN 0-7141-0630-5.

1.   Title   2.   Meredith-Owens, G.M.

Title proper needs explanation, so brief addition
is made as other title information – 1.1E6.

Work of an administrative nature emanating
from corporate body and dealing with the
resources of the body itself is entered under
heading for the body – 21.1B2(a). The phrase
'of an administrative nature' is a little
ambiguous. It could be argued that a catalogue
can be of an administrative nature only if it is
an inventory for the use solely of the staff of
the body and not a published work for general
use. However, the above item would be of use
to both the general public and members of
staff, and so it is treated as falling within the
compass of the rule. The examples: 'National
Gallery'; 'First National Bank of Chicago', and
'Royal Ontario Museum'; included in rule 21.4B1
appear to corroborate this interpretation. Added
entry under prominently named writer of a work
when main entry has not been made under that
heading – 21.30C1.

Pascal
from
BASIC

P. J. BROWN
University of Kent at Canterbury

ADDISON-WESLEY PUBLISHING COMPANY
in association with
ACORNS◆FT

Wokingham, Berkshire · Reading, Massachusetts
Menlo Park, California · Amsterdam · Don Mills, Ontario
Manila · Singapore · Sydney · Tokyo

43

BROWN, P.J.
Pascal from BASIC / P.J. Brown. –
[New ed.]. – Wokingham, Berkshire :
Addison-Wesley in association with
Acornsoft, 1984.
x, 182 p. ; 21 cm.
Previously published: Addison-Wesley,
1982.
Supplied free with Acornsoft ISO Pascal
(2 computer ROM chips for BBC B
microcomputer).
ISBN 0-201-13789-5.

1.   Title

First and subsequently named publisher are linked in a single statement and therefore both are named – 1.4D5(a). Publication area is recorded as if by a cataloguing agency in the United Kingdom. In the United States the area would read – 1.4C5:

> Wokingham, Berkshire ; Reading, Mass. : Addison-Wesley in association with Acornsoft, 1982.

in Canada:

> Wokingham, Berkshire ; Don Mills, Ont. : Addison-Wesley in association with Acornsoft, 1982.

and in Australia:

> Wokingham, Berkshire ; Sydney : Addison-Wesley in association with Acornsoft, 1982.

44

BURLIN, Robert B.
   The old English advent : a typographical commentary / by Robert B. Burlin. – New Haven : Yale University Press, 1968.
   xv, 202 p. ; 24 cm. – (Yale studies in English ; 168).
   A study of the Advent poem in the Exeter book, attributed to Cynewulf.
   Bibliography: p. 185-189.

   1.   Title   2.   Series

Entry under commentator, as chief source of information presents item as commentary – 21.13B1.

45

CAERNARVONSHIRE COUNTY
   RECORD OFFICE
   Caernarvonshire records : the Caernarvonshire Record Office, twenty-one years, 1947-1968 : a catalogue of an exhibition held at Caernarvon, 19-26 October 1968. – Caernarvon : County Record Office, 1968.
   71 p. : ill., facsim., map ; 22 cm.
   ISBN 0-901337-005.

   1.   Title

Other title information recorded in order indicated by sequence on chief source of information – 1.1E2.

Work of administrative nature emanating from corporate body and dealing with its resources is entered under heading for body – 21.1B2(a). See also example on p. 318 of AACR 2 : 'Rembrandt in the National Gallery of Art' – 21.4B1.

46

CAMPBELL, Patrick
   All ways on Sundays / by Patrick Campbell. – London : Sphere Books, 1967.
   190 p. ; 19 cm.
   Originally published: London : Blond, 1966.

   1.   Title

Author has title of nobility – 'Baron Glenavy'.* However, this is not recorded, as he is not commonly known by it and does not use it in his works – 22.6A1 and 22.12A1.

47

CARPENTER, Anne-Mary
   Human histology : a colour atlas / by Anne-Mary Carpenter. – New York ; Maidenhead : Blakiston Division of McGraw-Hill, 1968.
   96 p. : chiefly col. ill. ; 26 cm.
   Accompanied by: Text for "Human histology ..." 93 p. in pocket.

   1.   Title

Work consisting chiefly of illustrations – 2.5C6. Accompanying material recorded in note – 2.7B11.

Hyphen retained in given name – 22.1D2.

48

CARTER, Craig J.M.
   Ships of the Mersey / Craig J.M. Carter. – London : Record Books, 1966.
   79 p., 1 leaf of plates : ill. ; 20 cm. + 2 sound discs (analog, 33⅓ rpm, mono. ; 7 in.). – (Sound picture series).
   Discs, which are recordings of ships' sounds, in pocket.

   1.   Title   2.   Series

Sound recording accompanying textual material – 2.5E and 1.5E. Name and optionally the physical description of the accompanying material recorded at the end of the physical description – 2.5E1, 1.5E1(d) and 6.5. Location of accompanying material given in note – 2.5E2, 2.7B11 and 1.7B11.

49

CATHOLIC CHURCH
  [Ritual]
  Pocket ritual / [compiled by the Liturgical Commission of the Archdiocese of Glasgow]. – [New ed.]. – Glasgow : J.S. Burns, [1971].
    66 p. ; 13 cm.
    ISBN 0-900243-20-1.

  1. Title   2.   Pocket ritual
  3. Catholic Church. <u>Archdiocese of Glasgow. Liturgical Commission</u>

Liturgical work entered under the heading for the church to which it pertains – 21.39A1.* Well-established English title used as uniform title – 25.19A. In added entry, English form of name used for a diocese, etc. of the Catholic Church – 24.27C3.

50

CHAMBERS 20th century thesaurus : a comprehensive word-finding dictionary / edited by W.A. Seaton ... [et al.]. – Edinburgh : Chambers, 1986.
    ix, 750 p. ; 22 cm.
    ISBN 0-550-10559-X.

  1. Seaton, M.A.

Work produced under editorial direction entered under title – 21.7B1. If more than three editors, none of whom is given prominence, added entry is made under first named only – 21.7B1, 21.30A1 and 21.30D1.

CONVERSATIONS
between
The Church of England
and
The Methodist Church

AN INTERIM STATEMENT

LONDON
S · P · C · K
and
THE EPWORTH PRESS
1958

51

CHURCH OF ENGLAND
  Conversations between the Church of England and the Methodist Church : an interim statement. – London : S.P.C.K., 1958.
    vii, 49 p. ; 22 cm.

  1. Title   2.   Methodist Church †

Second publisher omitted because it does not fall within provisions (a), (b), (c) or (d) of rule 1.4D5.

Work emanating from corporate body and recording its collective thought is entered under heading for body — 21.1B2(c). Work emanates from two corporate bodies (21.6A1(d)) and principal responsibility is not attributed to either; entry is therefore under heading for one named first — 21.6C1. Body entered directly under the name by which it is commonly identified — 24.1A.

52

CHURCH OF ENGLAND. Liturgical
  Commission
The calendar and lessons for the Church's year : a report submitted by the Church of England Liturgical Commission to the Archbishops of Canterbury and York, November, 1968. — London : S.P.C.K., 1969.
  x, 95 p. ; 22 cm.
  ISBN 0-281-02323-9.

  1. Title

Work emanating from corporate body and recording its collective thought is entered under heading for body — 21.1B2(c). (See also example on p. 319 of AACR 2 : 'Capital and equality : report of a Labour Party study group' — 21.4B1.) Councils, etc. of single religious body entered as subheading of heading for religious body — 24.27A1. Full name of body is : 'Church of England. National Assembly. Liturgical Commission'. Intervening elements in hierarchy omitted unless needed to distinguish subordinate body — 24.14A.

53

CICRIS
  Cicris directory and guide to resources / compiled and edited by James W. Thirsk. — London : Cicris, 1968.
  [55] p. ; 21 cm.

  1. Thirsk, J.W.

Volume printed without pagination, so number enclosed in square brackets — 2.5B7.

Work of administrative nature emanating from corporate body and dealing with its resources is entered under heading for body — 21.1B2(a). Corporate body entered under name by which it is commonly identified; full stops omitted from

initialism in accordance with predominant usage of body — 24.1A. Variant forms of name found in items issued by body, so name as it appears in chief sources of information is used — 24.2B.

54

COMENIUS, John Amos
  Orbis sensualium pictus / by John Amos Comenius ; with an introduction by James Bowen. — 3rd ed. — Sydney : Sydney University Press ; London : Methuen, 1967.
  x, 43, 320 p. : ill., maps, port. ; 19 cm.
  Facsim. of: 3rd ed. London : S. Mearne, 1672.

  1. Title

Details of second publisher given, as it is in country of cataloguing agency — 1.4D5(d). Details of original of facsimile given in note — 1.11F.

Person's name which appears in different language forms (original name of author was Jan Amos Komensky) is given in form corresponding to language of most of works — 22.3B1. (A reference would be required.)*

55

CONFERENCE OF BRITISH
  TEACHERS OF MARKETING AT
  ADVANCED LEVEL (3rd : 1968 :
  Harrogate, England)
  Third Conference of British Teachers of Marketing at Advanced Level, Harrogate, June 1968 : conference proceedings. — Lancaster : University of Lancaster, Dept. of Marketing, [1969].
  51 leaves ; 30 cm.
  ISBN 0-901272-00-0.

  1. University of Lancaster.
      Department of Marketing

Conference as corporate body — 21.1B1 and 21.1B2(d). Words denoting number omitted from heading for conference — 24.7A1. Number, date and place where held added to heading — 24.7B1 (number — 24.7B2, date — 24.7B3, location — 24.7B4).

ELEMENTARY NUMERICAL ANALYSIS
An Algorithmic Approach

Third Edition

S. D. Conte
Purdue University

Carl de Boor
University of Wisconsin—Madison

INTERNATIONAL STUDENT EDITION

McGRAW-HILL INTERNATIONAL BOOK COMPANY

Auckland Bogotá Guatemala Hamburg Johannesburg Lisbon
London Madrid Mexico New Delhi Panama Paris San Juan
São Paulo Singapore Sydney Tokyo

56

CONTE, S.D.
Elementary numerical analysis : an algorithmic approach / S.D. Conte, Carl de Boor. – 3rd ed. International student ed. – Auckland ; London : McGraw-Hill International, 1981.
xii, 432 p. ; 21 cm. – (International series in pure and applied mathematics).
ISBN 0-07-012447-7

1. Title   2. De Boor, Carl
3. Series

Item has two edition statements. Both are considered important so both are recorded although there is no authority for this. They are given as found in the item – 1.2B1 and 2.2B1, using standard abbreviations – B.9. First named place of publication not in home country of cataloguing agency, therefore first named place that is in the home country is also given – 1.4C5. All other places omitted – 1.4C5. Date given in publication, distribution, etc. area is date of edition named in edition area – 1.4F1.

57

[CONVENTION ON INTERNATIONAL CIVIL AVIATION (1944) Protocols, etc., 1968 Sept. 24]
Protocol on the authentic trilingual text of the Convention on International Civil Aviation (Chicago, 1944), Buenos Aires, 24 September 1968. – London : H.M.S.O., 1969.
87 p. ; 25 cm. – (Treaty series ; no. 115, 1969) (Cmnd. ; 4198).
Text in English, French and Spanish.
ISBN 0-10-141980-5.

1. Title   2. Series

Numbering within the series is given in the terms used in the item and therefore the date is included – 1.6G1. This interpretation is supported by 1.6G3, which instructs that if the item has a designation other than a number, the designation is to be given as found. Separate series statements given when item belongs to two or more series – 1.6J1. Note on language of item – 2.7B2.

Separately published protocol entered under heading for basic agreement – 21.35E1. Uniform title consists of uniform title for original work, followed by 'Protocols, etc.' and the date of signing – 25.16B3.

CAMBRIDGE STUDIES IN INDUSTRY

———◄••►———

EFFECTS OF MERGERS
Six Studies

P. LESLEY COOK
WITH THE COLLABORATION OF
RUTH COHEN
University of Cambridge

Ruskin House

GEORGE ALLEN & UNWIN LTD

MUSEUM STREET LONDON

58

COOK, P. Lesley
  Effects of mergers : six studies /
P. Lesley Cook with the collaboration of
Ruth Cohen. – London : Allen & Unwin,
1958.
  458 p. ; 22 cm. – (Cambridge studies
in industry).
  Contents: The cement industry /
P. Lesley Cook – The calico printing
industry / P. Lesley Cook – The soap
industry / Ruth Cohen – The flat-glass
industry / P. Lesley Cook – The motor
industry / George Maxcy – The brewing
industry / John Vaizey.

1. Title   2. Cohen, Ruth
3. Series
4. Optionally, author and title
    analytical entries for each part †

Statement of responsibility recorded in form in
which it appears in the item – 1.1F1. No semi-
colon separating principal from secondary
author because both are named in single
statement – 1.1F4. (See also example 'A short-
title catalogue . . .' at 1.1F5.) Contents note –
2.7B18 and 1.7B18.

Entry under the principal author indicated by
both wording and layout – 21.6B1 (also
supported by information given in preface).

59

COTTON, G.B.
  Libraries in the North West / [G.B.
Cotton, D.H. Varley, G.R. Cliffe]. –
Manchester : Library Association, North
Western Branch, 1971.
  39 p. : ill. ; 23 cm.
  Special issue of: North Western
newsletter. No. 116.
  "Published on the occasion of the
Council Meeting of the International
Federation of Library Associations in
Liverpool, 27th August to 4th September,
1971".
  Contents: Public libraries in the North
West / G.B. Cotton – Academic libraries
in the North West / D.H. Varley –
Industrial libraries in the North West /
G.R. Cliffe.

1. Title   2. Varley, D.H.
3. Cliffe, G.R.
4. North Western newsletter
5. Library Association. North Western
    Branch
6. Optionally, author and title
    analytical entries for each part

Special number of a serial catalogued as a
separate item and treated as a related work –
21.28A1. Statement of responsibility appears
prominently in item but not in chief source of
information (i.e. on contents page not title page).
It is therefore recorded in statement of
responsibility area but enclosed in square
brackets – 1.1A2 and 1.1F1. Note on edition
and history, i.e. special issue of a serial – 2.7B7
and 1.7B7.

Related work under its own heading with added entry for work to which it is related – 21.28A1 and 21.28B1. Responsibility shared between three persons with principal responsibility not attributed. Main entry therefore under first named, with added entries for others – 21.6C1. Added entry for prominently named publisher whose responsibility extends beyond merely publishing work – 21.30E1.

60

COUNTRY magazine : book of the
    B.B.C. programme / compiled and
edited by Francis Dillon. – London :
Odhams Press, [1950?].
    256 p., [17] p. of plates : ill., music,
ports. ; 22 cm.

    1.   Dillon, Francis

Number of pages of plates recorded – 2.5B10. Music as illustrative matter – 2.5C2.

Related work under its own heading – 21.28B1. See 'Over the garden wall' example on p. 353. Work produced under editorial direction entered under title – 21.7A1(c) and 21.7B1. It is merely coincidence that the title of the book is the same as that of the radio programme.

See also examples no. 30, 335 and 346.

61

CROSBY CENTRAL LIBRARY
    Local maps & documents in the Local
History Library / Crosby Central
Library. – 2nd ed. – Crosby : The
Library, 1972.
    72 p. ; 21 cm.

    1.   Title

Work of administrative nature emanating from corporate body and dealing with its resources is entered under heading for body – 21.1B2(a). Body entered directly under the name by which it is commonly identified – 24.1A.

The Municipal Borough of Crosby became part of the Metropolitan District of Sefton in the local government reorganization of 1974. Explanatory references would therefore be needed to link each of the two headings :

Sefton Libraries and Arts Services and Crosby Central Library – 26.3C1.*

See also next example.

62

CROSBY in the past : a photographic
    record of the history of Crosby and
district / Sefton Libraries and Arts
Services. – Sefton : Libraries and Arts
Services, 1977.
    30 p. : chiefly ill., maps ; 21 cm.

    1.   Sefton Libraries and Arts Services

Work emanating from corporate body but not falling within any of the categories listed at 21.1B2 is entered under title – 21.1C1(c).

See also previous example.

63

CUNDALL, Arthur E.
    Judges / [Arthur E. Cundall]. Ruth /
[Leon Morris]. – London : Tyndale
Press, 1968.
    318 p. : maps, plans ; 19 cm. –
(Tyndale Old Testament commentaries).
    Bibliography: p. 49.
    ISBN 0-85111-622-1.

    1.   Title   2.   Morris, Leon
    3.   Ruth †   Ruth
    4.   Series

Item lacking a collective title and consisting of individually-titled works by different persons, in which no one part predominates, described as a unit – 1.1G2. Titles of the individually titled parts transcribed in the order in which they appear in the chief source of information or in the item – 1.1G3. Parts by different persons separated by full-stop and two spaces – 1.1G3. Statements of responsibility taken from source other than chief source of information enclosed in square brackets – 1.1F1.

Work lacking collective title entered under heading appropriate to first work named in chief source of information – 21.7C1. Added entry (name-title) made for other work.

DAILY Mail children's pictorial encyclopaedia. – London : Associated
Newspapers, [196-].
[76] p. : chiefly col. ill. ; 34 cm.

Work of unknown authorship entered under
title – 21.1C1(a) and 21.5A.

DANTE ALIGHIERI
[De monarchia. English]
On world government = De monarchia / Dante Alighieri ; translated by
Herbert W. Schneider ; with an
introduction by Dino Bigongiari. – 2nd
rev. ed. – New York : Bobbs-Merrill,
1957.
80 p. ; 19 cm.

1. Title   2. On world government
3. Schneider, Herbert W.

Translation entered under heading appropriate
to the original – 21.14A. For works created
before 1501, title in original language is used as
uniform title – 25.4A1. Language added if
different from original – 25.5C1. Added entry
under heading for translator, because work has
been translated into same language more than
once – 21.30K1(c).

DICKENS, Charles
[David Copperfield]
The story of David Copperfield / by
Charles Dickens ; abridged by
W. Jewesbury. – London : Pan, 1970.
128 p. : ill. (some col.) ; 20 cm.
Includes c.50 photographs, chiefly col.,
from the 20th Century-Fox film, 1970,
starring Richard Attenborough, Edith
Evans, Laurence Olivier, Wendy Hiller
and Ralph Richardson.
ISBN 0-330-02502-3.

1. Title   2. The story of David
                Copperfield
3. Jewesbury, W.

Note on physical description – 2.7B10 and
1.7B10.

Abridgement under heading for the original
work – 21.12A1. (Person responsible for original
is named in a statement of responsibility and it
also states in the item that it is told in Dickens'
own words.) Uniform title – 25.3A.*

Compare with example no. 222.

DIOCLES
The home medical encyclopedia / by
Diocles. – 4th large ed. – Kingswood,
Surrey : Right Way Books, 1956.
254 p. : ill. ; 20 cm.
"Including guide to the Health and
Insurance Service" – Dustjacket.

1. Title

Entry under single personal author – 21.1A1,
21.1A2 and 21.4A1. Basis of heading is name by
which person is commonly known – 22.1A –
determined from the chief source of information
of works by that person in his or her
language – 22.1B. Entry under pseudonym –
22.2B1.

DOS PASSOS, John
The best times : an informal memoir /
by John Dos Passos. – London : Deutsch,
1968.
ix, 229 p. : ill. ; 22 cm.
Originally published: New York : New
American Library, 1966.

1. Title

Entry under prefix for names in English
language – 22.5D1.*

DREXEL UNIVERSITY FACULTY
CLUB
Handbook / Drexel University Faculty
Club, Inc. – Philadelphia : The
University, [1973?].
12 p. ; 23 x 11 cm.
Cover title.

1. Title

Work of administrative nature emanating from corporate body and dealing with its policies is entered under heading for body – 21.1B2(a). Body entered directly under name – 24.1A. Term indicating incorporation omitted as it is not an integral part of the name nor is it needed to make clear that name is that of a corporate body – 24.5C1.

70

DUFFERIN AND AVA, Frederick
    Temple Hamilton-Temple Blackwood,
    Marquess
    Letters from high latitudes / Lord
Dufferin. – London : Dent, 1910.
    xv, 252 p. : ill. ; 18 cm. – (Every-
man's library).

    1.   Title

Statement of responsibility recorded in the form in which it appears in item – 1.1F1.

Entry under the proper name in the title of nobility for a person who uses his title in his works or is listed under his title in reference sources – 22.6A1. A reference would be required from the surname – 26.2A1. No added entry under heading for series, as items in series are related to each other only by common physical characteristics – 21.30L1(a).

71

E.R.P.B.
    Nursery rhymes of Gloucestershire / by
E.R.P.B. – Gloucester : British
Publishing Co., [1967].
    36 p. ; 19 cm.

    1.   Title

Name consisting of initials entered under initials in direct order. Name-title reference from inverted form beginning with last letter – 22.10A.*

72

EDUCATION and training for cataloguers
    and classifiers / Ruth C. Carter,
editor. – New York : Haworth, 1987.
    xv, 195 p. : ill. ; 23 cm.
    Also published as: Cataloging and
classification quarterly, v. 7, no. 4
(Summer 1987).

    1.   Carter, Ruth C.

Printed monograph also published as an issue of a serial. Note on the other manifestation of the same work – 1.7A4 and 1.7B16.

73

ELECTRONICS. – London :
    H.M.S.O., 1967.
    72 p., 2 folded leaves of plates : ill.,
forms ; 25 cm. – (Manpower studies ;
no. 5).
    Prepared by: Ministry of Labour.
Manpower Research Unit.

    1.   United Kingdom. Ministry of
        Labour. Manpower Research
        Unit

Statement of responsibility given in note – 1.1F2 and 1.7B6. Folded leaves described as such – 2.5B11.

Work emanating from corporate body but not falling into any of the categories listed at 21.1B2 is entered under title – 21.1C1(c). Intervening element in hierarchy included in added entry heading as name of subordinate body might be used by another body entered under heading for same higher body – 24.14A.

74

[ENCYCLOPAEDIA Britannica. Selec-
    tions]
    An anthology of pieces from early
editions of Encyclopaedia Britannica. –
London : Encyclopaedia Britannica, 1963.
    64 p. : ill. ; 26 cm.
    Extracts from the 1st ed., 1768-1771, to
the 8th ed., 1853-1860.

    1.   An anthology of pieces from early
        editions of Encyclopaedia
        Britannica

Collection of extracts from a work entered under the uniform title for the whole work followed by 'Selections' – 25.6B3. Optionally, a uniform title used as a main entry heading may be recorded without the square brackets – 25.2A.

EVANS, Gwynneth
    National Library news index = Index des nouvelles de la Bibliothèque Nationale : volumes 10-14 (1978-1982) / prepared by Gwynneth Evans, with the assistance of Gene Bodzin and Marie Duhamel. – [Ottawa] : National Library of Canada, [1983].
    11, 11 p. ; 28 cm.
    In English and French.

1. Title
2. Index des nouvelles de la
        Bibliothèque Nationale
3. National Library of Canada
        National library news

Index to a serial published separately described as a printed monograph. Other title information should be transcribed following the title proper or parallel title to which it pertains – 1.1E5. However, in this case, the other title information which follows the title proper is identical to the other title information which follows the parallel title and it is considered preferable therefore to record it once only following the parallel title.

Related work separately catalogued entered under its own heading – 21.28A1 and 21.28B1. Name-title added entry under work to which it is related – 21.28B1 and 21.30G1.

An alternative would be to describe this supplementary item dependently using one of the methods indicated in 1.9B. One of these methods is to record the item in the note area as illustrated in example no. 451.

FAIRLESS, Michael
    The roadmender and other writings / by Michael Fairless ; with a biographical note by M.E. Dowson ; an introduction by Frederick Brereton ; and wood engravings by Lennox Patterson. – New ed. / edited by G.F. Maine. – London : Collins, 1950.
    256 p. : ill. ; 25 cm.

1. Title   2. Maine, G.F.

Statement of responsibility relating to edition recorded – 1.2C1.

Whether the works of a person have appeared under one pseudonym (22.2B1) or, for a contemporary author, under more than one pseudonym or his or her real name and one or more pseudonyms (22.2B3), entry would be under the heading appearing in the particular work. A similar result would be obtained when a person has established separate bibliographic identities – 22.2B2. A reference would be required from the real name Margaret Fairless Barber.* Added entry for prominently-named editor – 21.30D1.

FARQUHAR, George
    The recruiting officer / by George Farquhar ; edited by Michael Shugrue. – London : Arnold, 1966.
    xxi, 137 p. ; 21 cm. – (Regents Restoration drama series).

1. Title   2. Shugrue, Michael †
3. Series

Not a work produced under editorial direction but single personal authorship – 21.1A2 and 21.4A1.

FILM guide for marketing executives / Sales and Marketing Executives-International ; edited by William Wachs. – New York : SME, 1966.
    xiii, 71 p. ; 28 cm. – (Research report).

1. Sales and Marketing Executives-
        International

Foreword states that this item is the result of staff research and enquiries made to a random selection of SME members. It consists, however, of a list of films and cannot be said to record the collective thought of the corporate body (see 21.1B2(c)). It is therefore entered under title – 21.1C1(c). If treated as a work produced under editorial direction (21.7A1(c)), entry would still be under title. Added entry is under the form of name which predominates in the chief source of information. A reference would be required from the alternative brief form of name (SME).

FIRST over Everest : the Houston-Mount Everest Expedition, 1933 / by P.F.M. Fellowes ... [et al.] ; with a foreword by John Buchan ; and an account of the filming of the flight by Geoffrey Barkas. – London : John Lane, the Bodley Head, 1933.

xix, 279 p., [50] leaves of plates (some folded) : ill., maps, ports. ; 24 cm. + 1 pair spectacles.

Spectacles, for viewing anaglyph in stereoscopic relief, in pocket.

1. Fellowes, P.F.M.
2. Houston-Mount Everest Expedition (1933)

Accompanying material recorded in physical description – 2.5E1 and 1.5E1(d). Additional details of accompanying material and its location given in a note – 2.5E2 and 2.7B11.

Work reporting the collective activity of an expedition is entered under heading for expedition as corporate body provided that the work emanates from body – 21.1B2(d). However, although all of the four authors named on the title page were members of the expedition, they were writing in a personal, not an official, capacity. Work is therefore treated as if no corporate body were involved, and, since it is by more than three personal authors, none of whom has principal responsibility, entry is under title – 21.6C2. An added entry may be made under the heading for the expedition as a prominently-named corporate body – 21.30E1.

... The FLYING Pallas, of 36 guns, at Plymouth, is a new and uncommonly fine frigate, built on purpose, and ready for an expedition as soon as some more good hands are on board : Captain Lord Cochrane ... commands her : the sooner you are on board the better. – London : H.M.S.O, 1974.

1 broadside ; 58 x 44 cm.

Recruitment notice.

Reproduction of early 19th cent. original in National Maritime Museum, England.

Description of broadsides. When item is without a title page and there is no other source to furnish a title proper, as many of the opening words of the text as are sufficient to identify the item uniquely are transcribed as the title – 2.14A. Appropriate term from supplied list chosen as specific material designation – 2.5B2. Height and width of a single sheet given – 2.5D4. Note on nature of item – 2.7B1. Note on original – 1.7A4.

FORT George National Historic Park, Ontario. – Ottawa : Parks Canada under the authority of the Minister of Indian Affairs and Northern Development, 1973.

13, 13 p. : ill., plan, ports. ; 21 x 9 cm. – (IAND publication ; no. QS-2073-000-BB-A3).

Text in English and French.

Cover title.

Pages numbered in opposite directions.

1. Series

Description of 'tête-bêche' work, that is one printed in opposite directions. Chief sources of information in more than one language – 1.0H. Not known which is original language of work – 1.0H1(d)(iii) therefore applies and source in English used as it is the language that occurs first in the list included in this rule. Pages numbered in opposite directions – 2.5B15. Width less than half the height – 2.5D2. Note on source of title when there is no title page as such – 2.0B1 and 2.7B3. Note on language of item and physical description – 2.7B2, 1.7B2, 2.7B10 and 1.7B10.

FOSS, Sam Walter
Song of the library staff / Sam Walter Foss. – Detroit : Gale Research, [19--].

5 broadsides.

Five stanzas originally read by the author (Librarian of Somerville, Mass.) at the 1906 Annual Meeting of the American Library Association and now republished by Gale.

Stanza 1: The cataloguer.

1 broadside : ill. ; 56 x 22 cm.

1. Title   2. The cataloguer

Multilevel description – 1.9B1(c) and 13.6. Choice of term 'broadside' – 2.5B2. Numeral which is the first word of a note that has not been quoted directly is spelled out – Appendix C.4A. Width recorded, as it is less than half the height – 2.5D2.

Entry under person responsible for intellectual content – 21.1A1 and 21.1A2.

83

FREEMAN, William
    Dictionary of fictional characters / by William Freeman. – London : Dent, 1963.
    ix, 458 p. ; 20 cm.
    "4500 references to over 2000 works of fiction from 500 British and American authors" – Dustjacket.

    Dictionary of fictional characters : author and title indexes / J.M.F. Leaper. – 1965.
    p. 461-532 ; 20 cm.

    1. Title   2. Leaper, J.M.F.

Supplementary item catalogued as a dependent work using a multilevel description – 1.9B1(c) and 13.6.

Alternatively, a supplementary item could be described independently as a separate item. The author and title indexes to Freeman's work could be catalogued in this way as illustrated in example no.147.

84

FREEMASONS. Grand Lodge (Sussex, England)
    The ritual of Craft Masonry as practised in the province of Sussex complete with the ceremony of installation / published with the authority of the Grand Lodge of Sussex. – 2nd ed. – London : A. Lewis, 1968.
    vii, 183 p. : 3 ill. ; 14 cm.
    ISBN 0-85318-000-8.

    1. Title

Number of illustrations specified if it can be easily ascertained – 2.5C4.

Work of administrative nature emanating from corporate body and dealing with its operations is entered under heading for body – 21.1B2(a). Name of body of ancient origin or that is international in character and that has become firmly established in English form is given in English – 24.3C2. Branch that carries out activities of corporate body in particular locality has name of locality added to it – 24.9A.

85

FREUD, Sigmund
    A psycho-analytic dialogue : the letters of Sigmund Freud and Karl Abraham, 1907-1926 / edited by Hilda C. Abraham and Ernst L. Freud ; translated by Bernard Marsh and Hilda C. Abraham. – London : Hogarth Press, 1965.
    xvii, 406 p., [2] leaves of plates : ports. ; 23 cm. – (The international psycho-analytical library / edited by John D. Sutherland ; no. 68).

    1. Title   2. Abraham, Karl
    3. Abraham, Hilda C.
    4. Freud, Ernst L.   5. Series

Work consisting of exchange between two persons is treated as work of shared responsibility – 21.6A1(c). Principal responsibility not indicated by wording or layout, so entry is under heading for first named – 21.6C1.

86

The FUTURE role of business in society : a special report of conference proceedings from The Conference Board / edited by Lillian W. Kay. – New York : The Board, 1977.
    v, 57 p. ; 23 cm. – (Conference Board report ; no. 710).
    ISBN 0-8237-0143-3.

    1. Kay, Lillian W.   2. Series

Conference without name (see definition – 21.1B1) entered under title – 21.5A. 'The future role of business in society' appears to be a general subject description rather than a specific appellation.

GALLICO, Paul
The snow goose / by Paul Gallico ;
illustrations by Peter Scott. – [New]
illustrated ed. – London : M. Joseph,
1946.
.55 p., [4] leaves of plates : ill. (some
col.) ; 26 cm.
First published: 1941.

1. Title   2. Scott, Peter †

Work which consists of text for which artist has
provided illustrations entered under the heading
appropriate to the text – 21.11A1. Added entry
under illustrator as illustrations are considered
an important feature of work – 21.30K2(c).

88

GALLOWAY, John
Origins of modern art, 1905-1914 / by
John Galloway. – New York ; London :
McGraw-Hill, 1965.
47 p. : ill. ; 20 cm. + 24 slides (col.)
Slides in pockets.

1. Title

If more than one place of publication is named
in the item, the first named place is always
recorded and the first of any subsequently
named places that are in the home country of
the cataloguing agency. 'London' would
therefore be omitted if the item were being
catalogued in the United States unless it was
given prominence by the layout or typography
of the source of information – 1.4C5. Slides
accompanying textual material – 2.5E1 and
1.5E1(d). Slides are standard 5 x 5 cm. size, so
no dimensions are recorded – 8.5D5. Location
of accompanying material given in note – 2.5E2
and 2.7B11.

89

GARRETT, John
Management by objectives in the civil
service / John Garrett and S.D. Walker. –
London : H.M.S.O., 1969.
16 p. ; 25 cm. – (CAS occasional
paper ; no. 10).
ISBN 0-11-630014-0.

1. Title   2. Walker, S.D.
3. Series

Title proper of series is recorded in accordance
with rules for title proper as instructed in
1.1B – 1.6B1. If title proper includes statement
of responsibility as an integral part of it, it is
transcribed as such – 1.1B2. If title proper
includes separate letters or initials without full
stops, these are recorded without spaces
between them – 1.1B6.*

Work of shared responsibility in which principal
responsibility is not indicated is entered under
heading for the person or body named first –
21.6C1.

90

GEOGRAPHIC encyclopaedia for
children / picture maps and illustrations
by Wilhelm Eigener and August
Eigener. – Rev. ed. – London : Hamlyn,
1967.
257 p. : col. ill., maps ; 35 cm.
One map on lining paper.

1. Eigener, Wilhelm
2. Eigener, August

Map on lining paper recorded in note – 2.5C5.

Work for which artist has provided illustrations
entered under heading appropriate for text –
21.11A1. Work of unknown authorship entered
under title – 21.5A. Added entry under heading
for illustrator if illustrations are considered
important feature of work – 21.30K2(c).

91

GEORGE FRY & ASSOCIATES
Study of circulation control systems :
public libraries, college and university
libraries, special libraries / George Fry &
Associates, Incorporated. – Chicago :
Library Technology Project of the
American Library Association, 1961.
vii, 138 p. ; 28 cm. – (LTP publica-
tions ; no. 1).
Published jointly with the Council on
Library Resources.
Partially thumb indexed.

1. Title   2. Series
3. American Library Association.
   Library Technology Project
4. Council on Library Resources

Title proper of series recorded as instructed in 1.1B – 1.6B1. Title proper includes initials without full stops; the letters are recorded without spaces between them – 1.1B6.

Work emanating from corporate body which records the collective thought of the body entered under the heading for the body – 21.1B2(c). Entry directly under name – 24.1A. Omission of 'Incorporated' – 24.5C1. Added entries under prominently named publishers when responsibility extends beyond that of merely publishing (the bodies named commissioned the work and assisted in the study) – 21.30E1.

92

GILBERT, Stuart
   James Joyce's Ulysses : a study / by Stuart Gilbert. – London : Faber, 1930.
   407 p. ; 22 cm.

   1.   Title
   2.   Joyce, James †
       Ulysses

Texts published with commentary – 21.13. Chief source of information ambiguous, but entry is under heading for commentator because work is described as commentary in preface and only selected passages from 'Ulysses' are included – 21.13D1. Rule 21.15A might also be relevant: text published with critical work and presented as critical work is entered under heading for critic – 21.15A.

93

GLAUERT, R.H.
   Trinity College / [photographs by R.H. Glauert ; text by R. Robson]. – Cambridge : Trinity College, 1967.
   [47] p. : chiefly ill. (some col.), map, plan ; 26 cm.
   Col. ill. reproduced from Ackermann's History of the University of Cambridge, 1815, and the endpapers from Loggans Cantabrigia illustrata, 1690.

   1.   Title   2.   Robson, R.

Unnumbered sequence of pages constitutes the whole of the item and exact number is enclosed within square brackets – 2.5B3. Note on important physical description details – 2.7B10.

Item appears to be a work of collaboration between an artist, i.e. a photographer, and a writer. Neither is given greater prominence and entry is therefore under heading for one named first (although the names appear in the colophon, not the chief source of information) – 21.24A. Item in fact emanates from a corporate body but it is not of an administrative nature and therefore falls outside the categories listed in rule 21.1B2.

94

GOETHE, Johann Wolfgang von
   [Faust]
   Urfaust : Johann Wolfgang Goethe's Faust in its original version (1775) / edited by R.H. Samuel. – 1st ed., Repr. – London : Macmillan, 1967.
   xxviii, 110 p. : 2 facsims. ; 20 cm.
   First ed. originally published : London : Allen and Unwin, 1951.
   Bibliography: p. 109-110.

   1.   Title   2.   Urfaust
   3.   Samuel, R.H.

Statement relating to reprinting of particular edition included because changes have resulted from reprinting – 2.2D1.

German name with prefix entered under part of name following prefix unless prefix consists of article or contraction of article – 22.5D1. Uniform title for work created after 1500 is title in original language by which work has become known – 25.3A.

95

GONZALES, Pancho
   How to play and win at tennis / by Pancho Gonzales & Dick Hawk ; edited by Gladys Heldman. – 1st British ed. – London : Souvenir Press, 1963.
   123 p. : 126 ill. ; 23 cm.
   Originally published: New York : Fleet Publishing, 1962.

   1.   Title   2.   Hawk, Dick †
   3.   Heldman, Gladys

Edition statement (in this instance, relating to first edition in one country) transcribed as it appears in item – 2.2B1.

Principal responsibility not indicated on chief source of information, so entry is under heading for first-named person – 21.6C1. Entry is under name by which person is commonly known (Gonzales' initials are 'R.A.') – 22.1A.*

96

GOOD Housekeeping's cookery book /
    compiled by Good Housekeeping
Institute. – Completely rev. and reset
ed. – London : Cookery Book Club,
1968.
    608 p., [24] p. of plates : ill. (some
col.) ; 26 cm.

    1.   Good Housekeeping Institute

In the chief source of information appears the statement 'Completely rewritten and with new colour plates and black and white photographs'. As this statement neither constitutes other title information nor forms part of the statement of responsibility, it is omitted – 1.1F15. There is no instruction to indicate this omission by the mark of omission, i.e. three dots.

Work emanating from corporate body but not falling within any of the categories listed at 21.1B2 entered under title – 21.1C1(c).

97

GORMAN, Michael
    The concise AACR2 : being a rewritten and simplified version of Anglo-American cataloguing rules second edition / prepared by Michael Gorman. – Chicago :
American Library Association, 1981.
    ix, 164 p. ; 23 cm.
    ISBN 0-8389-0325-8.

    1.   Title
    2.   Anglo-American cataloguing rules

This work is more than an abridgement; it is 'rewritten and simplified' and is therefore entered under the heading for the adapter – 21.10A. Added entry under original work – 21.10A and 21.30G1.

98

GOSLING, Peter E.
    Structured programming : a first course for students and hobbyists / Peter E.
Gosling. – London : McGraw-Hill, 1983.
    x, 139 p. ; 23 cm. + 1 computer
cassette ; in container 23 x 16 x 2 cm. –
(Linked software).

System requirements: BBC B.
Also available separately.
ISBN 0-07-84701-0.

    1.   Title   2.   Series

Computer file as accompanying material recorded at end of physical description – 1.5E1(d). Optionally, further detail given – 1.5E1(d).

99

GRANT, Alexander, <u>B. Com.</u>
    Modern method book-keeping ... / by
Alexander Grant. – Glasgow : R. Gibson,
c1934.
    152 p. ; 19 cm.
    "For day and evening classes".

    1.   Title

If dates are not available to distinguish between two identical names (see example no. 359) entered under surname, a term of address, title of position or office, initials of an academic degree, etc. are added – 22.19B1.

100

GREAT war stories. – [New ed.]. –
    [London] : Sundial, [198-].
    699 p. ; 22 cm.
    This ed. first published: London :
Octopus, 1978.
    Contents: The Colditz story / P.R.
Reid – The bridge on the River Kwai /
Pierre Boulle – The battle of the River
Plate / Dudley Pope – The dambusters /
Paul Brickhill.
    ISBN 0-904320-72-4.

    1.   Optionally, author and title
         analytical entries for each part

Chief source of information bears both a collective title and the titles of individual works. The collective title is given as the title proper and the titles of the individual works in a contents note – 1.1B10 and 1.7B18.

Collection of works by different persons with collective title is entered under the collective title – 21.7A1 and 21.7B1.

101

GREATER LONDON COUNCIL
  [Building acts]
  London building acts 1930-1939 :
constructional bylaws. – London : Greater
London Council, 1968.
  100 p. ; 30 cm. – (Publications /
Greater London Council ; 156).

  1. Title
  2. London building acts 1930-1939

Statement of responsibility relating to series
preceded by diagonal slash – 1.6A1 and 1.6E1.

Laws entered under heading for appropriate
corporate body – 21.1B2(b). Laws governing
one jurisdiction entered under heading for
jurisdiction governed by them – 21.31B1.
Uniform title for collection of laws is 'Laws, etc.'
unless they all deal with one subject, in which
case citation title is used – 25.15A1.

102

GREENBANK HIGH SCHOOL FOR
  GIRLS (Sefton, England)
  Parents' handbook / Greenbank High
School for Girls. – [Sefton : The School],
1978.
  11 leaves ; 26 cm.

  1. Title

Pagination recorded in terms of leaves – 2.5B2.

Work of administrative nature emanating from
corporate body and dealing with body itself is
entered under heading for body – 21.1B2(a).
Body entered directly under name – 24.1A.
Addition of local place name in which body is
located if body could be confused with others
of the same or similar names – 24.4C3 and
24.4C5. References would be required for
change of name – 26.3C1.* Until 1978, name of
school was Southport High School for Girls.

103

GROSSMITH, George
  The diary of a nobody / by George and
Weedon Grossmith ; with the original
illustrations by Weedon Grossmith. –
London : Heinemann Educational, 1968.
  180 p. : ill. ; 20 cm. – (New windmill
series ; 120).

  1. Title   2. Grossmith, Weedon
  3. Series

Same person named twice in successive
statements of responsibility but as such
statements are to be recorded as given in the
item – 1.1F1, both statements must be given
and name repeated.

Responsibility shared between two persons;
principal responsibility not attributed to either,
so entry is under heading for one named first –
21.6C1.

104

GUIDE to inns of character in
  Lancashire / D.G. Jackson Advertising
Service. – Halifax : Jackson, [1964?].
  63 p. : ill., maps ; 19 cm.

  1. D.G. Jackson Advertising Service

Work emanating from corporate body but not
falling within any of the categories listed at
21.1B2 is entered under title – 21.1C1(c). No
modification in added entry heading of name of
corporate body containing initials – 24.1A.*

105

A GUIDE to the better care of L.P. and
  stereo records : their mechanics and
maintenance / Cecil E. Watts Limited. –
2nd ed. – Sunbury-on-Thames : Watts,
1968.
  48 p. : ill. ; 22 cm.

  1. Cecil E. Watts Ltd.

Work emanating from corporate body but not
falling within any of the categories listed at
21.1B2 is entered under title – 21.1C1(c). Term
indicating incorporation included in added entry
heading to make it clear that the name is that of
corporate body – 24.5C1.

106

GUNSTON, Bill
  Aircraft of World War 2 / Bill
Gunston. – [St Michael ed.]. – London :
Octopus ; Marks and Spencer [distributor],
1981.
  207 p. : 600 col. ill. ; 28 cm.
  ISBN 0-86273-014-7.

  1. Title

Description of item produced exclusively for specific retail outlet. 'St Michael' appears on cover and is transcribed here as an edition statement – 1.2B1. Optionally, distributor's name follows name of publisher – 1.4D6 and, again optionally, a statement of function is added – 1.4E1. An alternative solution would be to make a note:

This ed. produced exclusively for Marks and Spencer Ltd.

Number of illustrations recorded in physical description area if it can be readily ascertained – 2.5C4.

107

HARRINGTON, Wilfred J.
  The Gospel according to St. Luke : a commentary / by Wilfred J. Harrington. – London : Chapman, 1968.
  vi, 297 p. ; 23 cm.
  Originally published: Westminster : Newman, 1967.
  Bibliography: p. 295-297.

  1. Title
  2. [Bible. <u>N.T. Luke. English. Revised Standard. 1946</u>]

Chief source of information presents item as commentary, and so it is entered as such, with added entry under heading appropriate to text – 21.13B1. In added entry heading, individual book entered as subheading of appropriate testament of Bible – 25.18A3.*

108

HARRIS, John, <u>b</u>. 1916
  Cotton's war : a novel of the Aegean campaign 1941 / John Harris. – London : Arrow, 1980.
  287 p. ; 18 cm.
  Previously published: London : Hutchinson, 1979.
  ISBN 0-09-922620-0.

  1. Title

Contemporary author using a real name and one or more pseudonyms (i.e. John Harris, Mark Hebden and Max Hennessy). Name appearing in each work is used as a basis for its heading – 22.2B3. The names would be linked by explanatory references – 26.2D1.* Dates added to heading to distinguish from headings which are otherwise identical – 22.17A. Optionally, dates may be added to any personal name, even if there is no need to distinguish between headings.

See also the next four examples, in relation to distinguishing between headings which are identical, and examples no. 114-5, in relation to the pseudonyms used by this author.

109

HARRIS, John (John P.), <u>b</u>. 1923
  Easy living in France : how to cope with the French way of life / John Harris. – London : Arrow, 1982.
  146 p. ; 18 cm.
  ISBN 0-09-928770-6.

  1. Title

Heading as prescribed by the rules does not contain all of the fuller form of name but, as this fuller form is known, it is added to the heading to distinguish it from other headings which are otherwise identical – 22.18A. Optionally, the fuller form may be added even if it is not needed to distinguish between headings. Also optionally, dates may be added – 22.17A.

110

HARRIS, John (John Frederick), <u>b</u>. 1931
  Georgian country houses / by John Harris. – Feltham : Country Life Books, 1968.
  64 p. : chiefly ill., plans ; 23 cm. – (Drawing series / Royal Institute of British Architects).
  Bibliography: p. 64.

  1. Title   2. Series

Heading as prescribed by the rules does not contain all of the fuller form of name but, as this fuller form is known, it is added to the heading to distinguish it from other headings which are otherwise identical – 22.18A. Optionally, dates may also be added – 22.17A.

111

HARRIS, John, <u>b</u>. 1942
  Reading children's writing : a linguistic view / John Harris and Jeff Wilkinson ; with contributions by Ronald Carter [et al.]. – London : Allen & Unwin, 1986.
  xiv, 218 p. ; 23 cm. – (Aspects of English).
  Bibliography: p. 206-211.
  ISBN 0-04-407021-7.

  1. Title   2. Wilkinson, Jeff
  3. Series

Dates added to heading to distinguish from headings which are otherwise identical – 22.17A.

112

HARRIS, John, <u>fl</u>. 1802-1814
  The recollections of Rifleman Harris / as told to Henry Curling. – New ed. / edited and introduced by Christopher Herbert. – London : Century, 1985.
  ix, 128 p. ; 22 cm. – (Century lives and letters).
  Originally published 1848; this ed. previously published: London : Leo Cooper, 1970.

  1. Title   2. Curling, Henry
  3. Herbert, Christopher
  4. Series

Dates added to heading to distinguish from headings which are otherwise identical – 22.17A. Years of birth and death unknown but some years of activity known so <u>fl</u>. (flourished) used – 22.17A (see also Abbreviations B.9). If years of activity were unknown, the term which indicates the person's rank could have been added – 22.19B1, i.e.:

  HARRIS, John, <u>Rifleman</u>

113

HAVELOK ; and, Sir Orfeo / translated into modern English by Robert Montagu. – Leicester : Ward, 1954.
  118 p., 4 leaves of plates : 6 ill. ; 19 cm. – (The golden legend series).
  Includes as appendix: Orpheus and Eurydice / Boethius ; translated by Alfred the Great.

  1. Sir Orfeo
  2. [Havelok the Dane. English]
  3. Montagu, Robert   4. Series
  5. Optionally, author and title analyticals for Orpheus and Eurydice

Collection of translations of works by different authors entered as general collection – 21.14B. Collection lacking collective title entered under heading appropriate to first work, with added entry under heading for other work – 21.7C1. Translation entered under heading appropriate to original – 21.14A. Work of unknown authorship entered under title – 21.5A. If added entry is required for basic story found in many versions, title that is established in English-language reference sources is used as uniform title; language of item is added – 25.12B.

114

HEBDEN, Mark
  A pride of dolphins / Mark Hebden. – London : M. Joseph, 1974.
  299 p. ; 21 cm.
  ISBN 0-7181-1230-X.

  1. Title

Contemporary author using a real name (John Harris) and one or more pseudonyms. Name appearing in each work is used as a basis for its heading – 22.2B3. The names would be linked by explanatory references – 26.2D1.

See also examples no. 108 and 115.

115

HENNESSY, Max
  The Lion at sea / Max Hennessy. – London : Hamilton, 1977.
  314 p. ; 23 cm.
  First of a trilogy; continued by: The dangerous years; and, Back to battle.
  ISBN 0-241-89745-9.

Note on edition, i.e. the first of a trilogy – 2.7B7.

Contemporary author using a real name (John Harris) and one or more pseudonyms. Name appearing in each work is used as a basis for its heading – 22.2B3. The names would be linked by explanatory references – 26.2D1.*

See also examples no. 108 and 114.

HERRMANN, Reinhard
    The wedding at Cana / illustrated by
Reinhard Herrmann. – [English ed.]. –
London : Methuen Children's Books,
1972.
    1 folded sheet ([16] p.) : chiefly col. ill. ;
95 mm. – (Zig zag books ; 15).
    "Based on John 2, I-XI".
    First published in West Germany: 1959.
Brief text on verso.
    ISBN 0-416-75220-9.

    1.   Title

Sheet designed to be read in pages when
folded is described as '1 folded sheet'. Number
of imposed pages and height of sheet when
folded given – 2.5D4.

HILTON, John Buxton
    [Death of an alderman / John Buxton
Hilton]. – London : National Library for
the Blind, 1969.
    3 v. of braille ; 35 cm.
    Previously published: London : Cassell,
1968.

    1.   Title

Description of work in braille – Ch.1 and Ch.2.
Title proper is given in braille, i.e. in symbols
that cannot be reproduced by the typographic
facilities available, and it is therefore romanized
by the cataloguer and given in square
brackets – 1.1B1 (see also 1.0E). The same
applies to the statement of responsibility –
1.1F9. Physical description for braille or other
raised types – 2.5B23. Note on history – 1.7B7
and 2.7B7.

Heading for name written in nonroman script is
romanized – 22.3C2.

See also example no. 225.

HIM, George
    Ann and Ben / artist George Him. –
London : Macmillan Educational, 1974.
    [12] p. : all col. ill. ; 97 mm. x
20 cm. – (The language project.
Language in action).
    "Core book at pre-literacy level, devised
to develop skill in left-to-right orientation
and ability to follow story sequence".
    ISBN 0-333-16565-9.

    1.   Title   2.   Series

Book consisting solely of illustrations – 2.5C6.
Height less than 10 cm. given in mm. – 2.5D1.
Width given as it is greater than height – 2.5D2.
Note on intended audience – 2.7B14 and
1.7B14.

Entry under heading for person responsible for
creation of intellectual or artistic content of
work – 21.1A1 and 21.1A2.

HINES, Barry
    A kestrel for a knave / Barry Hines. –
Harmondsworth, Middlesex : Penguin,
1969.
    160 p. ; 18 cm.
    Filmed under the cover title: Kes.
    Previously published: London :
M. Joseph, 1968.
    ISBN 0-1400-2952-4.

    1.   Title   2.   Kes

Description of a book which has been filmed
under another title. Note made of variation of
title – 2.7B4.

Added entry under variant form of title if
considered necessary for access – 21.2A1 and
21.30J.

HODIN, J.P.
  Edvard Munch / J.P. Hodin. –
London : Thames and Hudson, 1972.
    216 p. : 168 ill. (some col.) ; 21 cm. –
(World of art library. Artists).
    Bibliography: p. 211.

  1.   Title   2.   Munch, Edvard

Series and subseries recorded – 1.6H1.

Work consisting of reproductions of the works
of an artist and text about the artist. Entry is
under the heading for the writer, as he is
represented as the author of the work in the
chief source of information – 21.17B1. Added
entry under heading for artist.

Ministry of Public
Building and Works

THE CROWN JEWELS

at the
TOWER OF LONDON

BY MARTIN HOLMES, F.S.A.

LONDON
HER MAJESTY'S STATIONERY OFFICE
1968

HOLMES, Martin
  The crown jewels at the Tower of
London / by Martin Holmes. – 3rd ed. –
London : H.M.S.O., 1968.
    36 p. : ill. (some col.) ; 20 cm. –
(Ministry of Public Building and Works
official guide).
  At head of title: Ministry of Public
Building and Works.

  1.   Title   2.   Series
  3.   United Kingdom. Ministry of Public
        Building and Works

Title transcribed exactly as to wording, order
and spelling but not as to capitalization –
1.1B1. Not considered necessary to capitalize
'crown jewels' but 'Tower of London' capitalized
in accordance with A.16A. Her Majesty's
Stationery Office abbreviated – B.9.

Work emanates from a corporate body but does
not fall into any of the categories listed in rule
21.1B2 and is therefore entered under the
personal author – 21.1A2 and 21.4A1.

Compare with example no. 226.

HORN, Gladys M.
  Adventures with language / by Gladys
M. Horn ; illustrated by Roberta Paflin. –
Racine, Wis. : Whitman, 1961.
    80 p. : col. ill. ; 31 cm. – (Help
yourself series).
  ''Beginning workbook in English ...
planned so that a child can work indepen-
dently'' – Cover and inside cover.
    Pages are perforated to tear out.

  1.   Title   2.   Paflin, Roberta
  3.   Series

Name of state added to place of publication –
1.4C3, using abbreviation appearing in Appendix
B.14A. Note which is a quotation given in
quotation marks and source indicated – 1.7A3.
Note on physical description – 2.7B10 and
1.7B10.

Work for which artist has provided illustrations
under the heading appropriate to the text –
21.11A1. Added entry for illustrator because
name is given equal prominence in the chief
source of information – 21.30K2(a).

HOY, Peter
    Silence à minuit / par Peter Hoy ;
illustrations de Rigby Graham. –
Wymondham, Leics. : Brewhouse Press,
1967.
    1 portfolio (2 broadsides : ill.;
54 x 39 cm. folded to 17 x 20 cm.).
    French and English text.
    Second title page in English: Silence at
midnight.
    Limited ed. of 200 copies.

    1.   Title   2.   Graham, Rigby

Chief sources of information in 2 languages, but
as translation is not the purpose of the
publication, the source in original language is
taken as authority – 1.0H1(d)(ii). Choice of term
'portfolio' – 2.5B2 and 2.5B18. Specific
instructions for describing the contents of a
portfolio are not included in rules. Such contents
could be described in a note, but, if it is desired
to include fuller details in the physical
description area, a format similar to the one
illustrated here – adopted by analogy with rule
for 'monographs contained in more than one
volume' (2.5B20) – could be used. Both height
and width of single sheets recorded, including
dimensions when folded if sheet is designed for
issue folded – 2.5D4. Language of item and
variation in title recorded in notes – 2.7B2 and
2.7B4. Note relating to edition – 2.7B7.

HOYLAKE AMATEUR OPERATIC
    AND DRAMATIC SOCIETY
    ''A pair of silk stockings'' and ''The
man in the bowler hat'' : [programme of a
production] / presented by The Hoylake
Amateur Operatic and Dramatic Society
[at the] Winter Gardens, Hoylake, March
15th to 19th 1927. – [Hoylake : Winter
Gardens], 1927.
    [12] p. ; 23 cm.
    Chiefly advertisements.
    Cover title.

    1.   Title

Titles of individual parts of a work are separated
by a semi-colon – 1.1G3. However, in this
example, the two titles together constitute the
single title proper of the programme and so
there is no semi-colon. First world of every title

quoted is capitalized – A.4B1. If title proper
needs explanation, a brief addition is made as
other title information – 1.1E6.

Work emanating from corporate body and
recording collective activity of an event is
entered under heading for body – 21.1B2(d).

IAMBLICHUS, of Chalcis
    Iamblichus on the mysteries of the
Egyptians, Chaldeans and Assyrians /
translated from the Greek by Thomas
Taylor. – 3rd ed. – London : Stuart and
Watkins, 1968.
    xxvi, 365 p. : port. ; 23 cm.
    ISBN 0-7224-0081-0.

Name associated with responsibility for item
transcribed as part of title proper, so no further
statement relating to name is made – 1.1F13.

Name that does not include surname entered
under part of name under which person is listed
in reference sources. Phrase commonly
associated with name and denoting place of
origin is included – 22.8A1. No added entry
under translator unless work falls within one of
categories listed at 21.30K1. No added entry
under title because it is essentially the same as
main entry heading – 21.30J1(a).

[IMPERATORIS Iustiniani institutiones.
    English]
    The institutes of Justinian : text,
translation and commentary / J.A.C.
Thomas. – Amsterdam ; Oxford : North-
Holland Publishing, 1975.
    xviii, 355 p. ; 26 cm.
    Latin text, parallel English translation.
    ISBN 0-7204-8038-8.

    1.   Title
    2.   The institutes of Justinian
    3.   Thomas, J.A.C.
    4.   Justinian, Emperor of Rome

When more than one place of publication is
named in the item, the first is always recorded,
followed by the first of any subsequent ones in
the home country of the cataloguing agency –
1.4C5.

Texts published with commentary – 21.13. Chief source of information presents item as original work, so entry is under heading for that, with an added entry under the heading for the commentator – 21.13C1. Laws of ancient jurisdiction are entered under uniform title, which is established in accordance with the general rules for uniform titles for ancient works – 21.31C1 and 25.15B1. Uniform title for work created before 1501 is the title in the original language – 25.4A1. For work entered under uniform title, added entry is made under title proper – 25.2E1. Added entry under heading for person having relationship to work if heading provides important access point – 21.30F1. English form of name used for person entered under given name – 22.3B3. To the heading for a monarch is added a phrase consisting of the title in English and the name of the state governed – 22.16A1.

127

INTERNATIONAL EXHIBITION OF
WILD LIFE PHOTOGRAPHY
(2nd : 1950 : Westminster, England)
Wonders of wild life photography : being a selection of photographs from the second 'Country Life' International Exhibition. – London : Country Life, 1950.
96 p. : all ill. ; 26 cm.

1. Title   2. Country Life

Exhibition as corporate body – 21.1B1 and 21.1B2(d).* Entry directly under the name, which is given in a publisher's note as The Second International Exhibition of Wild Life Photography – 24.1A. Omission of number – 24.8A1. Addition to heading of number, date and place – 24.8B1.

128

INTERNATIONAL GARDEN
FESTIVAL (1984 : Liverpool, England)
International Garden Festival, Liverpool '84, 2nd May to 14th October : Festival guide / Merseyside Development Corporation. – Liverpool : Brunswick Printing and Publishing, 1984.
224 p. : ill. (some col.), maps, ports. ; 21 cm.

1. Merseyside Development
    Corporation

Event as corporate body – 21.1B1 and 21.1B2(d). Body entered directly under name by which it is identified – 24.1A. Date and location added – 24.7B1 and 24.8B1. England added – 23.4B1 and 23.4D2. No added entry under title as title is essentially the same as main entry heading – 21.30J1(a).

129

INTERNATIONAL SUNDAY SCHOOL
CONVENTION (11th : 1905 : Toronto,
Canada)
The development of the sunday-school, 1780-1905 : the official report of the Eleventh International Sunday-School Convention, Toronto, Canada, June 23-27, 1905. – Boston [Mass.] : International Sunday-School Association, 1905.
xx, 712 p. : ill., ports. ; 21 cm.

1. Title

Conference as corporate body – 21.1B1 and 21.1B2(d). Words denoting number omitted from heading for conference – 24.7A1. Number, date and place where held added to heading – 24.7B1 (number – 24.7B2, date – 24.7B3, location – 24.7B4).

130

INVENTAIRE général des bibliographies nationales rétrospectives / edité par Marcelle Beaudiquez = Retrospective national bibliographies : an international directory / edited by Marcelle Beaudiquez. – München : K.G. Saur, 1986.
189 p. ; 22 cm. – (IFLA publications, ISSN 0344-6891 ; 35).
Introduction to each country's publishing and bibliographic situation and annotations accompanying each bibliographic record in either French or English.
Contributors: Marcelle Beaudiquez, Barry Bloomfield, Chang Soo Choo, Richard Cheffins, Diana Grimwood-Jones, Frances Hinton, Maria Madsen, Guy Marco.
ISBN 3-598-20399-3 (München).
ISBN 0-86291-376-4 (Paris).

1. Beaudiquez, Marcelle   2. Series

Parallel titles recorded – 1.1D1. When item has parallel titles and statements of responsibility in more than one language, each statement is given after the parallel title or other title information to which it relates – 1.1F10. ISSN of series recorded if it appears in item – 1.6F1. Combined note on nature of item and language – 2.7B1, 1.7B1, 2.7B2 and 1.7B2. Note on statements of responsibility not recorded in the title and statement of responsibility area (if required by cataloguing agency) – 2.7B6 and 1.7B6. Optionally, more than one standard number given and qualifications added – 1.8B2.

Work with collective title consisting of contributions by various persons and produced under editorial direction is entered under title – 21.7A1(c) and 21.7B1.

131

JACOB, Naomi
    Four generations / Naomi Jacob. – [New ed.]. – London : Hutchinson, 1973.
    256 p. ; 20 cm. – (The Gollantz saga / Naomi Jacob ; 4th).
    Originally published: 1934.
    ISBN 0-09-114900-2.

    1.   Title   2.   Series

Edition statement should be transcribed as found on the item, using standard abbreviations – 1.2B1. However, this would, in this instance, result in the meaningless: 'This ed.' A brief edition statement has therefore been supplied and enclosed in square brackets – 1.2B4. Title of series and numbering within series should also be recorded as they appear in the item – 1.1B1 and 1.6B1 – but series statement on item is: 'Fourth of the Gollantz saga'. Numbering within a series is preceded by a semi-colon – 1.6A1 – so the statement has been inverted to make it conform with the usual format. There is no specific rule for common authorship of series and part of series. However, the examples at 1.6E1 and 2.6B1 suggest that the correct format is as shown above. A reference would be required – 26.4B2.*

An alternative method of cataloguing this work would be to make a multilevel description under the heading for the series – 13.6 – as illustrated in the next example.

JACOB, Naomi
    The Gollantz saga / Naomi Jacob. – [New ed.]. – London : Hutchinson, 1973.
    7 v. ; 20 cm.
    Originally published: 1930-1958.

    4th: Four generations.
    256 p.
    ISBN 0-09-114900-2.

    1.   Title   2.   Four generations

Multilevel description providing complete identification of both part and comprehensive whole in single record. At the first level only information relating to the item as a whole is recorded. At the second level, information relating to the individual part (or to a group of parts) is recorded – 13.6.

See also the previous example for an alternative method of cataloguing this work.

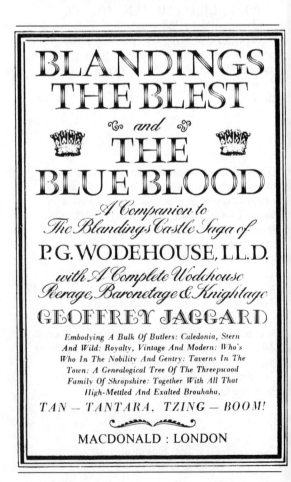

BLANDINGS THE BLEST and THE BLUE BLOOD

A Companion to The Blandings Castle Saga of

P. G. WODEHOUSE, LL.D.

with A Complete Wodehouse Peerage, Baronetage & Knightage

GEOFFREY JAGGARD

Embodying A Bulk Of Butlers: Caledonia, Stern And Wild: Royalty, Vintage And Modern: Who's Who In The Nobility And Gentry: Taverns In The Town: A Genealogical Tree Of The Threepwood Family Of Shropshire: Together With All That High-Mettled And Exalted Brouhaha,

TAN – TANTARA, TZING – BOOM!

MACDONALD : LONDON

JAGGARD, Geoffrey
   Blandings the blest and the blue blood : a companion to the Blandings castle saga of P.G. Wodehouse ... / Geoffrey Jaggard. – London : Macdonald, 1968.
   227 p., 1 folded leaf of plates : geneal. table ; 23 cm.
   ISBN 0-356-02319-2.

   1.   Title   2.   Wodehouse, P.G.

Abridgement of other title information indicated by mark of omission, i.e. three dots – 1.1E3. Genealogical tables treated as illustrative matter – 2.5C2.

Related work under its own heading – 21.28B1.

THE STORY OF RYLANDS BROTHERS LIMITED

Rylands of Warrington

1805 - 1955

HARLEY PUBLISHING COMPANY LTD., LONDON W.C.2

JANES, Hurford
   Rylands of Warrington : the story of Rylands Brothers Limited, 1805-1955. – London : Harley, [1956].
   141 p. : ill., coat of arms, facsims., ports. ; 22 cm.
   Written by Hurford Janes.

   1.   Title

Coat of arms designated – 2.5C2. Statement of responsibility does not appear prominently (see 0.8) in item, even though it is given in foreword, and so is recorded in note rather than statement of responsibility area – 1.1F2 and 1.7B6.

Work by personal author entered under heading for that person, whether named in item or not – 21.4A1.

JOHN XXIII, Pope
   Readings from Pope John ; edited by Vincent A. Yzermans. – London : Mowbray, 1968.
   xi, 99 p. ; 23 cm.

   1.   Title   2.   Yzermans, Vincent A.

Popes – a work which is not an official communication entered under personal heading – 21.4D2. Designation *Pope* added to heading – 22.16B1.

A work written by a Pope acting in an official capacity would be entered as a subheading under 'Catholic Church' – 24.27B2. In the above example an explanatory reference would be made from the corporate heading to the personal heading – 21.4D2 and 26.3C1.*

JOHN, Barry
   The Barry John story / by Barry John. – London : Collins, 1974.
   190 p., [16] p. of plates : 24 ill. ; 22 cm.
   ISBN 0-00-216011-0.

   1.   Title

Name associated with responsibility transcribed as part of title proper and repeated in statement of responsibility area, because separate statement of responsibility appears in chief source of information – 1.1F13.

John Dalton & the progress of science

Papers presented to a conference of historians of science held in Manchester September 19-24 1966 to mark the bicentenary of Dalton's birth

Edited by
D S L Cardwell

Manchester University Press

Barnes & Noble Inc, New York

137

JOHN Dalton & the progress of science :
 papers presented to a conference of historians of science held in Manchester, September 19-24, 1966, to mark the bicentenary of Dalton's birth / edited by D.S.L. Cardwell. – Manchester : Manchester University Press, 1968;
 xxii, 353 p., 5 p. of plates : ill., ports. ; 23 cm.
 Bibliography: p. 344.
 ISBN 0-7190-0301-6.

1. Cardwell, D.S.L.

Item contains 4 pages and 1 leaf of plates, so number is recorded in terms of whichever is predominant – 2.5B10. Contents note for bibliography – 2.7B18.

The typography of the title page, and the use of the indefinite article (see 21.1B1), indicate that this is a conference which lacks a name and therefore entry is under title – 21.5A.

138

JOHN, of the Cross, Saint
 Poems / by St. John of the Cross ; with a translation by Roy Campbell. – Harmondsworth : Penguin, 1968.
 109 p. ; 19 cm. – (Penguin classics).
 Spanish text, parallel English translation.
 This translation originally published: London : Harvill, 1951.

1. Campbell, Roy †

Note on language of text – 2.7B2. Note on bibliographic history – 2.7B7.

English form of name for person entered under given name – 22.3B3. Addition of words associated with name that does not include surname – 22.8A1. Addition of 'Saint' – 22.13A. Added entry under translator, because translation is in verse and also because it can be regarded as important in its own right – 21.30K1(a) and 21.30K1(b).

139

JOINT F.A.O./W.H.O. EXPERT COMMITTEE ON AFRICAN TRYPANOSOMIASIS
 African trypanosomiasis : report of a Joint F.A.O./W.H.O. Expert Committee. – Geneva : W.H.O., 1969.
 79 p. ; 24 cm. – (Technical report series / World Health Organisation ; no. 434) (Agricultural studies / Food and Agricultural Organisation ; no. 81).

1. Title   2. Series
3. Agricultural studies / Food and Agricultural Organisation

Statements of responsibility relating to series included if they are considered necessary for identification – 1.6E1. Two separate series statements recorded – 1.6J1.

Work emanating from corporate body and recording its collective thought is entered under heading for body – 21.1B2(c). Body made up of representatives of two or more bodies entered under its own name – 24.15A.*

KELLY, Stephen F.
　Forever Everton : the official illustrated history of Everton F.C. / Stephen F. Kelly. – London : Queen Anne Press, 1987.
　　192 p. : ill. (some col.), ports. ; 30 cm.
　　ISBN 0-356-15055-0.

　1.　Title

Item with both a publishing company and a division of that company given on title-page, ie:

Macdonald
Queen Anne Press

As the work is actually published by the division, Queen Anne Press is the name recorded in the publication area. This situation occurs quite frequently in, for instance, paperbacks, e.g.: Fontana/Collins, where the publisher would be recorded as Fontana. Rules 1.4D and 2.4D do not specifically refer to this problem but it is analagous to that covered by rule 6.4D2.

KENT, Mrs.
　The visit to Dolby Hall and what came of it; and, The mystery of a five-pound note / by Mrs. Kent. – London : Religious Tract Society, [1906].
　　125 p. : ill. ; 19 cm.

　1.　Title

Item lacking a collective title is here described as a unit and the titles of the individually titled parts are transcribed in the order in which they appear in the chief source of information, with the parts separated by a semi-colon, even if the titles are linked by a connecting word or phrase – 1.1G3.

Name by which person is commonly known consists only of a surname, so word associated with the name in works by the person is added – 22.15A. A reference would be required from the person's actual name if ascertainable, in this case Anna Kent – 26.2A2.

KFA
　Juelich Nuclear Research Center : facts and trends / edited and arranged by Helmuth F. Wust ; translated by Ralf Friese ; illustrations by Hans Schneider ; photographs by Karl Peters and Heinz Josef Ohling ; aerial photographs by Aerolux, Frankfurt ; plates by Walter Haarhaus, Cologne and Zerreiss & Co., Nuremberg. – Juelich : KFA, 1971.
　　102 p. : ill. ; 21 x 24 cm.

　1.　Wust, Helmuth F.

More than one statement of responsibility – 1.1F6. Width greater than height – 2.5D2.

Work is of an administrative nature in that it serves as an advertisement for the operations of the corporate body from which it emanates. It is therefore entered under the heading for the body – 21.1B2(a). Body entered directly under the name by which it is predominantly identified in items issued by that body in its language – 24.1A. (The Juelich Nuclear Research Center is commonly called KFA for Kernforschungs-anlage). References will be required from the alternative forms of name – 26.3A3. As title proper is essentially the same as a reference to the main entry heading, no added title entry is necessary – 21.30J1(a).

KING, Martin Luther
　Stride toward freedom : the Montgomery story / by Martin Luther King ; with a foreword by Trevor Huddleston. – London : Gollancz, 1959, c1958.
　　216 p. ; 21 cm.

　1.　Title

Latest date of copyright may optionally be given after the date of publication if they are different – 1.4F5.

Name containing compound surname is entered in accordance with the preferred or established form if this is known – 22.5C2. Surname is frequently followed by 'Jr'. Words indicating relationship are omitted (except when they are needed to distinguish between two or more identical names), unless the surname is Portuguese – 22.5C8.

[KORAN. al-Súrah 21-114. English]
The Koran interpreted. Volume two :
Suras XXI-CXIV / by Arthur J.
Arberry. – London : Allen and Unwin,
1955.
    367 p. ; 22 cm.
    Second of 2 v.

    1.   The Koran interpreted
    2.   Arberry, J.

If title proper for an item that is a section of
another item appears in two parts not
grammatically linked, the title of the main work
is recorded first, followed by a full stop and the
title of the section – 1.1B9.

Uniform title for sacred scripture is title by
which it is most commonly identified in English
language reference sources – 25.17A. Individual
chapters of the Koran are entered by name as a
subheading of the Koran in the form: KORAN.
Surat al-Baqarah. A reference is then made from
the súrah number in the form: KORAN. al-Surah
II – 25.18M1. There is no specific rule for
recording a sequence of chapters identified only
by numbers, but additions to uniform title may
be made as instructed in 25.5 and 25.6, so
the general rule for items consisting of consecutive parts of a work has been followed –
25.6B1. Numeric designation given in Arabic
numerals – 25.6A1. Language added – 25.5C1.

LAMB, Charles
    [Tales from Shakespeare]
    Ten tales from Shakespeare / Charles
and Mary Lamb ; pictures by
Grabianski. – London : J.M. Dent, 1969.
    223 p. : ill. (some col.) ; 24 cm.
    ISBN 0-460-05103-2.

    1.   Title
    2.   Ten tales from Shakespeare
    3.   Lamb, Mary
    4.   Grabianski, Janusz
    5.   Shakespeare, William

Version of an author's works presented in a
different literary form entered under the heading
for the adapter – 21.10A. Title by which work
created after 1500 has become known through
use and in reference sources used as uniform
title – 25.3A.

LAW COMMISSION
    Statute law revision : first report /
the Law Commission. – London :
H.M.S.O., 1969.
    42 p. ; 25 cm. – (Law Commission ;
no. 22) (Cmnd. ; 4052).
    "Draft Statute Law (Repeals) Bill
prepared under section 3(1)(i) of the Law
Commissions Act 1965''.

    1.   Title

Work emanating from corporate body and
recording its collective thought is entered under
heading for body – 21.1B2(c). Name of body
contains term normally implying administrative
subordination (i.e. 'Commission'), but name of
higher body is not required for identification –
24.13A (Type 2).* Body is therefore entered
directly under its own name – 24.12A.

LEAPER, J.M.F.
    William Freeman['s] dictionary of
fictional characters : author and title
indexes / by J.M.F. Leaper. – London :
Dent, 1965.
    p. 461-532 ; 20 cm.

    1.   Title
    2.   Freeman, William
                Dictionary of fictional characters

Supplementary item which is to be described
independently catalogued as a separate item –
1.9A1. If pages are numbered as part of larger
sequence, first and last numbers of pages are
given, preceded by appropriate abbreviation –
2.5B6.

Related work which is to be catalogued
separately is entered under its own heading –
21.28B1. Name-title added entry made under
heading for work to which it is related –
21.30G1.

An alternative solution is to catalogue a
supplementary item as a dependent work. This
would produce a more useful entry in this
instance. Supplementary items may be
described dependently in one of three ways
(see rule 1.9B1): a) as accompanying material; b)
in a note; c) using a multilevel description. The
above item is shown catalogued using the last
of these methods in example no. 83.

LIBRARY ADVISORY COUNCIL
  (England)
  A report on the supply and training of
librarians / Library Advisory Council
(England) [and] Library Advisory Council
(Wales). – London : H.M.S.O., 1968.
  viii, 64 p. ; 25 cm.
  ISBN 0-11-270006-3.

  1. Title
  2. Library Advisory Council (Wales)

Work emanating from corporate bodies and
recording their collective thought is entered
under heading for appropriate body – 21.1B2(c).
Work of shared responsibility emanating from
two corporate bodies – 21.6A1(d). Principal
responsibility not indicated by wording or
layout, so entry is under first-named, with
added entry under the heading for the other –
21.6C1. Government agency that does not fall
within any of the categories listed at 24.18A is
entered under its own name – 24.17A.* To
distinguish between two bodies with the same
name, the name of country is added – 24.4C2.

MARKHAM, Robert
  Colonel Sun : a James Bond adventure /
by Robert Markham. – London : Cape,
1968.
  255 p. : 2 maps ; 20 cm.
  Maps on lining papers.
  ISBN 0-330-02304-7.

  1. Title

Note of illustrations which appear on lining
papers – 2.5C5.

Pseudonyms – Robert Markham's real name is
Kingsley Amis but, for contemporary authors,
the basis of the heading to be used is the name
appearing in the particular work – 22.2B3.

MARTIN, Mrs. Herbert
  Cast adrift : the story of a waif / by
Mrs. Herbert Martin. – London : Gall
and Inglis, [1901].
  204 p., [9] leaves of plates : ill. ; 19 cm.

  1. Title

Term of address added to married woman who
is identified only by her husband's name –
22.15B1. A reference would be required from
the person's actual name, i.e. Mary Emma
Martin – 26.2A1.

McGARRY, K.J.
  Logic in the organisation of knowledge ;
and, Semantics in the organisation of
knowledge : a programmed text for
students of information retrieval / K.J.
McGarry & T.W. Burrell. – London :
Bingley, 1972.
  [64, 64] p. ; 23 cm. – (Programmed
texts in library and information science).
  Two separate but interrelated texts
printed in reverse format so that each
appears only on the right hand pages.
  Diagrams on lining papers.
  ISBN 0-85157-134-4.

  1. Title
  2. Semantics in the organisation of
        knowledge
  3. Burrell, T.W.   4. Series

Description of 'tête-bêche' work, that is one
printed in opposite directions. Item has two title
pages which are treated as if they were a single
source – 1.0H1(a). Item without collective
title – 1.1G2. Usually, for volume printed
without pagination, total number of pages is
ascertained and given in square brackets –
2.5B7. However, as this item has pages running
in opposite directions, pagination is recorded by
analogy with 2.5B13 and 2.5B15.

McGRAW, Eloise Jarvis
  The golden goblet / by Eloise Jarvis
McGraw ; illustrated by Owen Wood. –
Harmondsworth : Penguin, 1968.
  208 p. : ill. ; 18 cm. – (Puffin books).
  Originally published: New York :
Coward, McCann, 1961.

  1. Title

For married women whose surname consists of
maiden name and husband's surname, entry is
under husband's surname (unless the woman's
language is Czech, French, Hungarian, Italian or
Spanish) – 22.5C5.*

MEE, Arthur
   Worcestershire / by Arthur Mee. –
New ed. / fully revised and edited by Lord
Hampton and Richard Pakington ;
illustrated with new photographs by A.F.
Kersting. – London : Hodder and
Stoughton, 1968.
   194 p., 16 p. of plates : ill., map ;
21 cm. – (King's England).
   ISBN 0-340-00108-9.

   1.   Title
   2.   Hampton, Humphrey Pakington,
       Lord
   3.   Pakington, Richard
   4.   Series

Statement of responsibility relating to edition
follows edition statement, preceded by diagonal
slash; subsequent statement of responsibility
preceded by semi-colon – 1.2A1 and
1.2C1.

Work is a revision, but entry is under heading
for original author, as he is named in a
statement of responsibility in the item being
catalogued – 21.12A1(a). 'Lord' added to name
in added entry heading if it commonly appears
with name in person's works – 22.12B1.

MILLIGAN, Spike
   A book of bits, or, A bit of a book / by
Spike Milligan. – London : Tandem,
1967.
   95 p. : chiefly ill. ; 18 cm.

   1.   Title   2.   A bit of a book*

Alternative title preceded by *or*, with commas,
and first word of alternative title capitalized –
1.1B1.

Entry under name by which person is
commonly known – 22.1A. A reference would
be required from Milligan's real name (Terence
Alan Milligan).

MONBODDO, James Burnet, <u>Lord</u>
   Of the origin and progress of language /
by James Burnet. – Menston [Yorkshire] :
Scolar Press, 1967.
   6 v. ; 21 cm. – (English linguistics
1500-1800 : a collection of facsimile
reprints ; no. 48).
   Facsim of: 1st ed., London : Cadell,
1773-1792.

   1.   Title   2.   Series †

Number of volumes recorded – 2.5B17. Other
title information of series included, as it
provides valuable information identifying
series – 1.6D1.

Nobleman who uses his surname in his works
but is commonly known by his title and is listed
under this title in reference sources – 22.6A1.*
Author was Scottish ordinary lord of session, so
'Lord' is retained in title – 22.6B2.

The MUTINY and piratical seizure of
   the convict-brig Cyprus when on voyage
from Hobart-Town to Macquarrie
Harbour during August 1829 : being the
apprehension, trial, sentence, of the
mutineers, as reported by The Times of
Oct. 14th to Dec. 14th 1830. –
Mitcham : S.A. Spence, 1968.
   71 p. in various pagings, 2 leaves of
plates (1 folded) : ill., map ; 27 cm.
   Most alternate pages blank.
   Limited ed. of 75 copies.

   1.   The Times

This publication has an extremely complicated
pagination consisting mainly of leaves
numbered as pages, i.e. 1, 3, 5 ... 39, 41, 43
... through to 71. A few of the pages are
printed on both sides. One of the leaves is
numbered in roman, i.e. xi, and others in
asterisks, i.e. *, **, ***, etc. and b*, b**, etc. A
second sequence of leaves numbered as pages
in arabic, i.e. 13, 15, precedes p. 39. When a
volume has complicated or irregular paging, the
total number of pages may be given, followed
by 'in various pagings' – 2.5B8(a). (Rule 2.5B5
is relevant here too: if the numbering within a

sequence changes, the first part of the sequence is ignored.) Note on limited edition – 2.7B10.

Related work which is to be catalogued separately entered under its own heading – 21.28B1.

NATIONAL GALLERY (U.K.)
 Colour reproductions of pictures in the National Gallery. – London : National Gallery, Publications Department, [198-?].
 [17] p. : chiefly col. ill., plan ; 23 x 26 cm.
 Pictures illustrated in this catalogue are available for purchase as separate colour reproductions.

 1. Title

Work emanating from a corporate body describing its resources entered under the heading for the body – 21.1B2(a). Body entered directly under name by which it is commonly identified – 24.1A. To distinguish between bodies of the same name, a word or phrase is added – 24.4C1. For a body with a national character this addition is the name of the country – 24.4C2. Name abbreviated – B.14A.

See also example no. 203.

NATIONAL legislation and treaties
 relating to the law of the sea = Législation nationale et traités concernant le droit de la mer. – New York : United Nations, 1976.
 xxviii, 586 p. ; 24 cm. – (United Nations legislative series = Série législative des Nations Unies ; ST/LEG/SER.B/18).
 Text partly in English, partly in French.
 United Nations publication sales no.: E/F.76.V.2.

 1. Législation nationale et traités
      concernant le droit de la mer
 2. Series
 3. Série législative des Nations Unies

Parallel titles recorded in the order indicated on chief source of information – 1.1D1. Publication details appear in more than one language, so they are recorded in language of title proper – 1.4C1 and 1.4D2. Parallel titles of series

recorded as for parallel titles in a second level description (i.e. if there were three parallel titles, the third would not be recorded unless it were in English) – 1.6C1 and 1.1D2. Important number borne by item other than ISBN recorded in a note – 2.7B19 and 1.7B19.

Compilation of laws governing more than one jurisdiction and collection of treaties consisting of those contracted between more than three parties are both entered as general collections – 21.31B2 and 21.35F3. Collection with collective title entered under title – 21.7B1.

NETWORK analysis : a guide to the use
 of network analysis in programming and control of the design of construction works / prepared by joint working group of Royal Institute of British Architects ... [et al.]. – London : H.M.S.O., 1967.
 vi, 40 p. : ill., form ; 30 cm. – (Research and development building management handbooks ; 3).
 Cover title: Network analysis in construction design.
 At head of title: Ministry of Public Building and Works, Research and Development.
 One ill. on folded leaf in pocket.

 1. Royal Institute of British Architects
 2. United Kingdom. Ministry of Public
      Building and Works

Variation of title given in note – 2.7B4. Statement of responsibility not recorded in title and statement of responsibility area is given in note – 2.7B6. Illustrative matter issued in a pocket inside the cover of an item is included in the physical description; number of items and their location recorded in a note – 2.5C7 and 2.7B10.

Work emanating from corporate body but not falling within any of the categories listed at 21.1B2 is entered under title – 21.1C1(c). (Despite the wording of the title page, the foreword indicates, by the use of lower case letters etc., that the joint working group lacks a name, and so entry cannot be under name of body as instructed at 24.15A).

The NEW Oxford illustrated dictionary. – Sydney, Australia : Bay Books in association with Oxford University Press, 1976.

2 v. (xvi, 1920 p.) : ill. (chiefly col.), maps, ports. ; 29 cm.

Based upon the text of the Oxford illustrated dictionary / edited by J. Coulson . . . [et al.]; additional material derived from the Australian and New Zealand supplement to the Pocket Oxford dictionary, 5th ed., and from other sources; with many new illustrations.

Published in 40 weekly parts with loose-leaf binders; distributed in the U.K. by: City Magazines Ltd.

Contents: v.1. AAC-LEA – v.2. LEB-ZYM.

Description of item issued in weekly parts. Work in more than one volume – 2.5B17. Pagination continuous so given in parentheses, ignoring separately paged sequence of preliminary material in volumes other than first – 2.5B20. Note on edition and history – 2.7B7 and 1.7B7. Note on publication and distribution – 2.7B9 and 1.7B9. Contents note – 2.7B18 and 1.7B18.

It is appreciated that libraries and other agencies may wish to catalogue this work as an incomplete item when they receive the first parts. To do this, chapter 12 would be used as a guide to produce an open entry with the numeric designation of the first issue given, i.e.:

The NEW Oxford illustrated dictionary. –
   Pt. 1-   . – . . .

The specific material designation would be given alone, without the number of physical units, preceded by three spaces – 1.5B5, and followed by (loose-leaf), i.e.:

   pt. (loose-leaf)

A note about the method of publication would also need to be added – 1.7B9, e.g.:

   In progress; to be published in 2 v. (40 weekly parts).

Work of unknown authorship entered under title – 21.5A.

Robert Melville

NED KELLY

27 paintings by

SIDNEY NOLAN

Thames and Hudson · London

NOLAN, Sidney
   Ned Kelly : 27 paintings / by Sidney Nolan ; [text by] Robert Melville. – London : Thames and Hudson, 1964.
   60 p. : col. ill. ; 21 cm.

   1.   Title   2.   Melville, Robert †

Explanatory words added to statement of responsibility – 1.1F8. There are six unnumbered pages at the front of this book. However, unnumbered sequences are disregarded unless they constitute the whole or a substantial part of the work, or unless an unnumbered sequence includes a page or pages referred to in a note – 2.5B3. Illustrations in colour – 2.5C3.

Work consisting of reproduction of works of an artist and text about him is entered under heading for the artist, as he appears to be represented as the author in the chief source of information and the text is a minor element – 21.17B1. An added entry is made under the heading for the person who wrote the text – 21.17B1 and 21.30C1.

NORTH ATLANTIC TREATY
ORGANIZATION
The North Atlantic Treaty Organ-
ization : facts and figures. – 10th ed. –
Brussels : NATO Information Service,
1981.
376 p. : ill., maps, ports. ; 21 cm.
Previous ed.: 1978.

Work of administrative nature emanating from
corporate body and dealing with the body itself
is entered under the heading for the body –
21.1B2(a). Variant forms of name in chief source
of information; name that is presented formally
is used – 24.2D.*

O'BRIEN, Flann
The best of Myles : a selection from
'Cruisheen Lawn' / Myles na Gopaleen
(Flann O'Brien) ; edited and with a
preface by Kevin O Nolan. – London :
Pan, 1977.
400 p. : ill. ; 20 cm.
Articles originally appeared in: The Irish
times.
ISBN 0-330-24855-3.

1. Title   2. Irish times

Statement of responsibility recorded as it
appears in item – 1.1F1.

Author's works appear under more than one
pseudonym (real name is Brian O'Nolan); for
contemporary authors the name appearing in
the particular work is used as a basis for the
heading – 22.2B3. Added entry under heading
for related work – 21.30G1.

PARIS, Matthew
La vie de Seint Auban : an Anglo-
Norman poem of the thirteenth century /
edited by Arthur Robert Harden. –
Oxford : Blackwell for the Anglo-Norman
Text Society, 1968.
xxix, 85 p., [1] leaf of plates : facsim. ;
23 cm. – (Anglo-Norman texts ; 19).
Attributed to Matthew Paris.
ISBN 0-631-0480-1.

1. Title   2. Harden, Arthur Robert
3. Series

Statement of responsibility does not appear
prominently in item and so is given in note –
1.1F2 and 2.7B6.

Reference sources indicate that Paris is probable
author and so entry is made under heading for
him – 21.5B.

ENGINEERING WORKSHOP DRAWING

INCLUDING AN INTRODUCTION TO PLANE AND SOLID GEOMETRY
WITH SPECIAL REFERENCE TO THE NEEDS OF STUDENTS IN
MAJOR AND MINOR COURSES AND IN JUNIOR TECHNICAL SCHOOLS

BY

A. C. PARKINSON

A.C.P. (HONS.), F.COLL.H., ETC.

MEMBER OF THE ROYAL SOCIETY OF TEACHERS

LECTURER IN THE ENGINEERING DEPT., THE TECHNICAL COLLEGE, KINGSTON-UPON-THAMES

SOMETIME INSTRUCTOR, UNIVERSITY OF LONDON GOLDSMITHS' COLLEGE, ETC.

AUTHOR OF "A FIRST YEAR ENGINEERING DRAWING," "INTERMEDIATE ENGINEERING DRAWING"

"ENGINEERING INSPECTION," "BLUEPRINT READING SIMPLIFIED"

"SCREW THREAD CUTTING AND MEASUREMENT," ETC.

JOINT AUTHOR OF "LOGARITHMS SIMPLIFIED" AND "ENGINEERING MATHEMATICS"

FOURTH EDITION
(Thirteenth Impression—Reprinted with Revision and Additions)

LONDON
SIR ISAAC PITMAN & SONS, LTD.
1946

PARKINSON, A.C.
Engineering workshop drawing : including an introduction to plane and solid geometry ... / by A.C. Parkinson. – 4th ed., 13th impression, Repr. with revision and additions. – London : Pitman, 1946.
viii, 116 p. : ill. ; 22 x 28 cm. – (Technical school series).
"With special reference to the needs of students in major and minor courses and in junior technical schools".

1.   Title   2.   Series

Other title information which is lengthy is omitted from title and statement of responsibility area and given in a note – 1.1E3 and 1.7B5. Omission indicated by mark of omission (i.e. three dots) – 1.0C1 and 1.1E3. Omission of qualifications, etc. in statement of responsibility area – 1.1F7. Named revision of an edition transcribed following the edition statement – 2.2D1 and 1.2D1. Date in publication, etc. area is given as date of reissue only if reissue is specified in edition area (4th ed. was first issued in 1936) – 1.4F3. Width greater than height – 2.5D2.

PARLIAMENTARY AND SCIENTIFIC
    COMMITTEE
Report on collection, dissemination, storage and retrieval of scientific and technological information / Parliamentary and Scientific Committee. – London : The Committee, 1968.
24 p. ; 22 cm.

1.   Title

Work emanating from corporate body and recording its collective thought is entered under heading for body – 21.1B2(c). Name of body includes term implying administrative subordination (i.e. 'Committee'), but name of higher body is not required for identification of subordinate body – 24.12A and 24.13A (Type 2).

The PENGUIN book of French verse / [edited and introduced by Brian Woledge, Geoffrey Brereton and Anthony Hartley]. – Rev. ed. – Harmondsworth : Penguin, 1975.
xxxii, 664 p. ; 19 cm.
Text in French, with prose translations of each poem and introduction in English.
First published in 4 volumes, 1957-1961.
Contents: Twelfth to fifteenth centuries / introduced and edited by Brian Woledge – Sixteenth to eighteenth centuries / introduced and edited by Geoffrey Brereton – Nineteenth and twentieth centuries / introduced and edited by Anthony Hartley.
ISBN 0-14-042-182-3.

1.   Woledge, Brian
2.   Brereton, Geoffrey
3.   Hartley, Anthony

Title including name of publisher that is an integral part of title proper is transcribed in full – 1.1B2. Title page bears both collective title and titles of individual works; former is given as title proper and latter are given in contents note – 1.1B10 and 1.7B18. Statement of responsibility taken from cover, not chief source of information (i.e. title page) and so is enclosed in square brackets – 2.0B2.

Work produced under editorial direction entered under title – 21.1C1(b) and 21.7B1. Added entries made for up to three editors – 21.30A1 and 21.30D1.

PERKINS, Al
Doctor Doolittle and the pirates / Hugh Lofting ; adapted for beginning readers by Al Perkins ; illustrated by Philip Wende. – London : Collins and Harvill, 1968.
61 p. : col. ill. ; 24 cm. – (Beginner books. I can read it all by myself).
Published by arrangement with: New York : Random House.

1.   Title   2.   Lofting, Hugh
3.   Wende, Philip

More than one statement of responsibility – 1.1F6. Series and subseries recorded – 1.6H1. Note on publication – 2.7B9 and 1.7B9.

Adaptation under the heading for the adapter – 21.10A.

PHILIP, Prince, consort of Elizabeth II, Queen of the United Kingdom
The evolution of human organisations / by His Royal Highness the Prince Philip Duke of Edinburgh. – Southampton : University of Southampton, 1967.
27 p. ; 22 cm. – (Fawley Foundation lectures ; 1967).

1. Title   2. Series

Title added to name of consort of royal person followed by consort of and name of royal person – 22.16A3. Roman numeral associated with royal person treated as part of name – 22.1A. Title and name of state added – 22.16A1.

PLAUTUS, Titus Maccius
Miles gloriosus / T. Macci Plauti ; edited with an introduction and notes by Mason Hammond, Arthur M. Mack, Walter Moscalew. – 2nd ed. rev. / revised by Mason Hammond. – Cambridge, Mass. : Harvard University Press, 1970.
x, 208 p. ; 22 cm.
Latin text with introduction and notes in English.
ISBN 0-674-57436-2.

1. Title   2. Hammond, Mason
3. Mack, Arthur M.
4. Moscalew, Walter

Edition statement transcribed as it appears on item, except that standard abbreviations used and numerals in place of words – 1.2B1. Note on language of item – 1.7B2.

Roman living before 476 A.D. entered under part of name most commonly used as entry element in reference sources – 22.9A.

PLINY, the Elder
[Naturalis historia. Book 20-23. English]
Natural history : libri XX-XXIII / Pliny ; with an English translation [and introduction] by W.H.S. Jones. – Rev. and repr. – London : Heinemann, 1969.
xxvi, 532 p. ; 17 cm. – (Natural history / Pliny ; v. 6) (Loeb classical library).
Latin text, parallel English translation.
Complete work published in 10 v.

1. Title   2. Natural history
3. Loeb classical library

Numbering of first series as it appears on title page is: 'Volume VI'; this is recorded using standard abbreviations and substituting arabic for other numerals – 1.6G1. Note on language of item – 2.7B2.

Translation entered under heading appropriate to the original – 21.14A. Established English form of name used for Roman of classical times – 22.3B3.* Words normally associated with name added after comma and underlined, i.e. italicized – 22.8A1. Uniform title of work created before 1501 is title in original language – 25.4A1. Item consists of consecutive numbered parts of work, so designation of parts is given in singular as subheading of uniform title followed by the inclusive numbers of the parts – 25.6B1. Language added, if other than that of original – 25.5C1.

POLETTE, Nancy
Library skills for primary grades / Nancy Polette ; illustrated by Helen Hausner and Associates. – St. Louis : Milliken, 1973.
12 p., [36] leaves of plates : ill. (some col.) ; 28 cm. – (Milliken full-color transparency-duplicating books).
Plates consist of 12 full colour transparencies and 24 duplicating masters which may be detached and used to provide a complete and adaptable library programme for pupils in kindergarten and the primary grades.

1. Title
2. Helen Hausner and Associates
3. Series

Item which consists of text and a number of detachable graphics bound together in book format, here treated as a printed monograph. The detachable leaves are described as plates according to rule 2.5B10 and a note used to amplify the physical description (2.7B10) and to indicate the nature and scope of the item (2.7B1 and 1.7B1). It might be considered more appropriate to treat this item as a graphic (see example no. 255).

It is unclear whether this is a work for which an artist has provided illustrations (21.11A1) or a work that is a collaboration between a writer and an artist (21.24A). In either case the main entry heading would be 'Polette', under the former rule as the author of the text and under the latter as the first named (the artist is not given greater prominence).

173

[PRAJNAPARAMITA. English.
Selections]
Selected sayings from the Perfection of Wisdom / chosen, arranged and translated by Edward Conze. – 2nd ed. – London : Buddhist Society, 1968.
  131 p., [1] leaf of plates : ill. ; 23 cm.
  Translation from the Sanscrit.
  ISBN 0-901032-00-X.

  1. Title   2. Conze, Edward
  3. Buddhist Society

Work accepted as sacred scripture by religious group entered under title – 21.1C1(d) and 21.37A. Uniform title is title by which scripture is most commonly identified in English language sources – 25.17A. Language and 'Selections' added after uniform title by analogy with rules for other sacred scriptures in accordance with general rules for uniform titles – 25.5C1 and 25.6B3. Added entry under heading for translator because main entry is under title and because main entry heading may be difficult for catalogue-users to find – 21.30K1 and 21.30K1(e).

174

PRIESTLEY, Joseph
  [Historical account of the navigable rivers, canals and railways of Great Britain]
  Priestley's navigable rivers and canals : Historical account of the navigable rivers, canals, and railways throughout Great Britain / by Joseph Priestley ; with a new introduction by Charles Hadfield. – Newton Abbot : David and Charles, 1969.
  xv, 703, viii p., [1] folded leaf of plates : map ; 23 cm.
  Facsim. of: 1st ed., London : Longman, Rees, Orme, Brown and Green, 1831.
  ISBN 0-7153-4395-5.

  1. Title

Description of facsimiles – 1.11. Data relating to the original given in the note area only – 1.11A. If the facsimile has a title different from that of the original, the title of the facsimile is given as the title proper, and the original title is recorded as other title information if it appears on the chief source of information of the facsimile – 1.11B. Facsimile has publication details of both original and facsimile, but only those of facsimile are given in the publication area – 1.11C. Physical description of facsimile given in physical description area – 1.11D. ISBN of facsimile given in standard number and terms of availability area – 1.11E. All details of the original given in single note in the order of the areas of description – 1.11F.

For work created after 1500 and known by more than one title, uniform title is title in original language by which work is best known – 25.3A. If no one title predominates, the title of the original edition is used – 25.3B.

175

PROLE, Lozania
  The greatest nurse of them all / by Lozania Prole. – London : Hale, 1968.
  184 p. ; 21 cm.
  Based on the life of Florence Nightingale.

  1. Title

Work is the result of collaboration between two people (i.e. Ursula Bloom and Charles Eade) who have shared a pseudonym. Entry is under pseudonym with references from real names.* (If other works by either writer were entered under real name, a reference would have to be made to that name from this heading.) – 21.6D1.

176

PUTNAM, Sallie A.
[Richmond during the war]
In Richmond during the Confederacy / by a lady of Richmond (Sallie A. Putnam). – New York : McBride, 1961.
389 p. ; 21 cm.
Subtitle on facsim. of original t.p.: Four years of personal observation.
First published: New York : Carleton, 1867.

1. Title 2. In Richmond during the Confederacy

Numbering within sequence of pages changes from roman to arabic (i.e. i-xiv, 15-389 p.); numbering of first part of sequence is ignored – 2.5B5. Other title information not recorded in title and statement of responsibility area is given in note if considered important – 2.7B5.

Person commonly identified in reference sources by proper name is entered under that name, even if characterizing phrase appears in chief source of information. A reference would be made from that phrase – 22.11D.* (See also example no. 270). No single title established as being the one by which the work is best known, so uniform title is title proper of original edition – 25.3B.

177

REMINGTON, J.M.
Algebra / J.M. Remington. – 3rd ed. – London : Intercontinental Book Productions in conjunction with Seymour Press [distributor], 1974.
56 p. ; 13 cm. – (Pass GCE O level and CSE exams. Key facts ; 10).
Twenty-nine loose cards in plastic wallet.
ISBN 0-85047-201-6.

1. Title 2. Series

Description of item which, although containing numbered pages, actually consists of a series of cards. Note made of important physical details not already included in physical description area – 2.7B10.

Roads to Freedom

Essays in Honour of Friedrich A. von Hayek

Edited by

Erich Streissler
Managing Editor

Gottfried Haberler

Friedrich A. Lutz

Fritz Machlup

London   Routledge & Kegan Paul

ROADS to freedom : essays in honour of
Friedrich A. von Hayek / edited by
Erich Streissler ... [et al.]. – London :
Routledge & K. Paul, 1969.
  xix, 315 p., 1 leaf of plates : port. ;
26 cm.
  Bibliography: p. 309-315.
  ISBN 0-7100-6616-3.

  1. Streissler, Erich
  2. Hayek, Friedrich A. von † *

More than three persons have same degree of
responsibility for work, so all but first are
omitted and mark of omission and [et al.]
added – 1.1F5.

An example of a festschrift, here treated as a
work produced under editorial direction and
entered under title – 21.7B1. Added entry for
person honoured by festschrift – 21.30F1.

ROBERTS, James L.
  Hamlet : notes / James L. Roberts. –
Toronto : Coles, 1976.
  112 p. ; 22 cm. – (Coles notes ; 406).
  Cover title: Shakespeare Hamlet : notes.

  1. Title   2. Series

This work presents a discussion and
interpretation of 'Hamlet' but does not contain
any of the text of the play. It cannot therefore
be considered as a commentary (21.13) but
simply as a work of single personal authorship – 21.1A1, 21.1A2 and 21.4A1.

ROBINSON, John A.T.
  Honest to god / John A.T. Robinson. –
London : SCM Press, 1963.
  143 p. ; 19 cm.

  1. Title

Author is referred to on title page as 'John A.T.
Robinson, Bishop of Woolwich' but the title is
omitted from the statement of responsibility and
no mark of omission if necessary – 1.1F7.

Title is also omitted from heading – 22.15C.

RODIN MUSEUM
  Rodin Museum : handbook / by
John L. Tancock. – Philadelphia :
Philadelphia Museum of Art, 1969.
  103 p. : ill. ; 18 cm.

Work of administrative nature emanating from
corporate body and dealing with its resources is
entered under heading for body – 21.1B2(a). As
indicated in example no. 42, the phrase 'of an
administrative nature' is a little ambiguous but
the examples: 'National Gallery'; 'First National
Bank of Chicago'; and 'Royal Ontario Museum';
included in rule 21.4B1 appear to corroborate
this interpretation.

The ROMAUNT of the rose / edited by
  Frederick J. Furnivall. – London :
K. Paul, Trench, Trübner for the Chaucer
Society, 1911.
  ix, 101 p. ; 22 cm.
  "A reprint of the first printed edition by
William Thynne A.D. 1532".

  1. Furnivall, Frederick J.
  2. Chaucer Society
  3. [Roman de la rose. English
        (Middle English)]

If added entry is required for basic story found
in many versions, uniform title is title that is
established in English-language reference
sources; name of language is added – 25.12B.
Initial article omitted – 25.2C1. If language of
item is in an early form of a modern language,
name of modern language is added to uniform
title, followed by that of the early form in
parentheses – 25.5C1.

ROYAL COLLEGE OF SURGEONS.
  Museum
  Illustrated guide to the Museum of the
Royal College of Surgeons, England / by
Arthur Keith. – London : Printed for
The College and sold by Taylor and
Francis, 1910.
  vi, 132 p., [1] leaf of plates : ill., plans,
port. ; 22 cm.

  1. Title   2. Keith, Arthur

Inclusion in publication area of words indicating the function (other than solely publishing) performed by a body – 1.4D3(a).

Work of an administrative nature emanating from corporate body and dealing with its resources is entered under heading for body – 21.1B2(a). As indicated in example no. 42, the phrase 'of an administrative nature' is a little ambiguous but the examples noted in the annotation to this example and to example no. 181 appear to corroborate this interpretation. Name that includes the entire name of the higher body – 24.13A (Type 6). Name of the higher body omitted from subheading – 24.13A.

184

ROYAL COMMISSION ON LOCAL
   GOVERNMENT IN ENGLAND
   Local government reform : short version of the report of the Royal Commission on Local Government in England / presented to Parliament by command of Her Majesty June 1969. – London : H.M.S.O., 1969.
   vi, 22 p. : map ; 25 cm. – (Cmnd. ; 4039).
   Chairman: The Rt. Hon. Lord Redcliffe-Maud.

  1. Title
  2. Redcliffe-Maud, John Primatt
      Redcliffe Redcliffe-Maud, <u>Baron</u>

Abridgement under the heading for the original – 21.12A1. Work emanating from corporate body and recording its collective thought (in this case, the report of a commission) is entered under heading for body – 21.1B2(c). Body created by a government which does not need the name of the government for identification purposes entered under its own name – 24.17A and 24.18A (Type 2).

185

S.R. Ranganathan, 1892-1972 : papers
   given at a memorial meeting on Thursday 25th January 1973 / edited by Edward Dudley. – London : Library Association, 1974.
   40 p. : port. ; 22 cm.
   ISBN 0-85365-197-3.

  1. Dudley, Edward

If title proper includes initials with full stops between them, initials are recorded with full stops, but without spaces between them – 1.1B6.

Work emanating from body which is considered to lack a name (the indefinite article is used and 'memorial meeting' is relatively meaningless by itself) entered under title – 21.5A.

186

SALCOMBE and Kingsbridge :
   Dartmouth, Brixham, Paignton, Torquay and South Devon. – 5th ed. – London : Ward Lock, [1963].
   160 p., 11 p. of plates (some folded) : ill., maps, plans ; 18 cm. – (Red guides).

  1. Series

Volume which contains both leaves and pages of plates; number is recorded in terms of whichever is predominant – 2.5B10.

Work of unknown authorship entered under title – 21.5A.

187

SAN ANTONIO
   [La fin des haricots. English]
   The strangler / by San Antonio ; translated by Cyril Buhler. – London : Duckworth, 1968.
   144 p. ; 19 cm.
   Originally published: Paris : Editions Fleuve, 1961.
   ISBN 0-7156-0397-3.

  1. Title   2. The strangler

Entry under phrase – 22.11A. Apart from references needed in connection with the use of uniform title, a further reference would be required from the author's real name (Frederic Dard) – 26.1B1 and 26.2A1. No added entry under heading for translator because work does not fall into one of categories listed at 21.30K1.

188

SANGHARAKSHITA, *Bhikshu*
　The Three Jewels : an introduction to Buddhism / by Bhikshu Sangharakshita (Sthavira). – London : Rider, 1967.
　　xi, 276 p. ; 22 cm.

　　1.　Title

Vernacular term of address, etc. added to name of person of religious vocation – 22.16D1.

189

SCOTT, Robert
　The diaries of Captain Robert Scott : a record of the second Antarctic Expedition, 1910-1912. – High Wycombe : University Microfilms, 1968.
　　6 v. (ca. 2000 p.) : ill., ports. ; 21-26 cm.
　　Facsim. of: B.M. Add. Ms. 51024-41.
　　Includes facsim. of: South polar times. 1911.

　　1.　Title
　　2.　Scott Antarctic Expedition (2nd : 1910-1912)
　　3.　South Polar times

Rules for monographs in more than one volume do not give instructions on recording number of pages where work is printed without pagination – 2.5B17 to 2.5B22. However, estimate has been made in accordance with rule for single volumes – 2.5B7. If volumes in multivolume set differ in height by more than two centimetres, the smallest and largest size are given, separated by a hyphen – 2.5D3.

It might become necessary to distinguish this author from others with the same name. The fuller form of name could be added to the form by which this author is commonly identified – 22.18A, i.e.

　Scott, Robert (Robert Falcon)

An added entry under 'South polar times', as a related work, would be needed – 21.30G1 – unless it were decided to make an analytical entry – 13.5A. The added entry for the expedition is formulated by analogy with the rules for conferences. The footnote to the 'Challenger Expedition' example in rule 24.1A indicates that this is the method to follow.

190

SCOTT, Sir Walter
　[Novels. Selections]
　The Waverley pageant : the best passages from the novels of Sir Walter Scott ; selected, with critical introductions, by Hugh Walpole ; with notes by Wilfred Partington. – London : Eyre and Spottiswoode, 1932.
　　662 p. ; 20 cm.

　　1.　Title　　2.　The Waverley pageant
　　3.　Walpole, Hugh

Name associated with responsibility for the item is transcribed as part of other title information – 1.1E4. No further statement made – 1.1F13. Subsequent statements of responsibility recorded – 1.1F6 and preceded by semicolons – 1.1A1. An alternative solution would be to treat the statement of responsibility beginning with 'selected' as the first, and not a subsequent statement and precede it with a diagonal slash (see example no. 31).

Selections from the works of one personal author – 21.4A1. British title of honour inserted in heading – 22.12B1. If item consists of extracts from works of one person in a particular form, 'Selections' is added to collective title – 25.10A.

OKE'S
MAGISTERIAL FORMULIST

(A Companion Volume to Stone's Justices' Manual)

FORMS AND PRECEDENTS

SEVENTEENTH EDITION

BY

WILLIAM SCOTT, LL.B.(Lond.)
SOLICITOR ; CLERK TO THE JUSTICES FOR THE COUNTY
BOROUGH OF TEESSIDE.

LONDON
BUTTERWORTH & CO. (PUBLISHERS) LTD.
SHAW & SONS, LTD.

1968

SCOTT, William
    Oke's magisterial formulist ... : forms
and precedents. – 17th ed. / by William
Scott. – London : Butterworth, 1968.
    xii, 1088, 121 p. : forms ; 25 cm.
    "Companion volume to Stone's justices'
manual".
    Text on lining paper.
    ISBN 0-406-32603-7.

1.   Title   2.   Oke, George Colwell

Name associated with responsibility for item
transcribed as part of title and so no further
statement relating to that name needed –
1.1F13. Lengthy other title information omitted
from title and statement of responsibility area
and given in note – 1.1E3 and 1.7B5.
Statement of responsibility relating to edition
follows edition statement – 1.2C1. Two
publishers named on title page, but first only is
given, as second is not given prominence by
typography – 1.4D5. Date in publication area
refers to edition named in edition area – 1.4F1.
Number of pages in each numbered sequence
recorded – 2.5B2. Type of illustration
recorded – 2.5C2.

Edition that has been revised, updated, etc. is
entered under the heading for the reviser if the
wording of the chief source of information
indicates that the person responsible for the
original is no longer considered responsible for
the work (e.g. when the original author is
named only in the title proper and some other
person is named as being primarily responsible
in the statement of responsibility or in the
statement of responsibility relating to the
edition) – 21.12B1. A name-title added entry is
made under the heading for the original author.

SELECTIONS from the English novelists :
    an anthology of representative passages,
Henry Fielding to D.H. Lawrence / edited
by C.J. Lowe and R.J. Gates. –
London : Routledge and K. Paul, 1967.
    ix, 211 p. ; 20 cm.
    ISBN 0-7100-6031-9.

1.   Lowe, C.J.   2.   Gates, R.J.

Collection of a work produced under editorial
direction entered under title – 21.1C1(b).

SEMINAR ON THE DEVELOPMENT
    OF PUBLIC LIBRARIES IN ASIA
    (1955 : Delhi, India)
    Public libraries for Asia : the Delhi
Seminar. – Paris : Unesco, 1956.
    165 p., [9] p. of plates : ill. ; 22 cm. –
(Unesco public library manuals ; 7).

1.   Title   2.   Series

Conference not named on title page but name is
given in introduction and use of definite article
is taken as evidence of presence of name –
21.1B1. Access points are normally determined
from the chief source of information for the
item being catalogued but other statements
prominently stated may be taken into account
(21.0B1). 'Prominently stated' is defined (0.8) as
a formal statement found in one of the
prescribed sources of information for areas 1
and 2 of the item being catalogued. However,
information appearing in the content of an item
(e.g. the text of a book) may be used when a
statement appearing in the chief source of
information is ambiguous or insufficient (21.0B1).
'The Delhi Seminar' seems to be such an
ambiguous or insufficient statement and the
name of the conference given in the
introduction is therefore used. 'The Delhi
Seminar' is, however, a possible alternative
name from which a reference might be
required – 26.3A2.* The heading for this
reference would be:

Delhi Seminar (1955)

If the location is part of the name of a
conference, it is not repeated – 24.7B4.

SEUSS, Dr.
    One fish two fish red fish blue fish / by
Dr. Seuss. – London : Collins and
Harvill, 1960.
    63 p. : col. ill. ; 24 cm. – (Beginner
books. I can read it all by myself).
    Published by arrangement with: New
York : Random House.

1.   Title   2.   Series
3.   I can read it all by myself

Title included in statement of responsibility if
omission would leave only surname – 1.1F7(b).

Word or phrase associated with name added when name consists only of a surname – 22.15A. A reference would be required from the name in direct order.* If Seuss was not a real name entry would be under the phrase in direct order, e.g. Dr. X – 22.11A.

SHACKLETON, Keith
 Birds of the Atlantic Ocean / paintings by Keith Shackleton ; text by Ted Stokes ; foreword by H.R.H. The Prince Philip, Duke of Edinburgh. – Hamlyn for Country Life Books, 1968.
 156 p. : ill. (chiefly col.), maps ; 29 cm.

 1. Title   2. Stokes, Ted

Word of mixed responsibility resulting from the collaboration between an artist and a writer entered under the one named first unless the other's name is given greater prominence – 21.24A.

SHAKESPEARE, William
 [Plays. Selections]
 Shakespearian quotations in everyday use : a key to their source and context / by L.L.M. Marsden. – London : Witherby, 1927 (1964 printing).
 156 p. ; 18 cm.

 1. Title
 2. Shakespearian quotations in
     everyday use
 3. Marsden, L.L.M.

Optionally, date of printing can be given if found on the item and if considered important by the cataloguing agency – 2.4G2.

If item consists of extracts from works of one person in a particular form, uniform title consists of appropriate collective title, with the addition of 'Selections' – 25.10A.

SHAKESPEARE, William
 [Works]
 The complete works of William Shakespeare arranged in their chronological order / edited by W.G. Clark and W. Aldis Wright ; with an introduction to each play, adapted from the Shakespearian primer of Professor Dowden. – Garden City, N.Y. : Nelson Doubleday, [19--].
 2 v. (1140 p.) ; 22 cm.
 Two columns per page.

 1. Title
 2. The complete works of William
     Shakespeare
 3. Clark, W.G.
 4. Wright, W. Aldis

Number of volumes recorded – 2.5B17. Pagination given in parentheses if volumes continuously paged – 2.5B20. Note on important physical details not included in physical description area – 2.7B10 and 1.7B10.

Uniform titles – collective title 'Works' used for an item which consists of, or purports to be, the complete works of a person – 25.8A.

SHANKLAND, COX AND ASSOCIATES
 Ipswich draft basic plan : a consultants' proposals for the expanded town : a report to the Minister of Housing and Local Government and Ipswich County Borough / by Shankland, Cox and Associates. – London : H.M.S.O., 1968.
 151 p., [1] folded leaf of plates : ill. (some col.), maps, plans ; 30 cm.

 1. Title   2. Ipswich. Council
 3. United Kingdom. Ministry of
     Housing and Local Government

Work emanating from corporate body and recording its collective thought is entered under heading for body – 21.1B2(c). Ministry entered subordinately (in added entry heading) – 24.18A (Type 5). Ipswich is no longer a county borough; the Ministry of Housing and Local Government no longer exists. Appropriate references would have to be made – 26.1A.

Shop Stewards and Industrial Relations

by

T. W. Burrow   M. F. Somerton   T. G. Whittingham
N. Williams

Published by : The Department of Adult Education, University of Nottingham
and the Workers' Educational Association, East Midland District.

Printed by John Clough & Son, (Printers)
Blackstone Street Works
Nottingham
Tel. 83419

199

SHOP stewards and industrial relations /
   by T.W. Burrow ... [et al.]. –
Nottingham : University of Nottingham,
Dept. of Adult Education, 1968.
   98 p. ; 22 cm.
   Published jointly with the Workers'
Educational Association, East Midland
District.
   ISBN 0-802031-06-6.

1.   Burrow, T.W.
2.   University of Nottingham.
       Department of Adult Education
3.   Workers' Educational Association.
       East Midland District

More than three persons have same degree of
responsibility, so first only is recorded – 1.1F5.
Two publishers named on title page, but second
not recorded in publication area as it is not
given prominence by typography – 1.4D5. No
rule for recording publishing agency that
includes subordinate body, but example for
motion pictures and sound recordings has been
used as authority and subordinate and higher
body have been separated by comma – 7.4E1.
Note on publication details not included in
publication area – 2.7B9.

Responsibility is shared between more than
three persons and principal responsibility is not
attributed to any one, two or three, so entry is
under title – 21.6C2. Added entries for
prominently named publishers whose
responsibility extends beyond merely publishing
the work – 21.30E1.

200

SHOPPING in the United States / U.S.,
   Department of Commerce, United States
Travel Service. – [Washington?] : USTS,
1976.
   64 p. : ill. ; 23 x 11 cm.
   USTS-763 E.

1.   United States Travel Service

Work emanating from corporate body which
does not fall within any of the categories listed
in rule 21.1B2 and is therefore entered under
title – 21.1C1(c). In added entry, body created
or controlled by a government is entered under
its own name as it does not belong to any of
the types listed in 24.18A – 24.17A.

201

SINHA, Dharnidhar Prasad
   Culture change in an intertribal market :
the role of the Banari intertribal market
among the hill people of Chatanagpur / by
Dharnidhar Prasad Sinha. – London :
Asia Publishing House, 1968.
   xvi, 117 p., 14 p. of plates : ill.,
4 maps ; 22 cm.
   Bibliography: p. 109-112.
   ISBN 0-210-27031-4.

1.   Title

Entry under element of name which identifies
individual and functions as surname – 22.5B1.
Also applicable is rule for Indic name of person
flourishing after the middle of the nineteenth
century. Entry is under surname or the name
that the person is known to have used as a
surname – 22.25B1.

SMITH, John L.
Rail to Tenterden / by John L.
Smith. – Sutton [Surrey] : Lens of
Sutton, 1967.
  80 p. : chiefly ill., facsims., map ;
25 cm.

1. Title

Name of county given after place of publication
if considered necessary for identification –
1.4C3. (Name is not abbreviated, because list of
stipulated abbreviations of place names does
not include places in United Kingdom – B.14A.)

202

[SLOVO o polku Igoreve. English]
  The tale of the armament of Igor, A.D.
1185 : a Russian historical epic / edited
and translated by Leonard A. Magnus. –
London : Oxford University Press, 1915.
  lxiii, 122 p., [1] leaf of plates : map ;
23 cm. – (Publications of the Philological
Society).
  ''With revised Russian text, notes,
introduction and glossary''.
  Bibliography: p. 119-122.

1. Magnus, Leonard A.
2. The tale of the armament of Igor †
3. Series

Words in quoted notes not abbreviated – B.5A.

Original language of anonymous work created
before 1501 is not written in Greek nor in
roman script, so original title is used as uniform
title, since no established title exists in
English – 25.4C1. Name of language added to
title as it is different from original – 25.5C1.

205

The SPANISH Inquisition : a collection
  of contemporary documents / compiled
and edited by John Langdon-Davies. –
London : Jackdaw : Distributed by
J. Cape, 1966.
  16 pieces : ill. ; 21 x 22-42 x 37 cm. +
notes (1 sheet) in folder, 24 x 37 cm. –
(Jackdaw ; no. 44).
  Partial contents: A procession to an auto
de fe : engraving / by B. Schoonebeck –
A bond written by a nun making a pact
with the devil – The loyal martyrs : an
English ballad sheet.

1. Langdon-Davies, John
2. Series

Optionally, name of distributor may be given
following name of publisher – 1.4D6. Words or
phrase indicating function of distributor
retained – 1.4D3(a). Multipart item described in
terms of 'pieces' as 'v' (i.e. 'volume') is not
appropriate – 2.5B18 (rule 1.10C2(c) uses
'various pieces' for an item made up of a large
number of heterogeneous materials – see
example no. 6). Sizes of parts in multipart set
differing in size given here in similar manner to
differing volumes in multivolume set, i.e.
smallest size and largest size (when difference is
more than two centimetres) – 2.5D3.
Accompanying material recorded in physical
description – 2.5E1. Optionally, the container is
named and its dimensions given – 1.5D2.
Series statement recorded – 2.6B1 and 1.6B1,
with number given in terms used in the item –
1.6G1 (abbreviations – B.9 and numerals as
instructed in C.2B1).

203

SMART, Ted
  Art masterpieces of the National Gallery,
London / designed and produced by Ted
Smart and David Gibbon. – New York :
Crescent, 1978.
  [64] p. : chiefly col. ill. ; 28 cm. – (Art
masterpiece series).
  ISBN 0-517-25988-5.

1. Title   2. Gibbon, David
3. Series

Work which describes the resources of a
corporate body, but which does not emanate
from that body, entered under the heading for
the responsible person – 21.1A2. Principal
responsibility is not indicated and entry is
therefore under first named person – 21.6C1.

See also example no. 157.

SPENCER's decimal percentage and
    discount reckoner. – London :
J. Spencer, 1970.
    176 p. ; 18 cm.
    ISBN 0-85436-003-4.

1.   John Spencer & Co. (Publishers)

Publisher recorded in shortest form in which it
can be understood and identified internationally – 1.4D2. (Appears on title page as:
John Spencer & Co. (Publishers) Ltd.)

Work which appears to emanate from a
corporate body but which does not fall into any
of the categories listed in 21.1B2 is entered
under title – 21.1C1(c). An alternative
interpretation of the rules would be to treat it as
an anonymous work, but this would not alter
the entry – 21.1C1. If the first interpretation is
adopted, an added entry is needed under 'John
Spencer & Co. (Publishers)' as a prominently-
named corporate body; this entry would also be
needed for the second interpretation, as the firm
is a publisher whose responsibility extends
beyond that of merely publishing the work –
21.30E1.

STANDARD TELEPHONES AND
    CABLES
    What everyone who uses a telephone
should know about telecommunications /
Standard Telephone and Cables
Limited. – London : STC, [1976].
    [8] p. : col. ill. ; 30 cm.
    Brief survey of telecommunications in
general and STC's part in it in particular.
    Available also as wallchart (col. ;
62 x 89 cm.).

1.   Title

Same item available in different formats. Note
on the other format – 1.7B16.

Work is of an administrative nature in that it
serves as an advertisement for the operations of
the corporate body from which it emanates. It is
therefore entered under the heading for the
body – 21.1B2(a). Entry directly under name –
24.1A. 'Ltd' omitted from heading – 24.5C1.

STEPHEN BONE (Exhibition) (1986 :
    London, England)
    Stephen Bone : [an exhibition catalogue]
8th-31st October, 1986. – London : Sally
Hunter & Patrick Seale Fine Art, 1986.
    1 sheet : col. ill. ; 23 x 510 cm. folded
to 23 x 17 cm.
    With biographical notes.

1.   Bone, Stephen
2.   Sally Hunter & Patrick Seale Fine
      Art

Title proper needs explanation, therefore brief
addition supplied as other title information –
1.1E6. Single sheet described as '1 sheet' –
2.5B2. Height and width recorded, together with
dimensions when folded if sheet is designed for
issue folded – 2.5D4.

This work could be treated as a work emanating
from a corporate body which is of an
administrative nature dealing with the corporate
body itself – 21.1B2(a), or it could be treated as
an ad hoc event, an exhibition – 21.1B2(d). In
the former instance it would be entered under
the heading for the gallery and in the latter
under the name of the exhibition. As the name
of the exhibition is given greater prominence
and as this is not a catalogue of the resources
of the gallery (the paintings exhibited were
being sold by the Bone family), the
interpretation adopted here is to enter under the
name of the exhibition and to make an added
entry under the name of the gallery. As the
main entry heading does not convey the idea of
a corporate body, a general designation has
been added – 24.4B1. Date and location of
exhibition added – 24.8B1. No added title entry
as title proper is essentially the same as main
entry heading – 21.30J1(a).

STEVENSON, D.E. (Donald Edward)
    Metabolic disorders of domestic
animals / D.E. Stevenson and
A.A. Wilson. – Oxford : Blackwell
Scientific, 1963.
    xiv, 198 p. : ill. ; 23 cm.

1.   Title   2.   Wilson, A.A.

Work of shared responsibility between two persons. Principal responsibility is not attributed to either, so entry is under the heading for the one named first, with an added entry under the heading for the other – 21.6C1. Writer is known by surname and initials, but forenames in spelled out form are added and enclosed in parentheses to distinguish between names that are otherwise identical (see also next example) – 22.18A. Optionally, such additions may be made to other names containing initials.

210

STEVENSON, D.E. (Dorothy Emily)
  The house on the cliff / D.E. Stevenson. – 1st large print ed. – Anstey, Leicestershire ; Thorpe, 1977.
  480 p. (large print) ; 23 cm. – (Ulverscroft large print series).
  First published: London : Collins, 1966.
  ISBN 0-85456-537-X.

  1. Title   2.   Series

If item is in large print, statement of number of pages has (large print) added – 2.5B24. Edition statement transcribed as found on the item, using standard abbreviations – 1.2B1.

An added entry is not normally required for a series in which the items are related to each other only by common physical characteristics – 21.30L1. However, such an entry in this instance might well prove of convenience to users.

See also annotation following previous example.

211

STRAIGHT facts about sex and birth control. – London : Family Planning Information Service, [1977?].
  1 sheet (10 columns) ; 21 x 60 cm. folded to 21 x 10 cm.

  1. Family Planning Information Service

Although this item consists of one folded sheet, it contains ten numbered columns. This interpretation for the physical description has therefore been derived by using a combination of the appropriate terms from the supplied list – 2.5B2.

212

STREATFEILD, Noel
  Nicholas / by Marlie Brande ; translated by Elizabeth Boas ; adapted by Noel Streatfeild. – London : Benn, 1968.
  [29] p. : ill. (some col.) ; 20 x 24 cm.
  Originally published as: Nat ned Nikolaj. Copenhagen : Gyldendal, 1966.

  1. Title   2.   Brande, Marlie
  3. [Nat ned Nikolaj. English]

Pages are unnumbered so number is given in square brackets – 2.5B7. Width recorded as it is greater than height – 2.5D2. Note on other manifestation of same work – 1.7A4.

Adaptation entered under heading for adapter – 21.10A. Name-title added entry for the original work – 21.10A and 21.30G1.

213

SUMMER jobs abroad 1988. – 19th ed. / editor David Woodworth ; assisted by Heather Perry. – Oxford : Vacation Work, 1988.
  206 p. ; 21 cm.
  Verso of t.-p.: The directory of summer jobs abroad.
  ISBN 0-907638-80-5.

  1. Woodworth, David
  2. Perry, Heather

Item contains both an International Standard Book Number and an International Standard Serial Number. It could be described as a printed monograph, as illustrated here, or as a serial, as illustrated in example no. 458.

SYMPOSIUM ON ADVANCED
MEDICINE (4th : 1968 : Royal College
of Physicians of London)
Fourth Symposium on Advanced
Medicine / proceedings of a conference
held at the Royal College of Physicians of
London, 26th February-1st March, 1968 ;
edited by Oliver Wrong. – London :
Pitman Medical in association with the
Journal of the Royal College of Physicians
of London, 1968.
    xii, 420 p. : ill. ; 23 cm.
    Bibliography: p. 419-420.
    ISBN 0-272-79267-5.

1. Wrong, Oliver
2. Royal College of Physicians of
    London

Conference as corporate body – 21.1B1 and
21.1B2(d). Word denoting number omitted from
heading (i.e. not 'FOURTH SYMPOSIUM
ON·....') – 24.7A1. Number, date and place
where held added to heading – 24.7B1
(number – 24.7B2, date – 24.7B3, location,
which may be the name of an institution –
24.7B4).

215
SYMPOSIUM ON BIOTECHNOLOGY
FOR FUELS AND CHEMICALS
(5th : 1983 : Gallinburg, Tenn.)
Fifth Symposium on Biotechnology for
Fuels and Chemicals / proceedings of the
Fifth Symposium on Biotechnology for
Fuels and Chemicals, held in Gallinburg,
Tennessee, May 10-13 ; sponsored by the
Department of Energy and the Oak Ridge
National Laboratory ; editor Charles D.
Scott. – New York : Wiley, c1984.
    viii, 672 p. : ill. ; 23 cm. –
(Biotechnology and bioengineering
symposium, ISSN 0572-6565 ; no. 13).
    ISBN 0-471-88173-2.

1. Title   2. Scott, Charles D.
3. Series

Title and statement of responsibility given in the
form that they appear in item – 1.1B1 and
1.1F1. When a name associated with
responsibility for the item is transcribed as part

of the title proper, a further statement is not
made unless such a statement is required for
clarity, or unless, as in this case, a separate
statement of responsibility including that name
appears in the chief source of information –
1.1F13. ISSN of a series recorded – 1.6F1.

Conference as corporate body – 21.1B1. Work
which records the collective activity of a
conference entered under heading for that
body – 21.1B2(d). Entry directly under name –
24.1A. Addition of number, date and location –
24.7B1, 24.7B2, 24.7B3 and 24.7B4.

216
T.J. SMITH & NEPHEW LTD. Medical
Division
Elastoplast technique : a classified
reference to the use of Elastoplast in
modern surgery. – 10th ed. – Hull :
T.J.S. & N., 1942.
    87 p. : 86 ill. ; 23 cm.
    Prepared by: T.J. Smith & Nephew
Ltd., Medical Division.
    Issued to the medical profession only.

1. Title

A statement of responsibility is included in the
preface but, as this is not "prominent", the
relevant information is given in a note – 1.1F2
and 1.7B6. Number of illustrations recorded if it
can be easily ascertained – 2.5C4. Optional
note on terms of availability – 1.8D1.

Work emanating from a corporate body which is
concerned with the use of one of its products. It
seems reasonable, therefore, to consider the
item as being of an administrative nature and to
enter it under the heading for the body in
accordance with 21.1B2(a). 'Ltd' required to
make it clear that name is that of a corporate
body – 24.5C1. Subordinate body as
subheading of name of body to which it is
subordinate because name contains a term that
by definition implies that the body is part of
another – 24.13A (Type 1).

217

TALBOT MOTOR COMPANY.
    Franchising Department
    Peugeot/Talbot authorised dealers in the
United Kingdom and Eire / issued by
Franchising Department Talbot Motor
Company Limited. – 2nd ed. –
Coventry : Talbot, 1982.
    61 p. ; 22 cm.
    Ref.: C9628/1/25.

    1. Title

Work of an administrative nature emanating
from a corporate body and dealing with the
body itself is entered under the heading for the
body – 21.1B2(a).

218

TANNER, Ogden
    Stress / by Ogden Tanner and the
editors of Time-Life Books. – Authorized
British ed. – Nederland : Time-Life
International, 1977.
    176 p. : ill. ; 27 cm. – (Human
behaviour).
    Previously published: U.S. : Time-Life
Books, 1976.

    1. Title   2.   Time-Life Books
    3. Series

Name of country given as place of publication – 1.4C6.

Work of shared responsibility resulting from the
collaboration between a person and a corporate
body – 21.6A1(f). Principal responsibility is not
attributed to either one so entry is under the
heading for the one named first – 21.6C1.

219

TAYLOR, Frank
    The Comaneci story / by Frank Taylor ;
edited by Don Bate; cover and poster
photographs by Don Morley, Allsport ;
[other] photographs by Daily Mirror
photographers ... [et al.]. – London :
Mirror Group Newspapers, 1976.
    44 p. : ill., ports. ; 30 cm. + 1 poster
(col. ; 60 x 42 cm.).
    Cover title: Daily Mirror presents the
Comaneci story.

    1. Title   2.   Bate, Don
    3. Morley, Don   4.   Daily Mirror

Statements of responsibility recorded in the
order of their sequence in the chief source of
information – 1.1F6. Explanatory word
added – 1.1F8. Accompanying material
recorded in physical description area – 2.5E1
and 1.5E1(d). Note on variant title – 2.7B4.

220

TECHNICAL services for industry :
    technical information and other services
available from government departments
and associated organisations / Department
of Trade and Industry. – London : The
Department, 1970.
    302 p. ; 21 cm.

    1. United Kingdom. Department of
        Trade and Industry

Work emanating from corporate body but not
falling within any of the categories listed at
21.1B2 is entered under title – 21.1C1(c).
Added entry under corporate body – 21.30E1.
The Department of Trade and Industry was
formed by an amalgamation of the Ministry of
Technology and the Board of Trade in 1971. In
1974 the Department of Trade and Industry was
replaced by four separate bodies including the
Department of Industry and the Department of
Energy. This is a complex situation which would
require explanatory references to link the
various names – see 26.3C1(b) particularly the
United Kingdom. Ministry of Technology
example.

The Open University

Social Sciences : a second level course Urban development Unit 26

The new town idea

Prepared for the Course Team
by Ray Thomas and Peter Cresswell

The Open University Press

Other title information of series included if it provides valuable information identifying the series – 1.6D1; it is preceded by colon – 1.6A1. Subseries named and preceded by full stop – 1.6H1 and 1.6A1. Item belongs to two series; each statement enclosed in parentheses – 1.6J1.

Responsibility shared between two persons, neither of whom is attributed with principal responsibility. Entry is therefore under first-named – 21.6C1. Rules instruct that added entry be made under heading for series if it provides useful collocation – 21.30L1. For this example, an entry would appear to be useful under each series title and the subseries title.

See also example no. 259.

221

THOMAS, Ray
   The new town idea / prepared for the Course Team [of] The Open University by Ray Thomas and Peter Cresswell. – Milton Keynes : Open Univ. Press, 1973.
   64 p. : ill. ; 30 cm. – (Social sciences : a second level course. Urban development ; Unit 26) (DT 201 26).
   ISBN 0-335-01751-7.

1. Open University
2. Cresswell, Peter   3.   Series
4. Urban development
5. DT 201 26

STORIES FROM DICKENS

OLIVER TWIST, DAVID COPPERFIELD,

THE OLD CURIOSITY SHOP,

AND GREAT EXPECTATIONS

RETOLD FOR BOYS AND GIRLS

BY

RUSSELL THORNDIKE

RAPHAEL TUCK & SONS LTD.

Fine Art Publishers to Their Majesties the King and Queen and to Her Majesty Queen Mary

LONDON · NEW YORK · TORONTO

THORNDIKE, Russell
  Stories from Dickens / retold for boys
and girls by Russell Thorndike. –
London : R. Tuck, [194-].
    125 p. : ill. ; 20 cm.
    Contents: Oliver Twist – David
Copperfield – The Old curiosity shop –
Great expectations.

  1. Title   2. Dickens, Charles
  3. Optionally, analytical title entries
          for each part

Title page bears both collective title and titles of
individual works, so former is given as title
proper and latter are recorded in note – 1.1B10,
2.7B18 and 1.7B18. In the United States, the
publication, distribution, etc. area would be
given as:
    London ; New York : R. Tuck
and in Canada, as:
    London : Toronto : R. Tuck
– 1.4C5. Name of publisher given in shortest
form in which it can be understood and
identified – 1.4D2.

Adaptation for children entered under the
heading for the adapter – 21.10A.

Compare with examples no. 11, 66, 231.

THOSE Dutch Catholics / edited by
  Michel van der Plas and Henk Suer ;
preface by Desmond Fisher ; translated
from the Dutch by Theo Westow. –
London : Chapman, 1967.
    164 p. ; 23 cm. – ([Here and now]).

  1. Plas, Michel van der
  2. Suer, Hank   3. Series

Chief source of information for series of printed
monograph is the whole publication – 2.0B2.
However, series statement has been taken from
a source other than the prescribed source, and
so is enclosed in square brackets within
parentheses – 1.6A2.

Work produced under editorial direction entered
under title – 21.1C1(b). For Dutch surname with
prefix, entry is under part following prefix unless
prefix is 'ver' – 22.5D1.

THREE Restoration comedies / edited
  with an introduction by Gamini
Salgado. – Harmondsworth : Penguin,
1968.
    365 p. : 3 facsims. ; 18 cm. – (English
library).
    Contents: The man of mode / Sir
George Etherege – The country wife /
William Wycherley – Love for love /
William Congreve.

  1. Salgado, Gamini
  2. Optionally, author and title
          analytical entries for each part

Contents note – 2.7B18 and 1.7B18. Analytical
added entries may be made for parts when
comprehensive entry for larger work shows
parts either in title and statement of
responsibility area or in note area – 13.2A.

Entry under title for collection produced under
editorial direction – 21.1C1(b).

TOLSTOI, Alexei Nikolaevich, Count
  [Petr Pervyi : roman / A.N. Tolstoi ;
redaktor E. Romashkina]. – [Moskva :
Pravda], 1968.
    743 p. : ill. ; 21 cm. – ([Shkolnaya
biblioteka]).

  1. Title   2. Romashkina, E.
  3. Series

This item is printed in Cyrillic, in this case
Russian. The rules give no authority for
romanizing a title proper. The only relevant
statement appears in rule 1.1B1, where it
instructs that symbols in a title proper that
cannot be reproduced by the typographical
facilities available are replaced by a cataloguer's
description in square brackets. The same applies
to the statement of responsibility (1.1F9), the
publication details and the series statement (see
also 1.0E). Although square brackets have been
used in the above entry, in practice some
cataloguing agencies may wish to omit them.

Heading for name written in nonroman script is
romanized – 22.3C2. Title of nobility included in
heading if title commonly appears with name in
works by the person or in reference sources –
22.12A1.

The rules do recognize that there may be a need for romanization and make use of the ALA/LC rules when this is called for. The above example, however, has been formulated using British Standard BS 2979 : 1958.

See also example no. 117.

226

The TOWER of London / Ministry of
 Public Building and Works. – London :
H.M.S.O., 1967.
 55 p. : ill. ; 20 cm. + 1 plan (39 x 58
cm. folded to 20 x 12 cm.). – (Ministry
of Public Building and Works official
guide).
 Plan, scale 1:900, attached to inside
cover.

 1. United Kingdom. <u>Ministry of Public
   Building and Works</u>
 2. Series

Accompanying material recorded in the physical description area – 1.5E1(d). Optionally, dimensions of accompanying material given – 1.5E1. Note on the location of accompanying material and note on details not given in physical description area – 2.7B11.

Work emanating from a corporate body but not falling within any of the categories listed at 21.1B2 is entered under title – 21.1C1(c).

Compare with example no. 121.

227

TRANSPORT Act 1968 : a C.B.I.
 summary and assessment. – London :
C.B.I., 1969.
 42 p. ; 21 cm.
 ISBN 0-85201-001-X.

 1. C.B.I.
 2. United Kingdom
   [Transport Act (1968)]

Work emanating from corporate body but not falling within any of the categories listed at 21.1B2 is entered under title – 21.1C1(c). Variant forms of name appear on items issued by body (i.e. 'C.B.I.' or 'Confederation of British Industry'), but name as it appears in chief source of information is given as added entry heading – 24.2B. (A reference would be needed from form not used – 26.3A4.)

TRAQUAIR, Phoebe Anna
 Dante : illustrations and notes / [the
illustrations by Phoebe Anna Traquair ;
the notes by John Sutherland Black]. –
Edinburgh : T. & A. Constable, 1890.
 xcv, 83 p. : 21 ill. ; 23 cm.
 Ill. for Dante's Divine comedy.
 Notes comprise: A Dante chronology –
A short bibliography – Dante's library –
Index.

 1. Title
 2. Black, John Sutherland
 3. Dante Alighieri
   [Divina commedia]

This work consists principally of one artist's illustrations for a text, and they are entered under the heading for the artist as they are published separately from the text. A name-title added entry is made under the heading for the writer of the original work – 21.11B1. The work is also one of mixed responsibility resulting from a collaboration between artist and writer. Again, entry must be under the heading for the artist, as the one named first in the source of information. An added entry is made under the heading for the writer – 21.24A.

EUROPEAN
COMMUNITIES

Miscellaneous No. 5 (1972)

Treaty

establishing

The European Economic
Community

Rome, 25 March 1957

[The United Kingdom is not a party to the Treaty]

*Presented to Parliament
by the Secretary of State for Foreign and Commonwealth Affairs
by Command of Her Majesty
January 1972*

LONDON
HER MAJESTY'S STATIONERY OFFICE
£1 net

Cmnd. 4864

[TREATY OF ROME (1957)]
Treaty Establishing the European Economic Community : Rome, 25 March 1957 / presented to Parliament by the Secretary of State for Foreign and Commonwealth Affairs by command of Her Majesty, January 1972. – London : H.M.S.O., 1972.

vii, 170 p. ; 25 cm. – (Miscellaneous ; no. 5 (1972)) (Cmnd. ; 4864).

At head of title: European communities.
Signatories: Belgium, West Germany, France, Italy, Luxembourg, Netherlands.
ISBN 0-10-148640-5.

1. Treaty Establishing the European Economic Community

Names of treaties capitalized – A.20A. Two series statements recorded separately, the more specific one first – 1.6J1. Numbering within series recorded in terms given in the item – 2.6B1 and 1.6G1. Note on additional title borne by item – 2.7B4.

Treaty between more than three national governments entered under title – 21.35A2. Uniform title for treaty between more than three parties is name by which treaty is commonly known, with year of signing added in parentheses – 25.16B2. No added entry under 'United Kingdom', because, although it is both the home government and the publishing government, it is not a signatory of the treaty – 21.35A2.

HARALDR THE HARD-RULER AND HIS POETS

By

G. TURVILLE-PETRE

VIGFUSSON READER AND TITULAR PROFESSOR
OF ANCIENT ICELANDIC LITERATURE AND ANTIQUITIES
IN THE UNIVERSITY OF OXFORD

*The Dorothea Coke Memorial Lecture
in Northern Studies
delivered at University College London
1 December 1966*

PUBLISHED FOR THE COLLEGE
BY H. K. LEWIS & CO. LTD LONDON

TURVILLE-PETRE, G.
Haraldr the Hard-Ruler and his poets / by G. Turville-Petre. – London : H.K. Lewis for the [University] College, 1968.

20 p., 1 leaf of plates ; 26 cm. – (Dorothea Coke memorial lecture in northern studies ; 1966).

1. Title   2. Series

Two bodies named in publication area; both are included because they are linked in a single statement – 1.4D5(a). Numbering of series (in this instance, a chronological designation) given in terms used in item – 1.6G1.

Hyphenated surname entered under first element – 22.5C3.*

231

TWO satyr plays / translated with an introduction by Roger Lancelyn Green. – Harmondsworth : Penguin, 1957.
  95 p. ; 18 cm. – (Penguin classics).
  Contents: The cyclops / Euripedes – The searching satyrs / Sophocles.
  With: Appendix : two dithyrambs.

  1. Green, Roger Lancelyn
  2. Euripedes
       The cyclops
  3. Sophocles
       The searching satyrs
  4. The cyclops
  4. The searching satyrs

Title page has both collective title and titles of individual works, so former is given as title proper and latter are recorded in note – 1.1B10. Sophocles' play is named on collective title page as 'Ichneutai', but when a title is recorded formally in a note, the heading of the part of the item to which it refers is recorded – 2.7B18.

Collection of translations of works by different authors treated as general collection – 21.14B. Collection with collective title entered under title; added entry made for editor, and name-title added entries made for independent works, as there are not more than three – 21.7B1.

232

UNION OF SOVIET SOCIALIST REPUBLICS
  [Treaties, etc. United States, 1987 Dec. 8]
  Treaty Between the United States of America and the Union of Soviet Socialist Republics on the Elimination of Their Intermediate-range and Shorter-range Missiles. – London : United States Information Service, [1988].
  30 leaves ; 31 cm.

  1. Title   2. United States
  3. Treaty Between the United States
       of America . . .

Capitalization in title of treaties – A.20A.

Treaty entered under heading for appropriate corporate body – 21.1B2(b). For treaties between two national governments, entry is under first in alphabetical order, with added entry for the other – 21.35A1. Conventional name of government used – 24.3E1. English form of the name of the place which is the English form of the name of the government that has jurisdiction used – 23.2A1. Uniform title for single treaties – 25.16B1.

233

UNITED KINGDOM
  [British Library Act]
  British Library Act 1972. – London : H.M.S.O., 1972
  9 p. ; 24 cm.
  ISBN 0-10-545472-9.

  1. Title

Formal name of legislative act capitalized – A.20A.

Laws governing one jurisdiction entered under heading for jurisdiction governed by them – 21.31B1.[1] Official short title used as uniform title; date omitted because no other laws entered under same heading – 25.15A2.

---

[1] The conventional name (see rule 24.3E1) for the United Kingdom of Great Britain and Ireland is:

  United Kingdom

However, in large cataloguing agencies such as national libraries where, for many years, Great Britain has been used as a heading rather than United Kingdom, the cost of retrospective change may dictate that the former heading is retained. See also the explanatory reference example in rule 26.3C1(c)(ii).

234

UNITED KINGDOM
[Public Libraries and Museums Act (1964)]
Public Libraries and Museums Act 1964 : Chapter 75. – London : H.M.S.O., 1964.
ii, 22 p. ; 25 cm.

1. Title

Formal name of legislative act capitalized – A.20A.

Laws governing one jurisdiction entered under heading for jurisdiction governed by them – 21.31B1. Official short title used as uniform title; date added if several laws entered under same heading – 25.15A2.

235

UNITED KINGDOM. Army
Drill (all arms) / prepared under the direction of the Chief of General Staff. – London : H.M.S.O., 1965.
vi, 159 p. : ill. ; 19 cm.

1. Title

Work of administrative nature emanating from corporate body and dealing with its procedures is entered under heading for body – 21.1B2(a).

Principal armed service entered as direct sub-heading of name of government – 24.18A (Type 8) and 24.24A1. Geographical entity used as name of government – 23.1A. Subheading for government official not mentioned at 24.20 is that of agency that official represents – 24.20E1.

236

UNITED KINGDOM. Army. Lancashire Rifle Volunteer Regiment, Fifteenth
Fifteenth Lancashire Rifle Volunteer Regiment : prize list for 1877. – [Liverpool], 1877.
[12] p. ; 21 cm.

Work of administrative nature emanating from corporate body and dealing with its staff is entered under heading for body – 21.1B2(a). Principal armed service entered as direct subheading of name of government – 24.18A (Type 8) and 24.24A1. Component branch entered as direct subheading of heading for

principal armed service; numbering added after name in style found on item – 24.24A1.

237

UNITED KINGDOM. Committee of Inquiry into Trawler Safety
Trawler safety : final report of the Committee of Inquiry into Trawler Safety. – London : H.M.S.O., 1969.
x, 167 p. : ill., map ; 25 cm. – (Cmnd. ; 4114).
Committee appointed by the President of the Board of Trade and chaired by Sir Deric Holland-Martin.
ISBN 0-10-141140-5.

1. Title
2. Holland-Martin, Sir Deric

Work emanating from corporate body and recording its collective thought (in this case, the report of a committee) is entered under heading for corporate body – 21.1B2(c). Government agency containing name implying administrative subordination (i.e. 'Committee') entered subordinately – 24.18A (Type 2).* No specific rule for making added entry under heading for chairman of committee, but rule instructing that one be made for name having relationship to work that would provide important access point has been used as authority – 21.30F1.

238

UNITED KINGDOM. General Register Office
A digest of the results of the census of England and Wales in 1901 : arranged in tabular form, together with an explanatory introduction / compiled by William Sanders and produced under the general supervision of Thomas G. Ackland. – London : Layton, 1903.
xxxi, 131 p. ; 23 cm.

1. Title †   2. Sanders, William
3. Ackland, Thomas G.

Title page indicates that item is a digest of the 1901 census and the introduction repeats that the work 'claims to be nothing more than this; condensed from the voluminous folios recently issued by the Census office'. Entry is therefore under the heading for the original work – 21.12A1. The census was carried out by the Registrar-General and entry would therefore be made under the corporate heading for this official – 21.4D1 in the form indicated by rule – 24.20E1. Body entered subordinately, as name is general in nature – 24.18A (Type 3).*

agency whose name normally implies administrative subordination entered as subheading of heading for government, providing name of government is required for identification of agency – 24.18A (Type 2).

239

UNITED KINGDOM. Office of Arts & Libraries
Financing our public library service : four subjects for debate : a consultative paper / presented to Parliament by the Minister for the Arts, by command of Her Majesty, February 1988. – London : H.M.S.O., 1988.
21 p. ; 30 cm. – (Cm 324).

1. Title

Government official entered under the agency or office that the official represents – 24.20E1. An alternative interpretation might be to treat this work as an item emanating from a ministry that is identified only by the title of the official; entry would then be under the heading for the jurisdiction followed by the title of the official, i.e.:

UNITED KINGDOM. Minister for the Arts

In either case, the headings would need to be linked by references – 26.3A. Prior to 1983 the Office of Arts & Libraries was part of the Department of Education and Science and explanatory references linking these two bodies would also be required.

240

UNITED KINGDOM. Office of the Registrar of Restrictive Trading Agreements
Guide to the registration of goods under the Resale Prices Act 1964 : notes / by the Registrar of Restrictive Trading Agreements. – London : H.M.S.O., 1964.
5 p. ; 24 cm.

1. Title

Capitalization for legislative acts – A.20A.

Work emanating from corporate body and recording its collective thought is entered under heading for body – 21.1B2(c). Government

Public Libraries and Museums

A
B I L L

To place the public library service provided by local authorities in England and Wales under the superintendence of the Minister of Education, to make new provision for regulating and improving that service and as to the provision and maintenance of museums and art galleries by such authorities, and for purposes connected with the matters aforesaid.

Presented by Sir Edward Boyle
Supported by
Mr. Quintin Hogg, Mr. Secretary Heath, Sir Keith Joseph, Mr. Alan Green and Mr. Chataway

Ordered, by The House of Commons, *to be Printed*, 24 *January*, 1964

LONDON
PRINTED AND PUBLISHED BY
HER MAJESTY'S STATIONERY OFFICE
Price 1s. 6d. net
[Bill 67]   (37807)   42/5

UNITED KINGDOM. Parliament.
House of Commons
Public Libraries and Museums : a bill to
place the public library service provided by
local authorities in England and Wales
under the superintendence of the Minister
of Education ... / presented by Sir
Edward Boyle ; supported by Quintı
Hogg ... [et al.]. – London : H.M.S.O.,
1964.
iii, 17 p. ; 25 cm. – ([H.C.] Bill ;
[1963-64] 67).

1. Title   2. Boyle, Sir Edward

Long title may be abridged if this can be done
without loss of essential information – 1.1B4.

Legislative bill entered under heading for
appropriate legislative body – 21.31B3.
Legislative body entered as subheading of
heading for government – 24.18A (Type 6). For
legislature with more than one chamber,
chamber is entered as subheading of heading
for the legislature – 24.21A. No added entry is
required for Quintin Hogg but, if it were, the
heading would be:

Hailsham of St. Marylebone, Quintin Hogg,
Baron

and references would be required for changes
of name. See example in rule 22.6B3.

UNITED KINGDOM. Parliament. House
of Lords
Architects Registration (Amendment) :
a bill intituled An act to amend section 14
of the Architects (Registration) Act
1931 ... – London : H.M.S.O., 1969.
4 p. ; 25 cm. – ([H.L.] Bill ; [1968-69]
129).
Brought from the Commons 2nd July
1969.

1. Title

Legislative bill entered under heading for
appropriate legislative body – 21.31B3. For
legislature with more than one chamber,
chamber is entered as subheading of heading
for the legislature – 24.21A.

UNITED KINGDOM. Prime Minister
Statement on the findings of the
Conference of Privy Councillors /
presented to Parliament by the Prime
Minister. – London : H.M.S.O., 1956.
5 p. ; 25 cm. – (Cmnd. ; 9715).

1. Title
2. Conference of Privy Councillors
on Security

Official communications from heads of
government entered under corporate heading
for official – 21.4D1. Subheading for head of
government acting in official capacity consists
of title of official – 24.20C1. (Dates and name
are not added to subheading, unlike subheading
for head of state – 24.20B1). Head of
government entered subordinately – 24.18A
(Type 9). Added entry under heading for
prominently-named corporate body – 21.30E1.

UNITED KINGDOM. Royal Air Force.
Valley
RAF Valley open day, 1977. –
[Anglesey] : RAF Valley, 1977.
24 p. : ill. ; 24 cm.
Cover title.
Flying display programme as insert.

Item which emanates from a corporate body
and that records the collectivity activity of an
event entered under the heading for the
body – 21.1B2(d). Unit of an armed service
entered as a direct subheading of the heading
of the service of which it is part – 24.24A1.

It is appreciated that it would be feasible to
catalogue this item as a serial if such open days
were successive and were intended to be
continued indefinitely.

UNITED KINGDOM. Treasury.
Organisation and Methods Division
The design of forms in government
departments / compiled by the
Organisation and Methods Division of
Her Majesty's Treasury. – 2nd ed. –
London : H.M.S.O., 1962.
173 p. : ill. ; 28 cm.

1. Title

Work of administrative nature emanating from corporate body and dealing with procedures of body itself is entered under heading for body – 21.1B2(a). The fact that it relates to *all* government departments seems immaterial. Entry of a government agency as an *indirect* subheading as name could be used by another agency – 24.19A.

246

UNITED STATES
 [Trademark Act]
 Trademark laws / U.S., Dept. of Commerce, Patent Office. – Washington, D.C. : G.P.O., 1959.
   38 p. ; 24 cm.
   Contents: Trademark Act of 1946, as amended – Notes of other statutes – Patent Office, establishment, officers, functions.

   1. Title   2. Trademark laws
   3. United States. Patent Office

Government Printing Office abbreviated – B.9.

Laws governing one jurisdiction entered under heading for jurisdiction governed by them – 21.31B1. Uniform title for single law (this item contains only one act in full, although there are brief notes on others) is official short title – 25.15A2. Added entry under heading for body responsible for compiling and issuing the laws – 21.31B1. In added entry heading, intervening element in hierarchy is omitted, as name of subordinate body has not been used by another body entered under same higher body – 24.14A.*

247

UNITED STATES. Congress (85th, 1st session : 1957). House of Representatives. Committee on Ways and Means. Subcommittee on Foreign Trade Policy
 Foreign trade policy : hearings before the Subcommittee on Foreign Trade Policy of the Committee on Ways and Means ... – Washington, D.C. : G.P.O., 1958.
   vi, 865 p. ; 24 cm.
   "85th Congress 1st session pursuant to H. Res. 104, December 2, 3, 4, 5, 6, 9, 10, 11, 12 and 13 1957".

   1. Title

If legislature has more than one chamber, each is entered as subheading of heading for legislature – 24.21A. Committee entered as subheading of chamber – 24.21B. Legislative subcommittee entered as subheading of committee to which it is subordinate – 24.21C. If successive legislatures are numbered consecutively and if numbered sessions are involved, these details are added to the heading for the particular legislature – 24.21D.

248

UNITED STATES. Department of Defense
 A guide to resources and sources of information for acquisition research. – Washington, D.C. : Dept. of Defense ; G.P.O. [distributor], 1980.
   iv, 80 p. ; 27 cm.

   1. Title

Optionally, the name of the distributor may be given in addition to the name of the publisher – 1.4D6. Again optionally, a statement of function may be added – 1.4E1. Abbreviation for Government Printing Office – B.9.

Work emanating from corporate body which is of an administrative nature dealing with the body itself is entered under heading for body – 21.1B2(a). A government body which is a major executive agency is entered subordinately to the name of the government – 24.18A (Type 5). Conventional name of the government used, i.e. the geographic name of the area over which the government exercises jurisdiction – 23.1A and 24.3E1.

249

UNITED STATES. Department of State. Office of Public Communications
 Trade agreements. – [Washington, D.C.] : Dept. of State, Bureau of Public Affairs, Office of Public Communication, 1979.
   8 p. ; 27 cm. – (Current policy / Department of State ; no. 55).
   Reprinted from a background report released by the White House on Jan. 25 1979.

   1. Title   2. Series

Statement of responsibility appearing in conjunction with series title is considered to be necessary for identification of the series – 1.6E1.

Name of government agency that is likely to be used by another government agency has the name of the lowest element in the hierarchy that will distinguish between the agencies interposed – 24.19A.

250

UNITED STATES. President (1977-1981 : Carter)
Emergency aid in Kampuchean crisis / President Carter. – Washington, D.C. : Dept. of State, Bureau of Public Affairs, 1979.
7 p. ; 28 cm. – (Current policy / Department of State ; no. 100).
President Carter's announcement of assistance for Kampuchea and a press briefing by Father Theodore Hesburgh and Ambassador Henry Owen, Assistant to the President for Economic Conferences, and leaders from the private sector, on Oct. 24 1979.

1. Title   2. Series

Official communication from a head of state is entered under the corporate heading for the official – 21.4D1. Entry is made under the heading for the jursidiction followed by the title of the official, with the inclusive years of the incumbency and the name of the person in a brief form added – 24.20B1.

251

UNIVERSITY OF SHEFFIELD.
Congregation for the Conferment of Degrees (1974 May 3 : University of Sheffield, England)
University of Sheffield Congregation for the Conferment of Degrees, Firth Hall, Friday 3 May 1974, 7.30 p.m. – Sheffield : The University, 1974.
8 p. ; 21 cm.

Subordinate body, in this case an ad hoc event, with name that is general in nature entered under body to which it is subordinate – 24.13A (Type 3). A specific date is added to the year in

the heading as this is necessary to distinguish between this and other conferments in the same year – 24.7B3.

252

VALUE ENGINEERING ASSOCI-ATION. Conference (1st : 1967 : Stratford-on-Avon, England)
Proceedings of the 1st Annual Conference, Value Engineering Association, held at the Shakespeare Hotel, Stratford-on-Avon, 5-7th October 1967. – Stevenage, Herts. : Peregrinus, [1969].
73 p. : ill. ; 30 cm.
ISBN 0-901223-01-8.

Conference as corporate body – 21.1B1 and 21.1B2(d). Subordinate body with name (i.e. 1st Annual Conference), that is general in nature and does no more than indicate a numbered subdivision of a body entered under body to which it is subordinate – 24.13A (Type 3). (See also the Annual Conference of the Labour Party example at 24.13A (Type 6)). Added entry under title needed according to 21.30J1. However, entry beginning 'Proceedings . . .' is unhelpful to catalogue-users and so has been omitted in accordance with 21.29C.

253

VAN DER PLANK, J.E.
Disease resistance in plants / by J.E. Van der Plank. – New York ; London : Academic Press, 1968.
xi, 206 p. : ill. ; 24 cm.
Bibliography: p. 195-201.

1. Title

London would be omitted if item were being catalogued by U.S. agency – 1.4C5.

Surname with prefixes, rules for person's language, i.e. English, followed – 22.5D1.

254

WASHINGTON MEMORIAL CHAPEL (Valley Forge, Chester County, Pa.)
The Washington Memorial Chapel, Valley Forge. – Valley Forge : Wash. Mem. Ch., 1971.
32 p. : col. ill. ; 18 cm.
On endpapers: Brief history of events at Valley Forge, 1777-1778 – Washington's Prayer for the United States of America – Details of Church services.

Work emanates from a corporate body and describes the body and its resources, e.g. the organ, the lectern, the pulpit, a statue of Washington. It also has an administrative function in that it lists and describes services held. It therefore appears to fall within the scope of rule 21.1B2(a) and is entered under the heading for the body. Local church entered directly under its name – 24.1A. Location added in parentheses if needed for purposes of identification – 24.10B.

255

WATSON, T.F.
 Making sure of maths. 2 / T.F. Watson, T.A. Quinn. – Edinburgh : Holmes McDougall, 1974.
 24, [24] p. ; 28 cm.
 Twenty-four originals and 24 spirit-masters.
 ISBN 0-7157-1244-6.

1. Title   2. Quinn, T.A.

If title proper for an item that is a section of another item appears in two parts not grammatically linked, the title of the main work is recorded first, followed by a full stop and the title of the section – 1.1B9. Unnumbered sequence of pages recorded if it constitutes the whole or a substantial part of the publication – 2.5B3. When an item consists of a number of graphics packaged in 'book' format, it could be treated as a printed monograph as shown above and in example no. 172. However, it would seem more useful to describe the item as a graphic. Unfortunately, none of the specific material designations in rule 8.5B1 are appropriate. However, a specific name could be used by analogy with Ch. 10. The physical description would then be given as:

 24 spiritmasters ; 28 x 20 cm.

and the note would read:

 Packaged in book format with each master preceded by a print version.

256

WE, the people : the story of the United States Capitol, its past and promise / The United States Capitol Historical Society in cooperation with the National Geographic Society. – 9th ed. – Washington : U.S. Cap. Hist. Soc., 1974.
 144 p. : chiefly ill. (mostly col.) ; 26 cm.
 On endpapers: Constitution and Bill of Rights.

1. United States Capitol Historical Society
2. National Geographic Society

Work emanating from corporate body but not falling within any of the categories listed at 21.1B2 is entered under title – 21.1C1(c).

257

WHAT every director should know about automation : report of a one-day conference at the Connaught Rooms, London, 12 December, 1963. – London : Institute of Directors, 1964.
 71 p. : ill. ; 23 cm.

Conference without name (see definition 21.1B1) entered under title – 21.5A. 'A one-day conference' is not a particular name and 'what every director should know about automation' appears to be a general subject description rather than a specific appellation.

258

WILSON, John Rowan
 The side of the angels / by John Rowan Wilson. – London : Collins, 1968.
 351 p. ; 22 cm.

1. Title †

Nature of surname uncertain. As person's language is English, entry is under the last part of the name – 22.5C6.

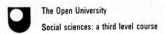

The Open University
Social sciences: a third level course

People and work   Block 1 (Units 1-3)

Work and society

Prepared by the course team

The Open University Press

259

WORK and society / prepared by the
   Course Team [of] The Open Univer-
sity. – Milton Keynes : Open Univ.
Press, 1976.
   120 p. : ill. ; 30 cm. – (Social sciences :
a third level course. People and work ;
Block 1 (Units 1-3)) (DE 351 1-3).
   Contents: Unit 1. The sociology of
work / by Graeme Salaman – Unit 2.
Work and social theory / by Peter
Hamilton – Unit 3. Capitalism and
industrial society in social theory / by Ben
Cosin.
   ISBN 0-335-07000-0.

1.   Open University   2.   Series
3.   People and work
4.   DE 351 1-3
5.   Optionally, author and title
       analytical entries for each part

Word added to make statement of responsibility
clear (by analogy with 1.1F8 and 2.1F2).

Work emanating from corporate body but not
falling within any of categories listed at 21.1B2
is entered under title – 21.1C1(c). Where the
added entry for The Open University is
concerned, the name of the Course Team could
be included as a subheading if this were
thought necessary by the particular cataloguing
agency, e.g.

   Open University. People and Work Course
      Team

If one alphabetical sequence of authors and
titles were required within the heading 'Open
University', this subheading would be omitted.

See also example no. 221.

260

WORKING PARTY ON COMPUTER
   FACILITIES FOR TEACHING IN
   UNIVERSITIES
   Report of a Working Party on
Computer Facilities for Teaching in
Universities. – London : Computer Board
for Universities and Research Councils,
1983.
   25, [21] p. ; 30 cm.
   Cover title.
   Chairman: Miss D.A. Nelson.
   Bibliography: p. [43].
   Includes: Specification for a student
workstation. p. [44-6].

1.   Title   2.   Nelson, D.A.

Cover used as chief source of information when
there is no title page as such – 2.0B1. Title
transcribed as it appears in this source – 1.1B1.
Name associated with responsibility is
transcribed as part of title so no further
statement made – 1.1F13. Note on Chairman of
Committee – 2.7B6. Notes on content –
2.7B18.

Work emanating from a corporate body and recording its collective thought is entered under heading for body – 21.1B2(c). The Working Party is subordinate to the Computer Board but it does not fall within any of the types listed in 24.13A and therefore is entered directly under its own name – 24.12A. A reference would be required from the name in the form of a subheading of the higher body.

261

WORKSHOP ON ANTHRACYCLINES (1979 : Norfolk, Va.)

Anthracyclines : current status and new developments / proceedings of a Workshop on Anthracyclines, which was held at Norfolk, Virginia, on June 14-15 1979 ; edited by Stanley T. Crooke and Steven D. Reich. – New York : Academic Press, 1980.

xiii, 444 p. : ill. ; 24 cm.
ISBN 0-12-197780-3.

1. Title   2. Crooke, Stanley T.
3. Reich, Steven D.

Workshop – conference as corporate body – 21.1B1 and 21.1B2(d).

262

The WORLD-WIDE encyclopedia in colour / edited by Colin Clark. – [New ed.]. – London : P. Hamlyn for Golden Pleasure Books, 1966.

301 p. : ill. (some col.), maps, ports. ; 30 cm.

1. Clark, Colin

Work produced under editorial direction entered under title – 21.7A1(c) and 21.7B1.

263

WORLOCK, Derek
You in your parish / by Bishop Worlock. – London : Living Parish Pamphlets, [1968].

20 p. ; 19 cm.

1. Title

Statement of responsibility recorded in the form in which it appears in item – 1.1F1.

Omission of 'Bishop' from heading – 22.15C. Titles such as Cardinal, Bishop, etc. are only used in headings when entry is *not* under surname – 22.8A1, *or* when they are required to distinguish between persons with identical names – 22.19B1.

264

WRITE now! : letter-pack / produced by BBC Television and The Letter-writing Bureau. – London : BBC Television, 1985.

11 lesson cards ; in envelope 17 x 23 cm.

''Aims to make letter-writing easier, more enjoyable, and more effective''.

Visibly indexed with subject headings.

1. BBC Television
2. Letter-writing Bureau

This is most certainly printed material but, physically, the item is difficult to describe precisely using Ch. 2. None of the terms given in rules 2.5B2 or 2.5B18 are appropriate. The most useful term for the specific material designation seems to be 'lesson card'. This term does not appear in the rules, although it does appear in a multi-media example in rule 1.10C2. Optionally, name of container and dimensions given – 1.5D2. Container dimensions can be given as the only dimensions if desired – 1.5D2.

Item emanates from corporate bodies but does not fall within any of the categories listed in 21.1B2 and is therefore entered under title – 21.1C1(c).

265

YORKSHIRE REGIONAL LIBRARY SYSTEM

Yorkshire Regional Library System : organisation and procedure. – Sheffield : Sheffield Central Library, 1958.

29 p. ; 22 cm.

Work of an administrative nature which emanates from a corporate body and deals with its procedures is entered under the heading for body – 21.1B2(a). Entry directly under name of body – 24.1A.

YUGOSLAVIA
[Ustav (1962). English]
The Constitution of the Federal Socialist
Republic of Yugoslavia : a preliminary
draft. – Beograd : Union of Jurists'
Associations of Yugoslavia, 1962.
   86 p. ; 21 cm.

1. Title
2. The Constitution of the Federal
      Socialist Republic of Yugoslavia

Place of publication recorded in form in which it
appears – 1.4C1.

Constitution entered under heading for
jurisdiction – 21.33A. Conventional name of
government used, and English form of name of
place – 24.3E1 and 23.2A1.* Uniform title is
title in original language – 25.3A. Date added in
parentheses if designation considered necessary
to distinguish between otherwise identical
uniform titles – 25.5B1. Language added –
25.5C1.

Chapter One and Chapter Two

Early printed monographs are, for the most part, pre-nineteenth century publications. In general, the instructions in Ch. 1 and Ch. 2 are followed for description of these materials but the additional rules:

2.12 to 2.18

are used when necessary

Anicius Manlius Severinus
B O E T I U S,

O F   T H E

CONSOLATION

O F

P H I L O S O P H Y.

In Five B O O K S.

Made *Englijh* and Illuftrated with N O T E S,
By the Right Honourable
R i c h a r d *Lord Vifcount* P r e s t o n.

The S e c o n d E d i t i o n Correӄed.

L O N D O N:
Printed for *J. Tonfon* in the *Strand*, and *J. Round*
in *Exchange-Ally*. MDCCXII.

Chief source of information for an early printed monograph is the title page if one exists – 2.13A. Statement of responsibility precedes title proper in chief source of information. This is transposed to the required position as it is not an integral part of the title proper – 1.1F3. Statement on title page which is separate from title proper omitted – 2.14C. Edition statement recorded as it appears on item, using standard abbreviations – 2.15A and 1.2B. Place of publication given as it appears on item – 2.16B. Details relating to publisher recorded as they are given in item, separating the parts of a complex publisher only if they are presented separately in the item – 2.16D. Date of publication given as found in the item, with roman numerals changed to Arabic – 2.16F. Pagination recorded – 2.17A1. Illustrations described – 2.17B1. Dimensions recorded, with format in abbreviated form added in parentheses – 2.17C1. Notes made as for ordinary monographs – 2.18A and 2.7. Additional note on special features of copy – 2.18F1.

English form of name chosen for Roman of classical times whose name has become well established in an English form – 22.3B3. For work created before 1501, uniform title is title in original language by which work is identified in modern reference sources – 25.4A1. Name of language added to uniform title – 25.5C1.

267

BOETHIUS
[De consolatione philosophiae. English]
Of the consolation of philosophy / Anicius Manlius Severinus Boetius ; made English and illustrated with notes by Richard Preston. – 2nd ed. corr. – London : Printed for J. Tonson in the Strand and J. Round in Exchange-Ally, 1712.
xlv, 273 p., [1] leaf of plates : port. ; 17 cm. (12mo.).
"In five books".
Calfskin binding, slightly rubbed and worn.
Bookplate and signature of Alex Leslie, Aberdeen.

1. Title
2. Of the consolation of philosophy

268

BRATHWAITE, R.
Drunken Barnaby's four journeys to the north of England. – [2nd ed.]. – London (under Searle's Gate, Lincoln's-Inn New Square) : Printed for S. Illidge, 1716.
151 p., [2] leaves of plates : 2 ill. (woodcuts) ; 14 cm. (8vo).
"In Latin and English verse".
Attributed to: R. Brathwaite.
Previously published as: Barnabae itinerarium / Corymbaeus.
With: Bessy Bell / Corymbaeus.
Calfskin binding.
Signed: Geo. Whitmore.

1. Title   2. Drunken Barnaby
3. Optionally, author and title
   analyticals for Bessy Bell

Chief source of information is the title page if one exists – 2.13A. Additions to title not treated as part of title proper – 2.14D. Optionally, edition statement supplied and enclosed in square brackets – 2.2B3 and 1.2B4. Place of publication given as it appears on item – 2.16B. Optionally, address of publisher may be added in parentheses – 1.4C7. Details relating to the publisher are recorded as presented in the item – 2.16D. Date of publication given as found in the item – 2.16F. Pagination recorded – 2.17A1. Illustrations described, with type optionally added in parentheses – 2.17B1. Dimensions recorded, with format in abbreviated form added in parentheses – 2.17C. Notes made as for ordinary monographs – 2.18A and 2.7; language of item – 2.7B2; statement of responsibility – 2.7B6; 'With' note – 2.7B21. Additional notes on special features of copy – 2.18F1.

Authoritative reference sources indicate that this work is by R. Brathwaite, so entry is made under the heading for him as author – 21.1A1, 21.1A2 and 21.5B. If responsibility is erroneously or fictitiously attributed to a person (i.e. 'Drunken Barnaby'), entry is made under the heading for the actual personal author – 21.4C1. An added entry is made under the heading for the person to whom authorship is attributed, unless he or she is not a real person. As the writer of the preface concludes that the work was written by Barnaby Harrington, an added entry is made under the heading for him. The basis for this heading is the form of name by which he is most commonly known, i.e. 'Drunken Barnaby' – 22.1A. For a phrase consisting of a forename preceded by words other than a term of address, entry is in direct order – 22.11A. References would be required from the forename followed by the initial word, i.e. Barnaby, Drunken – 22.11A,* from the other form of name, i.e. Harrington, Barnaby – 26.2A2, and from Brathwaite's earlier pseudonym Corymbaeus – 26.2A1.

BROWN, Josiah
Reports of cases upon appeals and writs of error in the High Court of Parliament : from the year 1701 to the year 1779 / by Josiah Brown. – Dublin (No. 6 Skinner Row and in the Four Courts) : Printed by E. Lynch, 1784.
7 v. (x, 555; 602; 586; 618; 610; 624; 558 p.) ; 22 cm. (fol.)
Rebound: 1969.

1. Title
2. United Kingdom. High Court of Parliament

Publisher statement may relate to a printer – 2.16A. Number of volumes in multi-volumed set recorded – 2.5B17. If volumes are individually paged, pagination of each volume may optionally be recorded – 2.5B21. Note on special feature of copy – 2.18F1.

Reports of one court which are ascribed to a reporter are entered under the heading for the court or the reporter according to whichever is used as the basis for accepted legal citation practice in the country where the court is located – 21.36A1. The example 'Common bench reports', included with this rule, appears to indicate that in the U.K. this would be the heading for the reporter. This is reflected in the above entry, although the legal experts whom the authors consulted seemed to be unsure whether there was such an accepted practice. However, when the practice is unknown, or cannot be determined, the entry for this item would still be under the heading for the reporter according to the same rule. An added entry is made for the court, entered as a subheading of the heading for the government – 24.18A (Type 7).

GENTLEMAN

The lion and fawn : a legend / by a gentleman. – London : Printed for the author, [1797?].

13 p. : coat of arms ; 23 cm. (4to).

"Presented on their marriage to the Right Honourable the Earl and Countess of Derby".

From the subject matter of the legend, it may be inferred that it refers to the marriage of the 12th Earl of Derby and Elizabeth Farren, the actress, on May 1, 1797.

1. Title

Statement of responsibility transcribed in the form in which it appears in the item – 1.1F1. Details relating to publisher recorded as given in the item – 2.16D. Approximate date given – 2.16G.

If name of personal author is unknown, and the only indication of authorship is the appearance in the chief source of information of a characterizing word or phrase, entry is under the phrase in direct order, with the initial article omitted – 21.5C and 22.11D.

HOPTON, Arthur

A concordancy of the yeares : containing a new, easier, and most exact computation of time, according to the English account : also the use of the English and Roman kalender with briefe notes, rules, and tables, as well as mathematicall and legal, as vulgar, for each private man's occasion. – [New ed.] / newly composed, digested and augmented by Arthur Hopton. – [London] : Printed by Nicholas Okes for Thomas Adams, 1615.

A1-A4, [3], 254 p. ; 18 cm. (8vo).

Previous ed.: Printed for the Company of Stationers, 1612.

Vellum binding.

1. Title

Title transcribed from chief source of information, i.e. the title page if there is one – 2.13A and 2.1B1 and 1.1B. Optionally, if item lacks an edition statement but is known to contain significant changes from other editions, an edition statement is supplied – 2.2B3. Statement of responsibility relating to a particular edition – 2.2C1, 1.2C and 2.1F. Publication details recorded as given in the item and, as the publication statement on the item includes the name of a printer, this is also recorded – 2.16D. Sequences of pages, etc. recorded as given in the item – 2.17A1. Note on special feature of copy being described – 2.18F1.

Chapter One and Chapter Three

For cartographic materials as accompanying material see examples no. 226, 293 and 394.

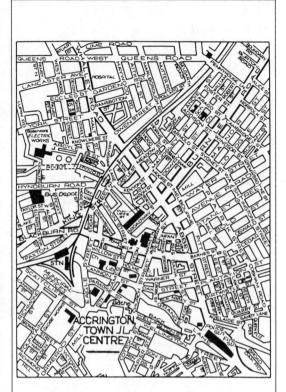

Published by Staples Printing Group Ltd., London.   1976
Copyright Staples Printing Group
Based upon the Ordnance Survey Map with the
sanction of the Controller of H.M. Stationery Office

272

ACCRINGTON town centre. – Scale [ca.
1:10,560]. – London : Staples, 1976.
1 map ; 17 x 14 cm.
"Based upon the Ordnance Survey".

Description of maps. Title transcribed as it
appears in chief source of information – 3.1B1
and 1.1B (chief source of information for a
cartographic material is the item itself –
3.0B2(a)). Scale is recorded as a representative
fraction; if no statement of scale is found on the
item, its container or accompanying material, it
is computed, e.g. by comparison with a map of
known scale, and given enclosed in square
brackets and preceded by 'ca.' – 3.3B1.
Publication details given – 3.4C1, 1.4C, 3.4D1,
1.4D, 3.4F1 and 1.4F. In the case of cartographic

materials other than atlases and globes, the
number of maps, etc. is given as the extent of
the item using one of the terms from a supplied
list – 3.5B1. Map is black and white so no
indication of colour is necessary – 3.5C3.
Dimensions of face of map (height and width)
given in centimetres to the next whole
centimetre up, measured within the neat line,
i.e. the inner border of the map – 3.5D1. Note
on edition and history – 3.7B7.

Work of unknown responsibility is entered
under title – 21.1C1(a).

273

BULLOCK, L.G.
   Historical map of England and
Wales / L.G. Bullock. – Scale
[ca. 1:58,000,000]. – Edinburgh :
Bartholomew, 1971.
   1 map : col. ; 94 x 63 cm. folded to
26 x 18 cm.
   Shows cathedrals, abbeys, castles,
historic and scenic features, Roman and
other pre-Conquest centres and sites,
battles and sieges (including air war
1940 – 1945).
   Insets: Coats of arms of England, Wales
and 142 towns and cities.
   ISBN 0-85152-550-4 (paper); issued also
in cloth.

   1.   Title

Note on nature of item – 3.7B1. Contents note
on insets – 3.7B18. Standard number recorded,
qualified, and combined with note on other
formats – 3.8B1, 3.7B16 and 1.7A5.

274

CANTERBURY Cathedral : plan and
   brief history. – Scale indeterminable. –
Canterbury : Cathedral Gifts, 1978.
   2 plans on 1 sheet ; 18 x 32 cm. folded
to 18 x 11 cm.
   Brief history with col. ill. on verso.
   ISBN 0-906211-02-6.

Item with one predominant component
described in terms of that component with
details of the subsidiary component given as
accompanying material in a note – 1.10B,
1.7B11 and 3.7B11.

Work of unknown authorship entered under
title – 21.1C1(a).

Château Dundurn Castle, *Hamilton Ontario*

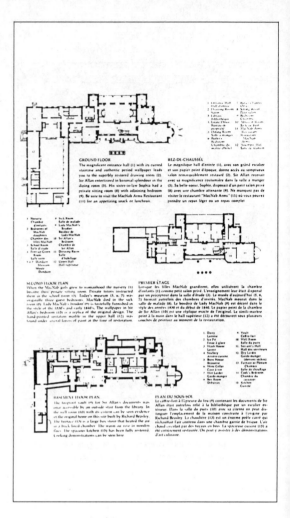

DUNDURN CASTLE

Château Dundurn = Dundurn Castle, Hamilton, Ontario. – Scale [ca. 1:400]. – Hamilton : The Castle, [197-?].

3 plans on 1 sheet ; 28 x 22 cm. folded to 10 x 22 cm.

Includes text in English and French.

On verso: Brief biography of Sir Allan Napier MacNab, the builder, a list of castle facilities and 2 ill., one a port.

Description of plans. Title as it appears on chief source of information is: Château Dundurn Castle. If a word appears only once but design of chief source of information makes it clear that it is intended to be read more than once, the word is repeated without the use of square brackets – 1.1B5. If there is more than one map, plan, etc. on a sheet, the number of maps, plans, etc. and the number of sheets are specified – 3.5B2. Sheet size is given as it is difficult to measure individual plans – 3.5D1. Sheet size in folded form also recorded – 3.5D1.

Work emanates from a corporate body and is considered to be of an administrative nature as it is intended to assist visitors when touring the building. It therefore appears to fall within the scope of 21.1B2(a) and is entered under the heading for the body. Name appears in two languages, both of which are official, so entry is under the English form – 24.3A1.* No title added entry because title is essentially the same as main entry heading and could be covered by a reference.

132

GAGE, Michael Alexander

This trigonometrical plan of the town and port of Liverpool : including the environs of Kirkdale, Everton, Low Hill, Edge Hill & Toxteth Park / from actual survey ... by ... Michael Alexander Gage. – Scale [ca. 1:3,200]. – Liverpool : Gage, 1836.

1 map ; 92 x 154 cm.

"Specially patronised by His Most Excellent Majesty William the Fourth and the Corporation of Liverpool" and dedicated to the Mayor and Common Council.

Engraved by Thomas Starling.

Survey completed: 1 Oct. 1835.

Insets include: Members of the Corporation and tidal information.

1. Title   2. Starling, Thomas

Title transcribed as it appears in chief source of information – 3.1B1 and 1.1B. The statement of responsibility has been abbreviated by analogy with 1.1F15, omitting statements that neither constitute other title information nor form part of the statement, i.e. a dedication to the Mayor and Common Council, and words such as 'their most obedient and humble servant'. The omissions are indicated by the mark of omission – 1.0C1. Dedication given in note and combined with note on patronization as descriptive information which cannot be fitted into other areas – 1.7A5. Note on responsibility – 3.7B6. Note on edition and history – 3.7B7. Note on insets – 3.7B18.

GEOGRAPHER'S A-Z MAP CO.

Map of central London / Geographer's A-Z Map Co. Ltd. – Ed. 8. – Scale [ca. 1:10,560]. – Sevenoaks, Kent : Geographer's, [198-].

1 map : col. ; 31 x 53 cm. folded to 15 x 10 cm.

Cover title: AZ handy map of central London.

Based upon the Ordnance Survey 1:10,560 and 1:2,500 maps.

Insets: West End theatres – Shopping centres – The London Underground – West End cinemas.

Index to streets on verso.

ISBN 0-85039-024-9.

1. Title
2. AZ handy map of central London

Map is adapted from Ordnance Survey maps and therefore the corporate body from which the map emanates appears to be responsible for more than mere publication and distribution and entry is made under the heading for the body – 21.1B2(f).

GEORGE PHILIP CARTOGRAPHIC SERVICES

Philips' world atlas. – 7th ed. / edited by B.M. Willett (cartographic editor). – Scales vary. – London : Philip, 1988.

1 atlas (32, 80, 64 p.) : col. ill., 62 col. maps ; 29 cm.

Includes an introductory section: The world today. 32 p.

ISBN 0-540-05546-8.

1. Title   2. Willett, B.M.

Description of atlases. Title transcribed as it appears in chief source of information, which, for an atlas, is the title page – 3.0B1 and 2.0B1. If maps are of three of more scales, 'Scales vary' is given – 3.3B6 (there is conflict and inconsistency between this rule and rule 3.3B3, where it states that the outside values should be recorded and 'Scale varies' given only if the scales are unknown). Publisher given in the shortest form in which it can be understood and identified internationally (full name is George Philip & Son Ltd) – 1.4D2. Number of physical units and the term 'atlas' given as specific material designation – 3.5B1. Number of volumes or pagination is added in parentheses – 3.5B3 and 2.5B. Number of maps given – 3.5C2 and 2.5C. Contents note – 3.7B18. Standard number recorded – 3.8B1 and 1.8B.

George Philip cartographic works are produced by George Philip Cartographic Services and, although the body is not named in this particular item, if a work probably emanates from a corporate body, entry is under that body – 21.5B. Responsibility goes beyond that of mere publication, distribution, etc. so rule 21.1B2(f) also applies.

H.M. GOUSHA CO.
California road map ... / H.M.
Gousha Co. – Scale [1:1,330,560]. 1 in.
= 21 miles. – San Jose, Ca. : Gousha,
[198-?].
1 map in 2 segments : col. ; on sheet
44 x 86 cm. – (Gousha/chek-charts).
Insets: Sacramento – San Diego. Scale
[ca. 1:247,100].
On verso: Los Angeles and vicinity.
Scale [ca. 1:323,136] – San Francisco
and Monterey Bay areas. Scale [ca.
1:465,500] – Mileage chart – Public
recreation areas.

1.   Title   2.   Series

If the scale found on the item is not expressed
as a representative fraction, it is given as a
representative fraction in square brackets –
3.3B1. Optionally, the scale found on the item is
also given – 3.3B2. If the maps, etc. are printed
in two or more segments designed to fit
together to form one or more maps, the number
of complete maps and the number of segments
are given – 3.5B2. Colour indicated – 3.5C3. If
it is difficult to determine the points for
measuring the height and width of the complete
map, only the height and width of the sheet is
given – 3.5D1. Note on insets – 3.7B18.

Item emanates from a corporate body which is
not merely responsible for publication,
distribution, etc. and entry is therefore under the
heading for the body – 21.1B2(f).

HELLAS = Greece : map = Griechen-
land : Karten = Grece : carte. – Scale
1:1,500,000. – [Greece] : N. & K.
Gouvoussis, [198-].
1 map : col. ; 55 x 77 cm. folded to
19 x 12 cm.

Parallel titles recorded in the order indicated by
their sequence on the chief source of
information – 3.1D1 and 1.1D1. Transcribe
other title information following the title proper
or parallel title to which it pertains – 1.1E5. No
added entries under parallel titles as not
necessary for access – 21.30J1.

Not known whether corporate body is merely
responsible for publication and because of this

doubt, item is treated as if 21.1B2 were not
applicable and therefore as a work of unknown
authorship entered under title – 21.1C1(a).

ILLUMINATED globe. – Scale [ca.
1:100,000,000]. – Florence, Italy :
Ricoglobus ; [United Kingdom] : House
Martin [distributor], [198-].
1 globe : col., plastic, on plastic stand ;
20 cm. in diam. in box 24 x 22 x 22 cm.
"Light off shows physical features; light
on shows political boundaries".
Title from container.
Requires 15 watt/220 volt bulb.

Description of globes. The chief source of
information (in order of preference) is (a) the
item itself and (b) its container, cradle and
stand – 3.0B2. In this instance, the title has
been obtained from the container, whilst other
detail has been obtained from the container and
the base of the stand. The scale has been
estimated from the size of the globe – 3.3B1.
Place of publication and name of publisher
recorded and, optionally, the place of
distribution and the name of the distributor –
3.4C1, 1.4C, 3.4D1 and 1.4D. Optionally, function
of distributor added – 3.4E1 and 1.4E. Number
of physical units given in the case of globes –
3.5B1. Indication that item is coloured – 3.5C3.
Material of which item is made given if
considered significant – 3.5C4. Mounting of
globe indicated – 3.5C5. Diameter of globe
given – 3.5D4. Note on nature and scope of
item – 3.7B1. Note on source of title proper –
3.7B3. Note on physical description, special
requirement – 3.7B10.

INSTITUTE OF HERALDIC AND
   GENEALOGICAL STUDIES
Lancashire parishes : with date of
commencement of registers / Institute of
Heraldic and Genealogical Studies. –
Scale [ca. 1:360,000]. – Canterbury : The
Institute, c1979.
1 map ; 39 x 31 cm.
Information on boundaries and dates
relate to the pre-1832 ancient parishes.
Boundaries only in colour.
Insets: List of parishes with dates.

1.   Title

Note on scope of item – 3.7B1. Note on physical description – 3.7B10.

The information contained in this item was collected from various record offices, etc. and the resulting map was produced by the Institute. Responsibility therefore goes beyond that of mere publication, distribution, etc. and entry is under the heading for the body – 21.1B2(f).

L & A RELIEF MAP CON-
STRUCTIONS
British Isles / made by L & A Relief Map Constructions Ltd. – Scale [ca. 1:274,000]. – London : L & A, [197-].
1 relief model : col., plastic ; 39 x 28 cm.

1. Title

Description of relief models. Scale estimated – 3.3B1. Number of units and appropriate term from a supplied list given as specific material designation – 3.5B1. Indication of colour – 3.5C1 and 3.5C3. Indication of material of which item is made – 3.5C1 and 3.5C4. Dimensions given – 3.5D3 (optionally the depth could be added).

Work emanates from a corporate body and responsibility goes beyond that of mere publication, distribution, etc. Therefore entry is under the heading for the body – 21.1B2(f). 'Ltd' is not needed to make clear that name is that of a corporate body – 24.5C1. (However, 'Ltd' must be included in statement of responsibility, which is transcribed as given on the item).

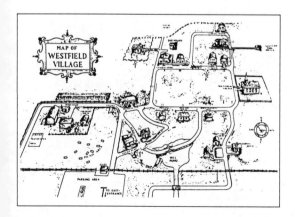

MAP of Westfield Village. – Scale indeterminable. – [Hamilton-Wentworth, Ont., 196-?].
1 view ; 20 x 29 cm.
Village is now named: Wentworth Pioneer Village.
On verso: ill., and descriptions of village buildings.

Description of views, in this case a bird's eye view. If scale cannot be determined, this is stated – 3.3B1. No publication details are given, so probable place of publication and approximate date are given in square brackets – 1.4C6 and 1.4F7. Specific material designation – 3.5B1. Map is black and white, so no colour statement is recorded – 3.5C3. Note of accompanying material on verso of item – 3.7B11 and 3.7B18.

ORDNANCE SURVEY
Ordnance Survey atlas of Great Britain. – Rev. ed. – Scale [1:250,000]. 4 miles to one inch. – Southampton : OS, 1988.
1 atlas (xvi, 186 p.) : col. ill., 60 col. maps ; 31 cm.
Published jointly with: Godalming, Surrey : Colour Library books; previous ed. published jointly with: Twickenham, Middlesex : Country Life Books, 1982.
Key to maps on endpapers.
Includes: The historical geography of Britain / R.A. Butlin. p. 122-135 ; with 7 additional maps [scale ca. 1:4,400,000] – Modern Britain / M.J. Wise. p. 136-157 ; with 12 additional maps [scale ca. 1:4,400,000] – Index: p. 158-187.
ISBN 0-86283-647-6.

Description of atlases. Title transcribed as it appears in chief source of information, which, for an atlas, is the title page – 3.0B1 and 2.0B1. Name associated with responsibility for the item is transcribed as part of the title proper and therefore no further statement necessary – 1.1F13. If name of publisher appears in the title and statement of responsibility area, it is given in the publication, distribution, etc. area in the shortest possible form – 1.4D4 (it is appreciated that the Ordnance Survey is given as 'The Survey' in the examples accompanying rule 3.0J1 but it seems preferable to use the abbreviation which appears on items issued by the body). The scale of the main maps is given – 3.3B6. Optionally, additional scale information found on the item is given – 3.3B2. Number of physical units and the term 'atlas' given as specific material designation – 3.5B1. Number of volumes or pagination is added in parentheses – 3.5B3 and 2.5B. Number of maps given – 3.5C2 and 2.5C (the number recorded here relates to the main 1:250,000 maps). Note on publication – 3.7B9 and 2.7B9. Note on physical description – 3.7B10. Contents note – 3.7B18 (it would seem clearer and more useful to indicate the additional maps which do not form part of the main sequence in a note and give their scale if possible).

Cartographic material emanating from a corporate body which is responsible for more than mere publication, distribution, etc. is entered under the heading for the body – 21.1B2(f). No added title entry as it would be essentially the same as the main entry heading – 21.30J1(a).

286

ORDNANCE SURVEY
   York / Ordnance Survey. – Ed. 6. – Scale 1:50,000. 1¼ in. to 1 mile. – Southampton : OS, c1986.
   1 map : col. ; 80 x 80 cm. folded to 23 x 14 cm. – (Ordnance Survey 1:50,000 landranger series ; sheet 105).
   Part of legend and tourist information in English, French and German.
   Cover title: York & surrounding area : the all purpose map with public rights of way and tourist information.
   Series title also given as: Ordnance Survey 1:50,000 second series ; sheet 105; and: Ordnance Survey series M 726 ; sheet 105.

   1. Title   2. Series

Title transcribed from the chief source of information, i.e. the map itself, and not from the container, i.e. the cover – 3.1B1, 1.1B and 3.0B2. Optionally, additional scale information that is found on the item may be given following scale expressed as a representative fraction – 3.3B2. Publisher abbreviated as it already appears in statement of responsibility

area – 1.4D4. Copyright date given – 1.4F6. More than one form of the series statement is given in the chief source of information, i.e. the map itself. Rule 1.6B does not address this problem; the series title chosen here is the one that is given prominence. The variant titles could be recorded in a note, if desired, as shown – 3.7B12 and 1.7B12. Note on language – 3.7B2 and 1.7B2. Note on variant title – 3.7B4 and 1.7B4.

Item which emanates from a corporate body and falls within categories listed in 21.1B2 is entered under the heading for the corporate body. The body is not merely responsible for publication or distribution – 21.1B2(f).

It should be noted that it is is possible to describe a whole collection of maps rather than to describe each part separately – 3.0J1, e.g.:

   ORDNANCE SURVEY
      Ordnance Survey 1:50,000 landranger series. – Scale 1:50,000. – Southampton : OS, [198-]-   .
      204 maps : col. ; 80 x 80 cm.

The instruction is that the scale is to be given even if it is already recorded as part of the title proper – 3.3B1. The inclusive dates would be given in the publication, distribution area if known.

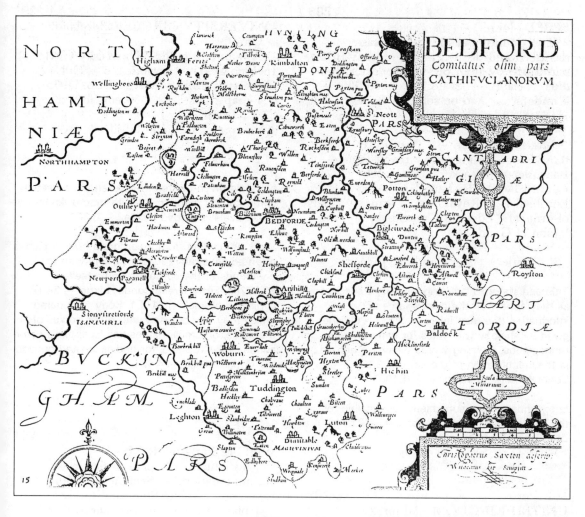

287

SAXTON, Christopher
   Bedford comitatus olim pars
Cathifuclanorum / Christophorus Saxton,
descrip.; Wilhelmus Kip, sculpsitt. – Scale
[ca. 1:300,000]. – [London : Orbis,
1976].
   1 map : col. ; 21 x 28 cm. – (Antique
maps of Britain ; no. 150).
   Reproduction of: 1607. Scale: [ca.
1:180,000].

   1. Title   2. Kip, William

Title and statement of responsibility transcribed
as they appear in chief source of information
(the map itself) – 3.1B1. However, 'V' is
transcribed as 'u' – 2.14E1. This item is a
reproduction of the original in a smaller size and
therefore the scales will differ. This is reflected
in the fact that an approximate scale of the
original is recorded in a note; the scale of the
reproduction is calculated and recorded in the
mathematical data area.

Entry under the person chiefly responsible for
the intellectual or artistic content – 21.1A1,
21.1A2 and 21.4A1.

SPEED, John
  The Countie pallatine of Lancaster :
described and divided into hundreds 1610 /
performed by John Speed ; Jodocus Hon-
dius, caelavit. – Scale [ca. 1:250,000] –
[London] : ... to be solde in Popes
Head Alley by G. Humbell ... , 1610.
  1 map : col. ; 38 x 50 cm.
  Insets: Lancaster – "Portratures of all
those Kings sprunge fro y royall families of
Lancaster and Yorke": Henry III, V, VI;
Edward IV, V; Richard III; Henry VII,
Elizabeth I – Royal coat of arms – Coats
of arms of "Edmond Crouckbak, E" and
"John of Gand, D".

  1. Title   2. Hondius, Jodocus

Title and statement of responsibility transcribed
as they appear on the chief source of
information (the map itself) – 3.1B1. Publisher
given by analogy with rules for early printed
monographs, omitting words which do not aid
in the identification of the item – 2.16D.
Contents note on insets – 3.7B18.

Entry under the person chiefly responsible for
the intellectual and artistic content – 21.1A1,
21.1A2 and 21.4A1.

UNITED KINGDOM. Admiralty
  Wales : Holyhead to Great Ormes
Head. – New ed. – Scale 1:75,000 :
Mercator proj. (W 04°53'00" – W 03°
48'42"/N 53°38'18" – N 53°13'00").
– London : Admiralty, 1973.
  1 hydrographic chart : blue & white ;
63 x 96 cm. – (Admiralty charts ; 1977).
  "From Admiralty surveys 1835-1971".

  1. Series

Description of hydrographic charts. Statement of
projection recorded if included on the item –
3.3C1. Co-ordinates recorded optionally –
3.3D1. Note on edition and history of item –
3.7B7.

UNIVERSITY CIRCLE (Cleveland,
Ohio)
  A map and guide / University Circle,
Incorporated. – Scale [ca. 1:6,750]. –
Cleveland, Ohio : Univ. Circle, [1975].
  1 map : col. ; 42 x 35 cm. folded to
23 x 11 cm.
  On verso: Key and 20 ill.

  1. Title

No scale given on item. Representative fraction
computed by comparison with map of known
scale. Scale preceded by 'ca.' – 3.3B1.

Work emanating from a corporate body which is
of an administrative nature dealing with the
operations of the corporate body itself –
21.1B2(a). Entry directly under name – 24.1A.
Omission of 'Inc' – 24.5C1. Body with name
which may be confused with other bodies of
the same, or similar names has local place name
added – 24.4C3 and, for bodies located outside
the British Isles, – 24.4C4.

WHITE Star Line R.M.S.
  "Adriatic" ... : plan of first class
accommodation. – Scale [ca. 1:250]. –
Liverpool : [White Star Line?], 1922.
  1 plan in 5 sections ; on sheet 57 x 89
cm. folded to 23 x 15 cm.
  Insets: Notes, 4 photos. of interior of
ship, 1 drawing of exterior.

Description of plans. Mark of omission – 1.0C1.
Conjectural interpolation (in this case the
probable publisher) given in square brackets
with question mark added – 1.0C. Scale does
not appear on item but has been estimated –
3.3B1. Sections of plan have irregular outlines,
so sheet size alone is given – 3.5D1. Sheet
contains panel designed to appear on outside
when sheet is folded, so sheet size folded is
given – 3.5D1. Inset material given in note –
3.7B18.

Chapter One and Chapter Four

292

ADAMS, Samuel
  [Letter] 1829 Dec. 8, Londonderry Gaol
[to] J. McCreery, Liverpool / Sam:
Adams.
  [1] leaf ; 25 cm.
  Holograph (transcript, typewritten),
original ([3] p. on 2 leaves) in Liverpool
City Libraries, available to researchers
under library restrictions.
  Title supplied by cataloguer.
  Summary: Reaction to William Roscoe's
Observations on penal jurisprudence, the
second and third parts of which Adams
had just received.

Description of manuscripts. The chief source of
information for a manuscript is the manuscript
itself – 4.0B1. If a manuscript lacks a title, one
is supplied and enclosed in square brackets –
4.1B2. (The title for a single letter is 'Letter'
and this is followed by the date of writing
(expressed as year, month, day), the place of
writing, the name of the addressee and the
place to which addressed. Statement of
responsibility transcribed in the form of which it
appears in item – 4.1F1 and 1.1F1. Date not
recorded as already included in title – 4.4B1.
Number of leaves or pages given – 4.5B1,
2.5B7. (Optionally, the number of leaves may be

added if this is different to the number of
pages, as shown in the note relating to the
original). Height given in centimetres to next
whole centimetre up – 4.5D1. A manuscript
handwritten by the author is recorded in note as
'Holograph' and, if the item being described is a
copy, appropriate terms are added to indicate
this – 4.7B1. Location of original recorded –
4.7B1. Source of title, if other than the chief
source of information, is given in a note –
4.7B3. Note on access (in this case combined
with the location of original note) – 4.7B14.
Brief objective summary given – 4.7B17 and
1.7B17.

Entry under heading for personal author, i.e. the
writer of the letter – 21.1A1 and 21.1A2. No
added entry under addressee, as it is a single
letter: an added entry would be made for a
collection of letters – 21.30F1. No added entry
for a title that has been composed by the
cataloguer – 21.30J1(b).

293

DAVIES, Harry
  [Letters] / Harry Davies. – 1916-1919.
  10 items : ill., plans, port.
  Conscientious objector. Letters to friend,
Edith, mainly relating to prison conditions
he was experiencing at various centres.
Includes detailed account of Wormwood
Scrubs (30 p.).
  Title supplied by cataloguer.
  Some pages of letters missing.
  Accompanied by hand-drawn plans of
Scrubs, Wakefield Centre and Dartmoor
and self-portrait.
  Also contains official regulations from
Scrubs concerning communications
between prisoners and visitors.

Collection of letters by individual given title
'[Letters]' – 4.1B2. Inclusive dates of
manuscript collection – 4.4B1. Number of items
recorded – 4.5B2. No instruction to record
dimensions when size of items is not uniform –
4.5D2. If in container (or containers of uniform
size) height, width and depth would be given –
4.5D2. Alternatively, the smallest and largest
size could be given by analogy with 2.5D3.
Information to identify writer recorded, followed
by summary – 4.7B1. Source of title – 4.7B3.
Additional physical description given – 4.7B10.
Accompanying material – 4.7B11. Further
contents recorded – 4.7B18.

294

INDENTURE, 1819 Nov. 1 between John Baron and John Hawkesley Thompson and William Hill, both of Liverpool, dry salters.

    1 leaf ; 38 cm. folded to 19 x 22 cm.

    Apprenticeship agreement: term 7 years.

    Open to researchers under library restrictions.

1. Baron, John
2. Thompson, John Hawkesley
3. Hill, William

For manuscript which lacks a title, one is supplied – 4.1B2. For legal documents, this consists of a word or brief phrase characterizing the document, the date of signing, the names of the persons concerned, and the occasion for the document if it can be expressed concisely; square brackets are not necessary as detail has been taken from the document – 4.1B2. Date not recorded as it is already included in the title – 4.4B1. Number of leaves or pages given – 4.5B1 and 2.5B. Height of single manuscript given and, as it is kept folded, dimensions when folded added – 4.5D1. Note on nature of item – 4.7B1. Note on access – 4.7B14.

Added entries under related persons if headings provide important access points – 21.30F1. These would not, of course, be required if names were used as subject headings in a catalogue in which name-title and subject entries are interfiled.

295

OWEN, Joseph

    [Will] 1777 May 28 / Joseph Owen.

    [4] p. ; 31 cm.

    Ms. (transcript, handwritten), original written in Lydiate, Lancashire.

    Title supplied by cataloguer.

    Witnesses: Henry Holland, Elizabeth Holland and John Molyneux.

Title supplied for legal document – 4.1B2. Date of signing legal document included as part of title – 4.1B2. Date not needed in date area because included already in title proper – 4.4B1. Details of copy given as note – 4.7B1. (Location of original should be added if it can be ascertained. In this instance, only the place where it was written is known). Note on

witnesses included as this is 'useful descriptive information that cannot be fitted into other areas' – 1.7A5.

296

PALMER, P.G.

    Archbishop Abbot and the woollen industry in Guildford / P.G. Palmer. – [1923?].

    66, a-g leaves ; 25 cm.

    Holograph.

    Bibliography: leaves a-g.

1. Title

Pagination recorded as for printed monographs – 4.5B1 and 2.5B. Lettered pages or leaves recorded as inclusive lettering – 2.5B2. Designation for manuscript handwritten by the author is 'Holograph' – 4.7B1.

297

THOMAS HILL AND CO.

    [Papers / relating to] Thomas Hill and Co. [and members of the firm]. – 1776-1849.

    22 items ; in folder 38 x 28 cm.

    Pot ash makers of Everton. Tax and rate bills, receipts, etc., indentures and apprenticeship, records of jury service and exemption from militia service, fire insurance papers, letter on sale of share in Liverpool Library, state lottery ticket, financial account for journey by stage coach, documents from London and North Western Railway Co. re. compensation for damage to firm's property by building of tunnel.

    Title supplied by cataloguer.

    Includes: cutting from Liverpool daily post, 28 Feb. 1966, on discovery of foundations of firm's chimney.

Title supplied for collection of manuscripts. Materials relating to corporate body would be described as 'Records', but a number of these items are personal and so term for miscellaneous personal or family material (i.e. 'Papers') is used – 4.1B2. Inclusive dates of manuscript collection given – 4.4B1. Extent given in terms of the number of items – 4.5B2. Dimensions of container recorded – 4.5D2 and 1.5D2. Note on nature of item – 4.7B1. 'Includes' note – 4.7B18.

Shared responsibility, but principal responsibility can be attributed in the chief source of information (i.e. the whole collection – 4.0B1) to the corporate body – 21.6B1. As many of the items are of an administrative nature dealing with the corporate body itself, entry is therefore under the heading for the body – 21.1B2(a).

Music

Chapter One and Chapter Five

Uniform titles are used whenever they are deemed appropriate but it should be noted that such titles are optional and can be applied according to the policy of the particular cataloguing agency.

For recorded music
see examples no. 319 – 22, 324 – 7, 333, 337 – 40
and, with video, 342 and 344

SAMUEL ADLER

CANTO VII

Tuba Solo

$2.00

BOOSEY & HAWKES
New York

---

consists of a list of titles). Other title information transcribed – 5.1E1 and 1.1E. Statement of responsibility transcribed as it appears in chief source of information – 5.1F1 and 1.1F. Place of publication, publisher and date of publication recorded – 5.4C1 and 1.4C, 5.4D1 and 1.4D, 5.4F1 and 1.4F. Copyright date given – 1.4F6. If this is found only on the first page of music, it is not enclosed in square brackets – 5.4F1. Extent of item recorded; if none of the terms given in the supplied list is appropriate, the pagination is given, followed by 'of music' (although the latter can optionally be omitted if general material designations are used) – 5.5B1. The term 'score' is not applicable, as the definition (see Appendix D) implies that two or more parts are aligned. Height in centimetres given to next whole centimetre up – 5.5D1 and 2.5D.

Entry under the heading for the personal author, i.e. the composer – 21.1A1, 21.1A2 and 21.4A1.

298

ADLER, Samuel
    Canto VII : tuba solo / Samuel Adler. – New York : Boosey & Hawkes, c1974.
        11 p. of music ; 30 cm.

    1. Title

Description of music. Title transcribed as it appears in chief source of information – 5.1B1 and 1.1B (chief source of information for music is the title page – 5.0B1, unless the title page

299

ANTHOLOGY of music : a collection of
    complete musical examples illustrating
the history of music / edited by K.G.
Fellerer. – Köln : Arno Volk.

    Vol. 1: Four hundred years of European ceyboard [sic] music / [edited with an introduction] by Walter
Georgii. – 1959.
        140 p. of music ; 31 cm.
        Partial contents: Praeludium in E-flat major / Johann Sebastian Bach – Capriccio in G minor / Georg Friedrich Händel – Adagio in B minor, K.540 / Wolfgang Amadeus Mozart – Small piece for piano, op. 19, no. 2 / Arnold Schönberg.

    1. Fellerer, K.G.
    2. Four hundred years of European ceyboard [sic] music
    3. Georgii, Walter
    4. Optionally, author and title analytical entries for each part

Multilevel description for identification of both part and comprehensive whole – 13.6. Inaccuracy or mis-spelled word transcribed as it appears, followed by [sic] or [i.e. keyboard] – 1.0F1. Place of publication recorded in the form in which it appears (i.e. 'Köln' not 'Cologne') – 1.4C1. None of listed terms is appropriate as specific material designation, so number of 'pages of music' is recorded – 5.5B1. Partial contents listed – 5.7B18.

Work produced under editorial direction entered directly under collective title – 21.7A1 and 21.7B1.

BACH, Johann Sebastian
  [Chorale preludes. Selections ; arr.]
  Organ choral preludes / J.S. Bach ; arranged for pianoforte by William Murdoch. – London : Schott, 1928.
  4 v. of music (14; 17; 18; 19 p.) ; 30 cm.
  Titles of individual pieces in German and English.
  Four pieces bound together.
  Partial contents: Liebster Jesu, wir sind hier – Herzlich thut mich verlangen – Jesus Christus, unser Heiland – Ein feste Burg ist unser Gott.

1. Title   2. Organ choral preludes
3. Murdoch, William
4. Optionally, analytical title entries
     for each part

No specific material designation is applicable, so number of volumes of music is given – 5.5B1. Pagination added, in accordance with rules for printed monographs – 1.5B3. If volumes in multi-volume set are individually paged, pagination of each volume may optionally be given in parentheses after the number of volumes – 2.5B21.

Arrangement of one or more works of one composer entered under heading for composer, with added entry under heading for arranger – 21.18B1. For a collection containing works of one type of composition, the name of that type is used for the uniform title – 25.34C2. For a collection that is incomplete 'Selections' is added – 25.34C3. Addition of 'arr.' – 25.35C1.

BACH, Johann Sebastian
  [Sonatas, violin, harpsichord, BWV 1014-1019]
  Sechs Sonaten für Klavier und Violine / Joh. Seb. Bach ; herausgegeben von Ferd. David. – Leipzig : Peters, [ca. 1889].
  1 score (2 v.) + 1 part (2 v.) ; 31 cm.
  Pl. no.: 7281-7282.

1. Title
2. Sechs Sonaten für Klavier und
     Violine
3. David, Ferdinand

Approximate date, estimated from plate number, given – 1.4F7. Number of volumes added to statement of extent – 5.5B2. Plate number recorded in note – 5.7B19.

Name of the type of composition used as a basis for uniform title – 25.26A and 25.27D1. Number omitted from initial title element – 25.28A(4). Accepted English form of name used – 25.29A1. Name given in the plural unless the composer wrote only one work of the type – 25.29A1. Addition of medium of performance, as this is not implied by title proper – 25.30B1. (The basis for the uniform title is the composer's original title in the language in which it was presented – 25.27A1; the use of the word 'Klavier' on the title page should not be interpreted as 'piano' for music before ca. 1775). English terms used for individual instruments using supplied list as a guide – 25.30B4. Addition of thematic index numbers in the case of certain composers (in the absence of, or in preference to, serial numbers and/or opus numbers) – 25.30C4. Bach composed other sonatas for harpsichord and violin not included in this publication. However, as the selections form a consecutively numbered group, the inclusive numbering is used instead of 'Selections' – 25.32B1 and 25.6B1.

302

BRITTEN, Benjamin
[Peter Grimes. Vocal score]
Peter Grimes : op. 33 : an opera in three acts and a prologue derived from the poem of George Crabbe / words by Montague Slater ; music by Benjamin Britten ; vocal score by Erwin Stein. – London : Boosey & Hawkes, c1945.
1 vocal score (379 p.) ; 31 cm.

1. Title   2. Slater, Montague
3. Stein, Erwin   4. Crabbe, George

Opus number treated as other title information because title proper does not consist of type of composition, medium of performance, etc. – 5.1B1.

Composer was created life peer but title is omitted as he is not commonly known by it – 22.6A1. Basis for uniform title is composer's original title in language in which it was presented – 25.27A1. Addition of vocal score – 25.35D1.

303

A COMPILATION of the litanies, vespers, hymns and anthems as sung in the Catholic Church / by John Aitken ; reissued in facsimile with a new introduction by J.C. Selner, Jules Baisnée, Albert Hyma. – Philadelphia : Musical Americana, 1956.
8, 136 p. of music ; 26 cm.
"Adapted to the voice or organ".
Facsim. reprint. Originally published: Philadelphia, 1787.

1. Aitken, John
2. Catholic Church

Note relating to bibliographic history of work – 5.7B7.

Liturgical music treated as general liturgical work – 21.22A. Liturgical work is normally entered under heading for church or denomination to which it pertains – 21.39A1. However, although the Catholic Church is named on the title page, this work appears to be a miscellany of Catholic and Protestant music, with no strict liturgical structure. It is

therefore considered to fall into one of the categories listed at 21.39A3 and is entered in accordance with the general rules, i.e. under collective title – 21.7B1.

304

ELGAR, Sir Edward
[Pomp and circumstance (Military march)]
Pomp and circumstance : military march no. 1, op. 39 / Edward Elgar. – London : Boosey & Hawkes, c1929.
1 miniature score (26 p.) ; 19 cm. – (Hawkes pocket scores).

1. Title

Term 'miniature score' is used as specific material designation for score reduced in size and not primarily intended for performance – 5.5B1 and ft. note 1. Optionally, a statement found in the chief source of information indicating the physical presentation of the music may be transcribed in a musical presentation area – 5.3B1 (see example no. 315). In this case such as transcription would result in the term 'miniature score' being recorded twice. Therefore, despite the fact that 'miniature score' is included as an example in 5.3B1, it would seem superfluous here. Note also the instruction in 5.3B2: 'If a musical presentation statement is an inseparable part of another area . . . do not repeat it'. Work is for orchestra so instruments involved not listed – 5.7B1.

As there are several compositions of this title, a uniform title with the addition of, in this example, a descriptive word or phrase enclosed in parentheses is used to resolve any conflict – 25.31B1. Alternatively a statement of the medium of performance could be added if this were thought sufficient to resolve the conflict. 'Sir' added to heading – 22.1C and 22.12B1.

305

FALLA, Manuel de
    El sombrero de tres picos = Le
tricorne = The three-cornered hat :
ballet / by Martinez Sierra ; after a story
by Alarcon ; [music by] Manuel de
Falla. – London : Chester, c1921.
    1 miniature score (xiv, 254 p.) ; 19 cm.
    Synopsis in English and French.
    Duration: 30 min.

    1.   Title †   2.   Le tricorne
    3.   The three-cornered hat † *
    4.   Sierra, Martinez

Parallel titles recorded in the order indicated on
chief source of information – 5.1D1 and 1.1D.
Work is for orchestra, so no note is made on
medium of performance – 5.7B1.

Musical setting for ballet entered under heading
for composer – 21.20A. Spanish name entered
under part following the prefix unless the prefix
consists of an article only – 22.5D1.

306

FINZI, Gerald
    By footpath and stile : for baritone solo
with accompaniment of string quartet /
poems by Thomas Hardy ; music by
Gerald Finzi. – London : Curwen, c1925.
    1 score (37 p.) + 4 parts ; 30 cm.
    Publisher's no.: 902902.

    1.   Title   2.   Hardy, Thomas

Pagination and number of parts added to
statement of extent – 5.5B2. Publisher's
number recorded in note – 5.7B19. Note on the
medium of performance is not required as it is
named elsewhere in the description – 5.7B1.

307

GLUCK, Christoph Willibald von
    [Alceste. Vocal score. English.
Selections ; arr.]
    Scenes from Alcestis / C.W. von Gluck ;
edited and arranged by Philip L. Baylis. –
London : Oxford University Press, 1957.
    1 vocal score (64 p.) ; 25 cm.
    For solo voices (SSMzMzMzAAA),
chorus and piano.
    "For stage or concert presentation by
female choirs and schools".

    1.   Title   2.   Scenes from Alcestis
    3.   Baylis, Philip L.

Note on medium of performance includes
parenthetical statement of component voice
parts, using prescribed abbreviations (i.e the
work is for two sopranos, three mezzo-sopranos
and three altos) – 5.7B1.

Arrangement of composer's work entered under
heading for composer – 21.18B1. German
whose name contains prefix which is not article
or contraction of article and preposition is
entered under the part following the prefix –
22.5D1. Uniform title for musical work is
composer's original title in language in which it
was presented – 25.27A1. For item consisting
of extracts from a work 'Selections' is added –
25.32B1 and 25.6B3. Addition of 'arr.' –
25.35C1. Addition of 'Vocal score' – 25.35D1. If
text is a translation, the name of language is
added – 25.35F1. Order of additions –
25.35A1.

308

GRAHAM, Colin
    A penny for a song : an opera in two
acts / [music by] Richard Rodney
Bennett ; libretto by Colin Graham ;
adapted from the play by John Whiting. –
London : Universal Edition, 1967.
    64 p. ; 21 cm.
    Libretto only.

    1.   Title
    2.   Bennett, Richard Rodney
    3.   Whiting, John

Other title information preceded by colon; each
subsequent statement of responsibility preceded
by semi-colon – 2.1A1. No specific material
designation for librettos, so details given in note
on artistic form – 2.7B1. (It would be evident to
a cataloguer that this item were a libretto, since
a score would always be recorded as such in
the physical description area. This would not be
clear, however, to most catalogue users. Where
a uniform title is used, the word 'Libretto' would
be added to the uniform title in accordance with
rule 25.35E1.)

Libretto as related work under its own heading
– 21.28A1 and 21.28B1. An alternative rule
(p. 351, footnote 7) permits entry under the
heading appropriate to the musical work which
is, in this case, the composer.

HANDEL, George Frederic
  [Messiah. Vocal score. Selections ; arr.]
  Unto us a child is born : music from
Handel's Messiah / arranged as a
Christmas cantata for two-part chorus
with optional ripieno chorus by Watkins
Shaw. – London : Novello, c1964.
  1 vocal score (40 p.) ; 16 cm.
  Duration: 20 min.

  1. Title   2. Unto us a child is born
  3. Shaw, Watkins

Duration of performance given if stated in the
item of music being described – 5.7B10.

Uniform title for musical work is composer's
original title in language in which it was
presented – 25.27A1. For item consisting of
extracts from a work 'Selections' is added –
25.32B1 and 25.6B3. Addition of 'Vocal score' –
25.35D1. Order of additions – 25.35A1.

MENDELSSOHN-BARTHOLDY, Felix
  [Symphonies, no. 5, op. 107, D minor]
  Symphony no. 5, D minor (Reforma-
tion), op. 107 / by Felix Mendelssohn-
Bartholdy ; foreword by Max Alberti. –
London : Eulenberg, [1960?].
  1 miniature score (iv, 90 p.) ; 19 cm.
  Foreword in English and German dated
1960.
  Pl. no.: E.E.6176.

  1. Title
  2. Symphony no. 5, D minor
      (Reformation), op. 107
  3. Reformation [symphony] † *

Type of composition treated as title proper –
5.1B1. Therefore, key and opus numbering
included in title proper and not separated by
colons – 5.1B1. (See also example no. 302).
Plate number recorded in note – 5.7B19.

Name of the type of composition used as a
basis for uniform title if composer's works with
titles that include the name of a type of
composition are also cited as a numbered
sequence of compositions of that type –
25.26A and 25.27D1. Accepted English form of

name used – 25.29A1. Name given in the plural
unless the composer wrote only one work of
the type – 25.29A1. Addition of serial
number – 25.30C2; opus number – 25.30C3;
key (for pre-twentieth century works) –
25.30D1.

The PARLOUR song book : a casquet of
  vocal gems / edited and introduced by
Michael R. Turner ; the music edited by
Antony Miall. – London : M. Joseph,
1972.
  x, 374 p. of music ; 27 cm.

  1. Turner, Michael R.
  2. Miall, Antony

Musical work that includes words is entered
under heading for composer – 21.19A1. This
item, however, is a collection with collective
title and so is entered under that title – 21.7B1.

PREVIN, André
  [The good companions. Vocal score.
Selections]
  The good companions : the musical of
the novel by J.B. Priestley : [vocal
selection / music by André Previn ; lyrics
by Johnny Mercer]. – London :
Chappell, c1974.
  1 vocal score (52 p.) : ill. ; 28 cm.

  1. Title   2. Mercer, Johnny
  3. Priestley, J.B.

Number of physical units recorded and an
appropriate term selected from a supplied list –
5.5B1. Pagination added in parentheses – 5.5B2
and 2.5B.

Musical work which contains words entered
under the heading for the composer – 21.19A1.

RIMBAULT, Edward F.

New instructions on the art of singing : comprising directions for the formation and cultivation of the voice after the methods of the best Italian masters ... chiefly selected from the celebrated tutor of Lablache / arranged and edited by Edward F. Rimbault. – New & rev. ed. – London : Chappell, [19--].

81 p. of music ; 36 cm.

Cover title: Rimbault's new singing tutor for soprano or tenor adapted from the valuable work of Lablache.

1. Title   2. Lablache, Luigi

Other title information abridged – 1.1E3.

Adaptation of music under heading for the adapter – 21.18C1.

RODGERS, Richard

[On your toes. Slaughter on Tenth Avenue]

Slaughter on Tenth Avenue : piano solo / by Richard Rodgers. – London : Chappell, c1956.

12 p. of music ; 28 cm.

1. Title

Note on medium of performance is not required as it is named elsewhere in the description – 5.7B1.

For a separately published part of a work, the uniform title for the whole work is used followed by the title of the part – 25.32A1. Although an arrangement, according to 25.35C2 'arr.' is not added.

A SELECTION OF

RODGERS & HART SONGS

Lyrics by
LORENZ HART

Arranged for Symphonic Band by
ERIK LEIDZÉN
Playing Time 8:50

Music by
RICHARD RODGERS

Conductor's Condensed Score

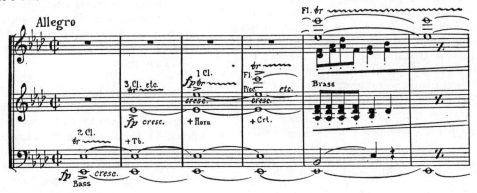

RODGERS, Richard
   [Songs. Selections ; arr.]
   A selection of Rodgers & Hart songs /
music by Richard Rodgers ; lyrics by
Lorenz Hart ; arranged for symphonic
band by Erik Leidzen. – Conductor's
condensed score. – New York : Chappell,
c1948.
   1 condensed score (14 p.) ; 31 cm.
Duration: 8 min., 50 sec.

   1.   Title   2. Hart, Lorenz
   3.   Leidzen, Erik

Optionally, a statement found in the chief
source of information indicating the physical
presentation of the music may be transcribed in
a musical presentation statement area – 5.3B1.
Number of physical units recorded and an
appropriate term selected from a supplied list –
5.5B1. Pagination added in parentheses – 5.5B2
and 2.5B. Note of duration of performance if it
is stated in the item – 5.7B10.

For a collection containing works of one type,
the name of that type is used for the uniform
title – 25.34C2. Addition of 'Selections' –
25.34C3. Addition of 'arr.' as this is a vocal work
arranged for instrumental performance –
25.35C2.

ROSSINI, Gioacchino
   [Il barbiere di Siviglia. Vocal score.
English & Italian]
   The barber of Seville = Il barbiere di
Siviglia : a lyric comedy / adapted from
the French of Pierre Augustin Caron de
Beaumarchais ; and rendered into English
from the Italian by J. Wrey Mould ; the
music composed by Gioacchino Rossini ;
revised from the orchestral score by W.S.
Rockstro. – London : Boosey, 1848.
   1 vocal score (viii, 16, 370 p.) ;
24 cm. – (The standard lyric drama ;
v. 3).
   Preface and libretto in English, followed
by the music with words in English and
Italian.

   1.   Title   2. The barber of Seville
   3.   Beaumarchais, Pierre Augustin
       Caron de
   4.   Mould, J. Wrey
   5.   Rockstro, W.S.   6. Series

Opera entered under heading for composer –
21.19A1. Uniform title for musical work is
composer's original title in language in which it
was presented – 25.27A1. 'Vocal score' added
to uniform title – 25.35D1. Names of languages
added – 25.35F1 and 25.5C.

VANHAL, Johann Baptist
   [Concertos, oboe, strings, F major ; arr.]
   Concerto for oboe and strings / J.C.
Vanhall ; freely adapted by Vilem
Tausky. – London : Oxford University
Press, c1957.
   1 score (18 p.) + 1 part ; 32 cm.
For oboe and piano.
Duration: about 12 min.

   1.   Title
   2.   Concerto for oboe and strings
   3.   Tausky, Vilem

Medium of performance named in note if it
does not appear in the rest of the description –
5.7B1. (In this example, the title statement
refers to the complete work.) If duration of
performance is stated in item, this is given in
note in abbreviated form – 5.7B10.

Although the words 'freely adapted' appear on
the title page, the musical material appears to
be 100% Vanhall. Since there is doubt as to the
work's status, it is treated as an arrangement
and entered under heading appropriate to
original work – 21.18C1 and 21.18B1. Person is
known by more than one name. Name by which
he is most commonly known or which appears
most frequently in his works cannot be
determined. Entry is therefore under name
appearing most frequently in reference sources
– 22.2A1(b).

Name of the type of composition used as a
basis for uniform title – 25.26A and 25.27D1.
Accepted English form of name used –
25.29A1. Name given in the plural unless the
composer wrote only one work of the type –
25.29A1. Medium of performance added –
25.30B1. English terms used for individual
instruments using supplied list as a guide –
25.30B4. Term selected from supplied list for a
group of instruments – 25.30B5. Addition of
key (for pre-twentieth century works) –
25.30D1. Addition of 'arr.' – 25.35C1.

Sound recordings

Chapter One and Chapter Six

For sound recordings as accompanying material see example no. 48.

For sound recordings as part of multimedia items see examples no. 2–4.

For serials in the form of sound recordings see example no. 457.

CAEDMON

JAMES AGEE: A PORTRAIT

James Agee reading

TC 2042 A   Side 1
                                                      13:02

1. James Agee, Theme with Variations
2. James Agee, *White Mane*
3. A. E. Housman, Mercenary Soldiers
4. Shakespeare, from *King Lear*
5. The Lord's Prayer

LONGPLAYING · 33⅓ RPM · MICROGROOVE

CAEDMON
A 2 RECORD ALBUM TC 2042

JAMES AGEE: A PORTRAIT

James Agee reads from his work
Father Flye reads from Agee's work and reminisces about the author

SIDE 1	TIMING
James Agee reading	
1. James Agee, Theme with Variations	4:14
2. James Agee, *White Mane* (Agee's English translation of the French film, *Crin Blanc*)	6:58
3. A. E. Housman, Mercenary Soldiers	:27
4. Shakespeare, from *King Lear*	:26
5. The Lord's Prayer	:32

SIDE 2	TIMING
James Agee reading	
1. Letter to a friend (dictated)	17:58

SIDE 3	TIMING
Father Flye reading from James Agee's works	
1. *A Death in the Family* p. 11 ff. "We are talking now of summer evenings . . ." p. 13 ff."Now is the night one blue dew . . ."	5:55
2. *The Morning Watch* p. 126 ff. "The ferment of the hogpen . . ."	7:40
3. *Let Us Now Praise Famous Men*	

	TIMING
p. 87 ff. "By now it is full glass light . . ." p. 91 "and the breakfasts ended . . ."	7:19
4. Collected Short Prose p. 125 ff. "Now as Awareness . . ."	5:21
Poems	
5. Delinquent	:54
6. A Lullaby	1:03
7. Rapid Transit	:41
8. Sonnet, "Now on the world and on my life as well"	1:01

SIDE 4	TIMING
Father Flye reminisces about his friendship with James Agee	
1. Early days at St. Andrews · travels · visits and correspondence	5:36
2. Agee's three marriages · Days on Fortune · Of the writing of *Let Us Now Praise Famous Men*, *The Morning Watch* and *Death in the Family*	11:42
3. Misfortunes and final hours	4:37
4. A summing up · Agee's insight, compassion and unfailing humor	5:00

CAEDMON TC 2042   JAMES AGEE: A PORTRAIT

CAEDMON TC 2042   JAMES AGEE: A PORTRAIT

AGEE, James

James Agee : a portrait / James Agee reading [from his work ; Father Flye reads from Agee's work and reminisces about the author]. – New York : Caedmon, 1971.

2 sound discs (ca. 90 min.) : analog, 33⅓ rpm, stereo. ; 12 in.

Contents: Side 1. James Agee reading: Theme with variations (4 min., 14 sec.). White mane (7 min.). A.E. Housman, Mercenary soldiers (27 sec.). Shakespeare, from King Lear (26 sec.). The Lord's prayer (32 sec.) – Side 2. James Agee reading: Letter to a friend (dictated) (18 min.) – Side 3. Father Flye reading from Agee's work: A death in the family (6 min.). The morning watch (8 min.). Let us now praise famous men (8 min.). Collected short prose (6 min.). Poems (3 min., 39 sec.) – Side 4. Father Flye reminisces about his friendship with James Agee: Early days at St. Andrews (6 min.). Agee's three marriages (12 min.). Misfortunes and final hours (4 min., 37 sec.). A summing up (5 min.).

Caedmon: TC 2042.

1. Flye, James Harold †
2. Optionally, author and title analytical entries for any particular part

Description of sound recordings (in this case a sound disc). Title transcribed as it appears in the chief source of information (i.e. the disc and label – 6.0B1) – 6.1B1 and 1.1B1. Labels on various sides are treated as if they were a single source – 1.0H1(a). Statements of responsibility are recorded in the form in which they appear on the item – 1.1F1. That part of the statement that is not taken from the prescribed chief source of information is enclosed within square brackets – 1.1F1. The participation of Flye goes beyond that of mere performance and his name can therefore be recorded in the statement of responsibility area – 6.1F1. The number of physical units and an appropriate term from a supplied list given as the specific material designation – 6.5B1. Optionally, approximate duration added – 6.5B2 and 1.5B4. Other physical details required are: type of record-ing – 6.5C2; speed in rpm – 6.5C3; number of sound channels – 6.5C7; and diameter of disc – 6.5D2. (The examples in the relevant

rules give the diameter in inches but rule 0.28 permits it to be recorded in metric if metric measurement is considered the normal measurement). Contents note – 6.7B18 and 1.7B18. Duration of individual pieces given – 6.7B18. Note of publisher's alphabetic and/or numeric symbol preceded by label name – 6.7B19.

Work by a single personal author, i.e. that person responsible for the creation of the intellectual or artistic content, entered under heading for that person – 21.1A1, 21.1A2 and 21.4A1. Also applicable is rule for sound recording of works by the same person – 21.23B1. Added entry under Flye as collaborator – 21.30B1. Omission of "Father" from heading – 22.15C. No added title entry as title proper is essentially the same as the main entry heading – 21.30J1(a).

BEE GEES

How deep is your love / Bee Gees. – [London] : RSO Records, p1977.

on 1 side of 1 sound disc (ca. 3 min.) : analog, 45 rpm, stereo. ; 7 in.

"From the Paramount/Robert Stigwood motion picture: Saturday night fever".

RSO: 2090 259.

With: Night fever.

1. Title   2. Saturday night fever

Separate description for separately titled work on sound recording lacking a collective title – 6.1G1, 6.1G4, 6.5B3 and 6.7B21. The members of the group (B., R., and M. Gibb) are also named in the chief source of information (the label) but they can be omitted from the statement of responsibility area – 6.1F2. They could be given in a note if considered important enough. Phonogram (copyright) date recorded – 6.4F1 and 1.4F6. 'With' note – 6.7B21 and 1.7B21.

Sound recording resulting from the collective activity of a performing group as a whole is entered under the heading for the group where the responsibility of the group goes beyond that of mere performance, execution, etc. – 21.1B2(e). The Bee Gees fall into this category since they write and produce their own music.

BEETHOVEN, Ludwig van
  Symphony no. 3, E flat, op. 55
"Eroica" = Symphonie nr. 3, Es-Dur,
op. 55 "Eroica" / Ludwig van
Beethoven. – [S.l.] : Sonata, [198-].
  1 sound disc (49 min., 58 sec.) : digital,
stereo. ; 4¾ in.
  Slovak Philharmonic Orchestra, Zdenek
Kosler, conductor.
  Sonata: CD 91004.

  1. Title   2. Eroica (symphony)
  3. Slovak Philharmonic Orchestra

Description of compact discs. Title transcribed
as instructed in 6.1B1 and 1.1B1, with data
included as for musical items – 5.1B. If a title
consists of the name of a type of composition
and one or more of medium of performance,
key, date of composition and number, the type
of composition, medium of performance, etc., is
treated as the title proper – 5.1B1. Parallel title
transcribed – 6.1D1, 1.1D and 5.1D. If no place
or probable place of publication can be given,
the abbreviation s.l. (sine loco) is used – 1.4C6.
If the playing time is on the item, give this time
as stated – 1.5B4(a).

Optionally, a uniform title could have been used
according to Ch. 25, i.e:

  [Symphonies, no. 3, op. 55, E flat]

A sound recording of one work is entered
under the heading appropriate to that work –
21.23A1.

BERLIOZ, Hector
  Symphonie fantastique : op. 14 /
Berlioz. – England : Philips, p1975.
  1 sound disc : analog, 33⅓ rpm,
stereo. ; 12 in.
  Concertgebouw Orchestra, Amsterdam,
Colin Davis, conductor.
  Philips: 6500 774.

  1. Title
  2. Concertgebouw Orchestra

Title transcribed as instructed in 6.1B1 and
1.1B1, with data included as for musical
items – 5.1B. If a number is found in the chief
source of information it is treated as other title

information – 5.1B1 and 5.1E1. When the
participation of a performer is confined to
performance, execution or interpretation (as is
commonly the case with "serious" or classical
music) the statement of responsibility is given in
the note area – 6.1F1 and 6.7B6.

Optionally, a uniform title could have been used
(see examples no. 310 and 320).

A sound recording of one work is entered under
the heading appropriate to the work – 21.23A1.

CHICAGO (Musical group)
  If you leave me now / P. Cetera ;
[performed by] Chicago. Together again /
L. Loughnane ; [performed by]
Chicago. – [London] : CBS, p1976.
  1 sound disc (8 min.) ; analog, 45 rpm,
stereo. ; 7 in.
  "Taken from the LP Chicago".
  CBS: S CBS 4603.

  1. Title   2. Cetera, P.
  3. Together again
  4. Loughnane, L.
         Together again

Sound recording without a collective title and
with no one part predominating described as a
unit – 6.1G1 and 1.1G2. Titles of the individual
parts transcribed in the order in which they
appear in the chief source of information –
6.1G2 and 1.1G3. If the participation of the
person or body named in a statement found in
the chief source of information goes beyond
that of performance (as is commonly the case
with "popular" music) such a statement is given
as a statement of responsibility – 6.1F1. The
format adopted here is that shown in the
Limmie & Family Cookin example provided in
rule 6.1G2.

Sound recording with no collective title containing works by different persons is entered
under the heading for the performer if the
participation goes beyond that of performance – 21.23D1. A suitable designation is
added to the heading if the name alone does
not convey the idea of a corporate body –
24.4B1.

An alternative solution would be to treat the
title on the 'A' side as the predominant part and

record the title on the 'B' side in a note – 1.1G1 and 1.7B18. Such a solution would mean that the main entry would then be made under the heading for Cetera, i.e. the heading appropriate to the separate, predominant part – 21.23A1 (see also example no. 325).

323

CHURCHILL, Winston S.
    I can hear it now : speeches / Sir Winston Churchill ; edited by E.R. Murrow and F.W. Friendly. – [Croydon] : Philips, [195-].
    1 sound disc (ca. 40 min.) : analog, 33⅓ rpm, mono. ; 12 in.
        Narration by Edward R. Murrow.
        Philips: SPL 100.

    1. Title   2. Murrow, Ed
    3. Friendly, F.W.

When the participation of a person found in a statement in the chief source of information is confined to performance, such a statement is given in a note – 6.1F1 and 6.7B6.

Entry under the heading for the person responsible for the intellectual content – 21.1A1, 21.1A2 and 21.4A1. Entry under the name which appears most frequently in the person's works – 22.2A1(a). This takes preference over the name that appears most frequently in reference sources, i.e.: Churchill, *Sir Winston Leonard Spencer*. Added entry for Murrow is made under the form of name by which he is commonly known – 22.2A1.

324

DAVRATH, Netania
    Songs of the Auvergne / arr., Joseph Canteloube. – New York : Vanguard ; London : RCA [distributor], 1972.
    2 sound discs (ca. 80 min.) : analog, 33⅓ rpm, stereo. ; 12 in. – (Vanguard recordings for the connoisseur).
        "Sung in the original dialect – Full translation inside" – Container.
        Netania Davrath, soprano ; Pierre de la Roche, conductor.
        Vanguard: VSD 713/714

    1. Title   2. Canteloube, Joseph
    3. Series

When the publisher is not in the home country of the cataloguing agency, a subsequently named distributor which is in the home country is added – 1.4D5(d). Optionally, statement of function of distributor may be added – 6.4E1 and 1.4E1. Where a sound recording is concerned, if the participation of persons found in a statement in a chief source of information is confined to performance, execution or interpretation, such a statement is given in a note – 6.1F1 and 6.7B6. (But see also example no. 322).

Entry is under the heading for the principal performer for a sound recording containing musical works by different persons which has a collective title – 21.23C1.

325

HUPFIELD, Herman
    As time goes by / Herman Hupfield ; [sung by] Dooley Wilson, with the voices of Humphrey Bogart and Ingrid Bergman. – London : United Artists, [1977].
    on 1 side of 1 sound disc (3 min., 10 sec.) : analog, 45 rpm, mono. ; 7 in.
        Edited from original soundtrack of the film: Casablanca, cWarner Bros., 1943.
        With: I'll string along with you / Harry Warren, Al Dubin ; sung by Dick Powell.
        United Artists: UP 36331A.

    1. Title   2. Wilson, Dooley

Separate description for separately titled work on sound recording lacking a collective title – 6.1G1, 6.1G4, 6.5B3 and 6.7B21.

When an item has been described separately, entry is made under the heading appropriate to that work – 21.23A1, which, in this instance, is that of the composer of the music – 21.1A1, 21.1A2 and 21.4A1.

An alternative solution would be to describe the item as a unit. Such a solution would mean that main entry would then be under the heading for Wilson as the principal performer on a sound recording with no collective title containing musical works by different persons – 21.23C1 (see also examples no. 322 and 324).

KHACHATURIAN, Aram
The ''Onedin Line'' theme ; Sabre dance / Khachaturian. – London : Decca, p1971.
1 sound disc (ca. 8 min.) : analog, 45 rpm, stereo. ; 7 in.
Vienna Philharmonic Orchestra, Aram Khachaturian, conductor.
First item consists of ''Music from ''Spartacus'' as adapted for the BBC-TV series by Anthony Isaac''.
Decca: F 13259.

1. Title   2. Sabre dance
3. Vienna Philharmonic Orchestra
4. Isaac, Anthony †

Sound recording without a collective title described as a unit – 6.1G1, 6.1G2 and 1.1G3.

Sound recording of two or more works all by the same person under the heading appropriate to those works – 21.23B1.

LAST, James
Love must be the reason / James Last [and his orchestra] ; produced and arranged by James Last. – [London] : Polydor, p1972.
1 sound disc (ca. 40 min.) : analog, 33⅓ rpm, stereo. ; 12 in.
Issued also as stereo cassette and 8-track stereo cartridge.
Partial contents: Wedding song / Stookey – Heart of gold / Young – I don't know how to love him / Lloyd Webber – Love must be the reason / Schuman.
Polydor: 2371-281.

1. Title
2. Optionally, author and title analyticals for each part

Same item available in different formats. Note on the other formats – 6.7B16 and 1.7B16.

Sound recording with collective title containing works by different persons entered under the person represented as principal performer – 21.23C1. The collective title is, in this instance, the same as that of one of the parts. A reference would be necessary from Last's real name (Hans Last).

McKENZIE, Robert
The modern election : a critical appraisal / Robert McKenzie and David Butler. – London : Audio Learning, 1971.
on 1 track of 1 sound cassette (ca. 28 min.) : analog, mono. + 1 pamphlet (22 p. ; 21 cm.) in box 21 x 14 x 3 cm. – (Audio Learning discussion tapes. Politics ; POAOO3).
Supplementary pamphlet by Maurice Willatt.
With: The modern electoral system : the alternatives / Robert McKenzie and David Butler.

1. Title   2. Butler, David
2. Series   4. Willatt, Maurice

See annotation following next example.

McKENZIE, Robert
The modern election : a critical appraisal ; The modern electoral system : the alternatives / Robert McKenzie and David Butler. – London : Audio Learning, 1971.
1 sound cassette (ca. 56 min.) : analog, 2 track, mono. + 1 pamphlet (22 p. ; 21 cm.) in box 21 x 14 x 3 cm. – (Audio Learning discussion tapes. Politics ; POAOO3).
Supplementary pamphlet by Maurice Willatt.

1. Title
2. The modern electoral system
3. Butler, David   4. Series
5. Willatt, Maurice

Sound recording lacking a collective title may be described as a unit (329) or a separate description is made for each separately titled part (328) – 6.1G1.

Optionally, if an item is in a container, the container is named at the end of the physical description area and its dimensions given – 1.5D2.

330

O'CONNOR, Tom
   "Alright mouth" / Tom O'Connor. –
Liverpool : Stag Music, p1974.
   1 sound disc (ca. 40 min.) : analog,
33⅓ rpm, stereo. ; 12 in.
   Stag music: SG.10063.

   1.   Title

Title transcribed in accordance with rule 1.1B1;
quotation marks are retained as the title proper
is a quote from the item's content. Work
consists of a performance by a comedian who
is also responsible for the material; his
contribution therefore goes beyond that of mere
performance and his name is recorded as a
statement of responsibility – 6.1F1.

Entry is under the heading for the single person
responsible for the artistic content – 21.1A1,
21.1A2 and 21.4A1. Entry under name by which
person is commonly identified – 22.1A. Name
with prefix which is not article, preposition or
combination of the two entered under prefix –
22.5D2.

331

PLANNING for cataloguing : proceedings
   of a meeting of the Cataloguing and
Indexing Group of the Library Association,
held at Liverpool on 11th June, 1970. –
Liverpool : College of Commerce, Dept. of
Library and Information Studies, 1970.
   1 sound tape reel (ca. 90 min.) : analog,
3¾ ips, mono. ; 7 in.
   J. Watters, S. Fellows and A.C. Bubb,
principal speakers.

   1.   Library Association. Cataloguing
        and Indexing Group

Description of sound tape reels. No indication of
duration appears on item but approximate time
can readily be ascertained – 6.5B2 and
1.5B4(b). Number of tracks given only if other
than standard – 6.5C6. Diameter of reel given
but width of tape only given if other than
standard – (¼ in.) – 6.5D6. Note of persons
considered to be important who were not
named in the statement of responsibility –
1.7B6 and 6.7B6.

Item consists of the proceedings of a meeting

but the meetings lack a name (the name of the
organizing corporate body is *not* the name of
the meeting) and entry is therefore under
title – 21.5A.

332

POWELL, Sandy
   The lost policeman : humorous sketch /
Sandy Powell (comedian) ; assisted by
Little Percy. – [London?] : Broadcast,
[193-?].
   1 sound disc (ca. 5 min.) : analog,
78 rpm, mono. ; 8 in.
   Broadcast: 429.

   1.   Title   2.   Little Percy

Statement of responsibility recorded in the form
in which it appears on the item – 1.1F1.
Contribution of person which goes beyond that
of mere performance and so name can be
recorded as a statement of responsibility –
6.1F1. Probable place of publication – 1.4C6
and probable date – 1.4F7.

Entry under the heading for the principal person
responsible, which is indicated by the wording
and the layout of the chief source of information – 21.1A2 and 21.6B1. Entry under name
by which person is commonly identified –
22.1A. Added entry under collaborating person
– 21.30B1 and heading for that person involves
entry under phrase which is entered in direct
order as it consists of a forename preceded by
a word other than a term of address or a title of
position or office – 22.11A.

SCHOLA HUNGARICA ENSEMBLE
Magyar Gregorianum : a karácsonyi ünnepkör dallamai. – [Budapest] : Hungaraton, [1976].
1 sound disc : analog, 33⅓ rpm, stereo. ; 12 in.
Container notes in Hungarian, English, German and Russian.
Title on container: Gregorian chants from Hungary : medieval Christmas melodies.
Schola Hungarica Ensemble, Janka Szendrei, László Dobszay, leaders.
''This recording was made at the medieval church at Besa'' – Container.
Hungaraton: LPX 11477.

1. Title
2. Gregorian chants from Hungary †

Title proper appears in two languages but the version chosen is that which appears on the chief source of information (i.e the disc and label) – 6.0B1 and 6.0B2.

Note made of container title[1] – 1.7B4 and 6.7B4. When the participation of a body found in a statement in the chief source of information is confined to performance, such a statement is given in a note – 6.1F1 and 6.7B6. (But see also example no. 322).

Sound recording with collective title containing musical works by different persons entered under the heading for the principal performer – 21.23C1.

---

[1] "Container" is the umbrella term for a sound recording's sleeve, box, etc. (see 6.0B1) and this is the term which appears in the examples included in rules such as 6.7B4.

SHAKESPEARE, William
Hamlet / [directed by Michael Redgrave ; script adapted by Michael Benthall]. – Modern abridged version. – London : Oldbourne Press, c1964.
1 sound disc (ca. 50 min.) : analog, 33⅓ rpm, mono. ; 12 in. + 1 text (42 p. ; 31 cm.). – (Living Shakespeare).
Cast: Michael Redgrave, Margaret Rawlings, John Phillips.
Credits: Musique concrete, Desmond Leslie ; narrator Michael Benthall.
Text includes acting version, complete play, notes and glossary.
Oldbourne: DEOB 1AM.

1. Title*   2. Redgrave, Sir Michael
3. Benthall, Michael   4. Series

No statement of responsibility in the chief source of information of a sound recording (i.e. the disc and label) so information taken from the container, i.e. the sleeve, and enclosed in square brackets – 6.0B2 and 1.0A1. Shakespeare is not given as a statement of responsibility on either the label or the sleeve and cannot therefore be included – 1.1F2. The presence of the word *version* is taken as evidence of edition statement – 1.2B3. Two names appear on the label but the trade name "Living Shakespeare" appears to be the name of a series rather than a publishing subdivision – 6.4D3. It is also presented as a series on the accompanying text. Accompanying material recorded in physical description area – 1.5E1(d) and 6.5E1 (rules 1.9B1 and 1.10B are also relevant). Optionally, the physical description of the accompanying material is added. Notes on cast and credits – 1.7B6, 6.7B6 and by analogy with 7.7B6. Note on accompanying material – 1.7B11 and 6.7B11.

Sound recording of one literary work under the heading appropriate to that work – 21.23A1. Item is treated as an abridgement – not an adaptation – and entry is made under the heading for the original author – 21.12A1.

SPENCER, Peggy

Step this way : an introduction to modern dancing / by Peggy Spencer ; music by the Burt Rhodes Orchestra. – London : BBC ; Pye [distributor], p1979.

1 sound disc : analog, 33⅓ rpm, stereo. ; 12 in.

From the BBC TV series.

Contents: Side 1. 1. Disco. 2. Music. 3. Samba. 4. Music. 5. Cha cha cha. 6. Music – Side 2. 1. Jive & rock 'n roll. 2. Music. 3. Social foxtrot. 4. Music. 5. Social quickstep. 6. Music.

BBC: REC 374.

1. Title   2. Burt Rhodes Orchestra

Related work under its own heading – 21.28B1. No added entry under related work as the title of the BBC TV programme is the same as the title of the recording.

STANBURY, Jacqueline
    Come love with me : poems for people in love / selected by Christine Westwood. – [London] : Times Newspapers, p1975.
    1 sound cassette (55 min.) : analog, stereo. – (World of literature).
    Read by Jacqueline Stanbury, Peter Jeffrey and Ian Gelder.
    Times Newspapers: WLA 003.

1. Title   2. Westwood, Christine
3. Jeffrey, Peter   4. Gelder, Ian
5. Series

Description of sound cassettes. Title transcribed as it appears in the chief source of information (i.e. the cassette and label – 6.0B1) – 1.1F6. Statement of responsibility recorded in the form in which it appears on item – 1.1F1. Where a sound recording is concerned, if the participation of persons found in a statement in the chief source of information is confined to performance, such a statement is given in a note – 6.1F1 and 6.7B6. (But see also example no. 322). Phonogram (copyright) date recorded – 6.4F1 and 1.4F6. Playing speed and number of tracks not required as they are standard (i.e. 1⅞ ips and 4) – 6.5C3 and 6.5C6. Cassette is of standard dimensions (3⅞ x 2½ in.) and tape is of standard width (⅛ in.), so this information is also omitted – 6.5D5. Tape is Dolby processed; it is optional whether to include this following "stereo" in the physical description – 6.5C8.

Sound recording with collective title containing literary works by different persons entered under the principal performer or, as in this instance, under the first named when there are two or three principal performers – 21.23C1.

SULLIVAN, Sir Arthur
    Patience / [Gilbert & Sullivan]. – London : London, p1961.
    2 sound discs : digital, stereo. ; 4¾ in.
    D'Oyly Carte Opera Company and the New Symphony Orchestra of London, Isidore Godfrey, conductor.
    London: 414429-2.

1. Title   2. Gilbert, W.S.
3. D'Oyly Carte Opera Company
4. New Symphony Orchestra

Description of compact discs. Statement of responsibility taken from outside prescribed source of information (i.e. the disc and label) is enclosed in square brackets – 6.1F1 and 1.1F1. When a sound recording bears both the name of a publishing company and the name of a subdivision of that company or a trade name or brand name used by that company, the name of the subdivision or trade name or brand name is given as the publisher – 6.4D2. (In this instance the disc bears both the trade name London and the name of the publisher Decca Record Company). For a sound disc, the manner in which the sound is encoded on the item, i.e. analog or digital, is given – 6.5C2. When participation of performers is confined to performance, execution or interpretation, the statement of responsibility is given in the note area – 6.1F1 and 6.7B6.

A sound recording of one work is entered under the heading appropriate to that work – 21.23A1. A musical work that includes words is entered under the heading for the composer – 21.19A1.

338

TEXAS country / Willie Nelson ... [et al.]. – Los Angeles : United Artists, c1976.
    2 sound discs : analog, 33⅓ rpm, stereo. ; 12 in.
    Recordings by Willie Nelson (side 1), Bob Willis and his Texas Playboys (side 2), Asleep At The Wheel (side 3), and Freddie Fender (side 4).
    United Artists: LA574-H2.

    1.   Nelson, Willie

This item is included in AACR 2 as an example of a performing body whose contribution goes beyond that of mere performance and which is therefore recorded as a statement of responsibility – 6.1F1. All but the first body omitted when more than three bodies are named; omission is indicated and "et al." added in square brackets – 1.1F5. Playing time may be omitted if it cannot readily be ascertained – 1.5B4. Note of names of performers not already named in the statement of responsibility – 6.7B6.

Sound recording with collective title containing musical works by different persons or bodies performed by more than three principal performers entered under title – 21.23C1. If four or more persons or bodies are involved an added entry is stipulated for the first named only – 21.30B1. However, in this instance, the names of the other performers could be considered to provide "important access points" – 21.30H1. Headings such as Asleep At The Wheel would require the addition of a suitable designation in order to convey the idea of a corporate body (as illustrated in example no. 322).

339

The WORLD of your hundred best tunes : the top ten – London : Decca, p1970.
    1 sound disc (ca. 45 min.) : analog, 33⅓ rpm, stereo. ; 12 in.
    Container title.
    Based upon the 10 most frequently requested tunes from the BBC radio programme: Your hundred best tunes.
    Contents: Finlandia / Sibelius – Nuns' chorus from Casanova / Strauss – Intermezzo from Cavalleria rusticana / Mascagni – Don't be cross from Der Obersteiger / Zeller – Final movement from Symphony no. 6 (Pastoral) / Beethoven – Piano sonata no. 14 (Moonlight) / Beethoven – Chorus of the Hebrew Slaves from Nabucco / Verdi – Violin concerto no. 1 in G minor / Bruch – Cantata no. 147 (Jesu Joy) / Bach – Nimrod from Enigma variations / Elgar.
    Decca: SPA 112.

    1.   Optionally, author and title analytical entries for each part †

Collective title is on container, i.e. sleeve only; this is therefore treated as chief source of information – 6.0B1. A note of the source is made – 6.0B1 and 6.7B3. Titles and statements of responsibility for individual works contained on a sound recording given in a contents note – 6.7B18.

Related work under its own heading – 21.28B1. Sound recording with collective title containing musical works by different persons performed by more than three principal performers (each of the ten tunes is performed by a different person and/or body) is entered under title – 21.23C1.

340

YOUNG, Faron
    It's four in the morning / Faron
Young. – [London] : Mercury, [197-].
    1 sound cartridge (ca. 29 min.) : analog,
stereo.
    Partial contents: After the fire is gone /
White – Trip to Tijuana / Harden – I'll
take the time / Cochran – It's four in the
morning / Chesnut.
    Mercury: 7708-045.

1. Title
2. Optionally, author and title
    analytical entries for each part

Description of 8-track stereo sound cartridges.
Playing speed and number of tracks given only
if other than standard – 6.5C3 and 6.5C6.
Cartridge is of standard dimensions (i.e. 5¼ x
3⅞ in.) and tape is of standard width (i.e. ¼ in.)
and so this information is also omitted from
physical description – 6.5D4.

Sound recording with collective title containing
works by different persons entered under the
person represented as principal performer –
21.23C1. The collective title is, in this instance,
the same as that of one of the parts.

Motion pictures and videorecordings

Chapter One and Chapter Seven

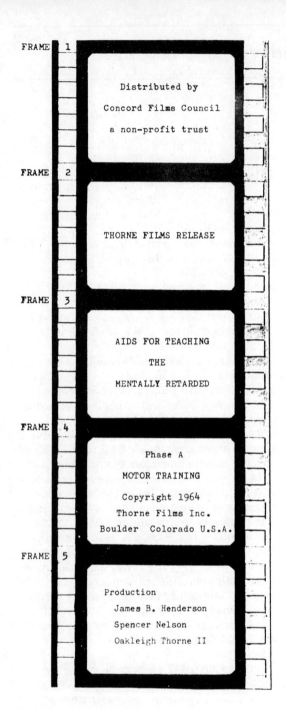

FRAME 1

Distributed by
Concord Films Council
a non-profit trust

FRAME 2

THORNE FILMS RELEASE

FRAME 3

AIDS FOR TEACHING
THE
MENTALLY RETARDED

FRAME 4

Phase A
MOTOR TRAINING
Copyright 1964
Thorne Films Inc.
Boulder Colorado U.S.A.

FRAME 5

Production
James B. Henderson
Spencer Nelson
Oakleigh Thorne II

CONCORD
FILMS COUNCIL
Nacton, Ipswich, Ipswich 76012

AIDS FOR TEACHING
THE MENTALLY RETARDED
PHASE A : MOTOR TRAINING

Please do NOT rewind
Please return films
promptly

341

AIDS for teaching the mentally retarded /
  production, James B. Henderson,
Spencer Nelson, Oakleigh Thorne II. –
Boulder, Colo. : Thorne Films ; Ipswich :
Concord Films [distributor], c1964.
  5 film reels (ca. 40 min.) : sd., col. ;
16 mm.
  One phase per reel.
  Contents: Phase A. Motor training –
Phase B. Initial perceptual training –
Phase C. Advanced perceptual training –
Phase D. Integrated motor perceptual
training – Phase E. Sheltered workshop.

  1. Henderson, James B.
  2. Nelson, Spencer
  3. Thorne, Oakleigh
  4. Optionally, analytical title entries
        for each part

Description of motion pictures (in this case film
reels). Title transcribed as it appears in chief
source of information – 7.1B1 and 1.1B1 (chief
source of information for a motion picture is the
film itself – 7.0B1). Names of persons credited
in the chief source of information with
participation in the production of a film who are
considered to be of major importance are given
in the statement of responsibility area – 7.1F1.
Place of publication, distribution, etc. and
publisher recorded in the form in which they
appear in item – 7.4C1, 1.4C, 7.4D1 and 1.4D.
Optionally, the distributor, releasing agency, etc.
may also be given – 7.4D1, and a statement of
function added – 7.4E1 and 1.4E. Number of
units and an appropriate term from a supplied

list given as the specific material designation –
7.5B1. Duration in minutes added (if no
indication appears on the item, optionally an
approximation is made) – 7.5B2 and 1.5B4.
Other physical details required are: sound
characteristics (i.e. 'sd' or 'si') – 7.5C3; colour –
7.5C4; and gauge (i.e. width) of the film in
millimetres – 7.5D2. Speed in frames per
second is only given if this information is
considered important – 7.5C5. Other physical
details given in a note – 7.7B10(k). Individual
works contained in the motion picture listed in
contents note – 7.7B18.

The producers, although named in the
statement of responsibility area, are not
considered primarily responsible for the
intellectual or artistic content. Item is therefore
treated as a work of which the personal
authorship is unknown and diffuse and entry is
under title – 21.1C1(a). Added entries would be
made under the producers according to rule
21.30F1, unless the cataloguing agency did not
consider that they provided important access
points.

BUSH, Kate
    The whole story / Kate Bush. –
[London] : Polygram, c1986.
    1 videodisc (ca. 55 min.) : sd., col. ;
12 in. – (Polygram music video).
    Photography, John Carder Bush; a
Picture Music International release.
    PAL TV, stereo digital sound.
    Contents: Intro. – Wuthering heights –
Cloudbusting – The man with the child
in his arms – Breathing – Wow –
Hounds of love – Running up that hill –
Army dreamers – Sat in your lap –
Experiment IV – The dreaming –
Babooshka – The big sky – Credits.
    PAL 0805041.

1.   Title
2.   Optionally, title analytical entries
     for each part

Description of videorecordings, in this case a
videodisc. Title and statement of responsibility
transcribed as they appear in chief source of
information – 7.1B1 and 1.1B1. Chief source of
information for a videorecording is the item
itself – 7.0B1 (in this case the label from the
disc has been used). Appropriate term from
supplied list chosen as specific material
designation and preceded by number of parts –
7.5B1. Playing time given – 7.5B2 and 1.5B4.
Sound character and colour indicated – 7.5C3
and 7.5C4. Diameter in inches given – 7.5D4.
Credits note for photography combined with
note on releasing agency – 7.7B6, 7.7B9 and
1.7A5. Releasing agency could, optionally, have
been given in publication, distribution, etc.
area – 7.4D1. Note in videorecording system
and other physical detail if desired – 7.7B10.
Contents note – 7.7B18. Note on important
number borne by item – 7.7B19.

Entry is made under principal performer by
analogy with rule for sound recording with
collective title containing works by different
persons or bodies – 21.23C1.

CHILDREN of a lesser god / Paramount
Pictures presents ; a Burt Sugarman
production ; a Randa Haines [director]
film. – [London] : CIC Video, 1988.
  1 videocassette (115 min.) : sd., col.
  Cast: William Hurt, Marlee Matlin,
Piper Laurie, Philip Bosco.
  Credits: Screenplay, Hesper Anderson
and Mark Medoff; music, Michael
Convertino; director of photography, John
Seale.
  Based on the stage play by Mark
Medoff.
  c1986: Paramount.
  VHS Hi-fi.
  Suitable only for persons 15 years and
over.
  VHB 2234.

  1. Paramount Pictures
  2. Sugarman, Burt
  3. Haines, Randa

Description of videorecordings, in this case a
videocassette. Title and statements of
responsibility transcribed from chief source of
information – 7.1B1, 1.1B1, 7.1F1 and 1.1F1.
The chief source of information for a
videocassette is, in order of preference, (a) the
item itself (e.g. the title frames) and (b) the
container and its label as the container is an
integral part of the piece – 7.0B1. Statements
of responsibility can include those persons or
bodies credited with participation in the
production of a film (e.g. as producer, director,
etc.) – 7.1F1. Word added to a statement of
responsibility if the relationship to the title is not
clear – 7.1F2. Publication details relate to the
physical item itself, i.e. the videocassette, and
not to the original film. Notes on cast and
credits – 7.7B6. Note on history – 7.7B7. Note
on publication, distribution – 7.7B9. Note on
videorecording system – 7.7B10(f). Note on
intended audience – 7.7B14. Note on number
borne by item – 7.7B19.

Entry under title when work emanates from
corporate body but does not fall within any of
the categories given in 21.1B2 and personal
authorship is diffuse – 21.1C1(c) and (a). Added
entries for up to three collaborating persons or
bodies – 21.30B1. Further added entries could
be made for any other persons or bodies having
a relationship to the work if such entries were
considered to be important access points –
21.30F1.

DIAMOND, Neil
  I'm glad that you're here with me / Neil
Diamond. – Utrecht, Netherlands :
Vestron, c1987.
  1 videocassette (ca. 53 min.) : sd., col.
  VHS Hi-fi stereo.
  Made in 1977.
  Partial contents: Sweet Caroline – You
don't bring me flowers – Song sung
blue – Desiree.
  VHS MA 11062.

  1. Title
  2. Optionally, title analytical entries for
      each part

Description of videorecordings. Title and
statement of responsibility transcribed as they
appear in chief source of information – 7.1B1
and 1.1B. Chief source of information for
videocassette is, in order of preference, (a) the
item itself (e.g. the title frames) and (b) the
container and its label as the container is
an integral part of the piece. Copyright date
given – 7.4F1 and 1.4F6. Appropriate term from
list chosen as specific material designation and
preceded by number of parts – 7.5B1. Playing
time given – 7.5B2 and 1.5B4. Sound
characteristic and colour indicated – 7.5C3 and
7.5C4. Note on date of publication – 7.7B9.
Note on videorecording system if desired –
7.7B10(f). Partial contents note – 7.7B18. Note
on important number borne by item – 7.7B19.

Entry is made under principal performer by
analogy with rule for sound recording with
collective title containing works by different
persons or bodies – 21.23C.

FIONA & Martyn's wedding / Devereux
    Video. – [Southport] : Devereux, 1988.
    1 videocassette (ca. 90 min.) : sd., col.
    VHS.
  Summary: Marriage ceremony of Fiona
and Martyn Jackson on 20th Feb. 1988 at
the Parish Church of St. John, Ainsdale,
and reception at Martin Inn, Burscough.

  1. Devereux Video

Title and statement of responsibility transcribed from chief source of information (in this case the title frames of the item – 7.0B1) – 7.1B1 and 1.1B. Item was published in that multiple copies were produced for sale and therefore publication details are required. Place of publication is known but does not appear on item and is therefore enclosed in square brackets – 1.0A1 and 1.4A2. Publisher given in shortest possible form as it has already appeared in title and statement of responsibility area – 1.4D4. Note on videorecording system – 7.7B10(f). Brief objective summary given – 7.7B17.

Item emanates from corporate body but does not fall within any of the categories listed in 21.1B2 and is therefore entered under title – 21.1C1(c).

346

INTRODUCING information. – 1987.
   1 videocassette (18 min.) : sd., col.
   BBC 2 television programme:
Information world, broadcast on 29 Apr. 1987, presenter: Carol Leader.
   VHS.
   Summary: The nature of information and the use made of the computer by public libraries.
   For educational non-commercial use only.

   1.   Information world

Title transcribed from chief source of information (in this case the title frames of the item itself – 7.0B1) – 7.1B1 and 1.1B. Place of publication and publisher not recorded for unpublished item – 7.4C2 and 7.4D2. Date of creation given – 7.4F3. Note on nature of item and note of presenter – 7.7B1 and 7.7B6. (Two notes or more may be combined when appropriate – 1.7A5). Brief objective summary given – 7.7B17. Note on restrictions that apply recorded by analogy with 4.7B14 as this is 'useful descriptive information that cannot be fitted into other areas' – 1.7A5.

Related work under its own heading – 21.28B1. Work of unknown authorship entered under title – 21.1C1(a). Added entry under work to which item is related – 21.30G1.

347

RAISING the ''Empress of Canada'' in Gladstone Dock, Bootle, 3 March, 1954 / made by Bootle Fire Brigade. – Bootle : The Brigade, 1954.
   1 film reel (10 min.) : si., b&w ; 16 mm.
   Summary: Shows how the ship was raised after she rolled over and sank owing to the effects of a fire on board.

   1.   Bootle (<u>Lancashire, England</u>)
      <u>Fire Brigade</u>

Brief objective summary given – 7.7B17.

Work emanating from corporate body but not falling within any of the categories listed at 21.1B2 is therefore entered under title – 21.1C1(c). Heading for added entry distinguishes Bootle, Lancashire (now Sefton, Merseyside) from Bootle, Cumbria. The name of a geographical entity is used to distinguish between corporate bodies of the same name – 23.1A. This is the name of the larger place, England – 23.4D2 but, if this is not sufficient, as in this case, the name of an appropriate smaller place is also given before the name of the larger place – 23.4F1.

348

RASMUS, Carolyn J.
   Agility / Carolyn J. Rasmus. – Cambridge, Mass. : Ealing, 1969.
   1 film loop (3 min., 35 sec.) : si., col. ; super 8 mm. – (Functional fitness).
   Consultants: The American Association for Health, Physical Education and Recreation.
   ''Licensed only for direct optical projection before a viewing audience'' – Box.
   Notes on box.

   1.   Title   2.   Series

Description of film loops. Duration added to specific material designation – 7.5B2 and 1.5B4. Sound characteristic given – 7.5C3. Indication of colour – 7.5C4. Gauge given in millimetres; 'super', etc. added as appropriate, since the film is 8 millimetres – 7.5D2. Note on restrictions that apply recorded by analogy with 4.7B14 as this is 'useful descriptive information that cannot be fitted into other areas' – 1.7A5.

349

SIMON Simon / Denouement Films ;
   producer, Peter Shillingford ; director, Graham Stark. – London : Tigon Film Productions [distributor], 1970.
   1 film reel (30 min.) : sd., col. ; 35 mm.
   Cast: Graham Stark, John Junkin, Norman Rossington, Julia Foster.
   Credits: Photography, Derek van Lynt and Harvey Harrison, Jr. ; sound, John Wood ; editor, Bunny Warren ; music, Denis King.
   Summary: Mixed comedy involving two municipal workmen, a blonde typist and a hydraulic platform truck.

1. Shillingford, Peter
2. Stark, Graham

Persons or bodies credited in the chief source of information with participation in the production of a film who are considered to be of major importance are recorded in the statement of responsibility area – 7.1F1. Alternatively, a production company, releasing agency, etc. may be named in the publication, distribution, etc. area – 7.4D1 (see example no. 341). Other statements of responsibility are given in notes, i.e. cast and credits – 7.7B6.

If a film emanates from a corporate body it is unlikely to fall within the categories listed in 21.1B2. The producers, by definition (see Appendix D) are not responsible for the artistic or intellectual content. Personal authorship is usually, as in this case, uncertain or diffuse and entry is therefore under title – 21.1C1(a). Further added entries could be made under any of the other bodies or persons named in the entry if the cataloguing agency considered that they provide important access points.

350

VISIT to London. – London : Walton, [197-?].
   1 film reel (ca. 12 min.) : si., col. ; standard 8 mm. – (Walton home movies).
   Available in col. or b&w as standard 8 si. and super 8 si.

1. Series

Gauge recorded in millimetres; if film is 8 mm., the number is preceded by single, standard, super, or Maurer as appropriate – 7.5D2. Note on other available formats – 7.7B16.

Graphic materials

Chapter One and Chapter Eight

For graphic materials as accompanying material see examples no. 88 and 219.

For graphic materials as part of multimedia items see examples no. 1, 3, 5, 6 and 7.

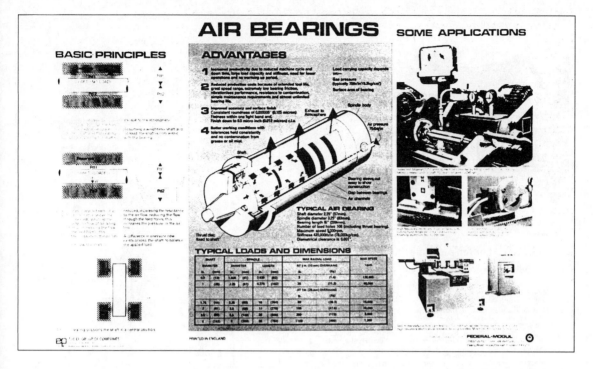

351

AIR bearings : some applications / The
  EP Group of Companies, Educational
Productions Limited. – Wakefield,
Yorkshire : EP, c1973.
  1 wall chart : col. ; 51 x 76 cm.
  "Produced in collaboration with Federal-
Mogul, Westwind Air Bearings Ltd."
  EP: C1180.

1.   Educational Productions
2.   Federal-Mogul

Description of wall charts. Title proper
transcribed as it appears in chief source of
information (i.e. the item itself – 8.0B1) –
8.1B1 and 1.1B. Other title information
transcribed – 8.1E1 and 1.1E. Statement of
responsibility transcribed in the form in which it
appears on item – 8.1F1 and 1.1F. Place of
publication, publisher and date of publication
given – 8.4C1, 8.4D1 and 8.4F1. Number of
physical units and an appropriate term from a
supplied list given as the specific material
designation – 8.5B1. Indication of colour
given – 8.5C2. Dimensions (height x width)
recorded – 8.5D1. Statement of responsibility

not recorded in the statement of responsibility
area given in a note – 8.7B6. Important number
borne by the item given in a note – 8.7B19.

Work of unknown authorship entered under
title – 21.1C1(a) and 21.5A.

352

The ARCADE, Cleveland, Ohio. –
  Cleveland : W. Evans, [197-?].
  1 postcard : col. ; 9 x 14 cm.
  "The largest of its type in the world ...
a street under an arched glass roof".

Description of postcards. Number of physical
units and an appropriate term from a supplied
list given as the specific material designation –
8.5B1. Indication of colour given – 8.5C2.
Dimensions (height x width) recorded – 8.5D1.
Note which is quotation from item given in
quotation marks. Source of quotation is not
included, as it is the chief source of information – 1.7A3. (Chief source of information for
graphic material is the item itself – 8.0B1).

Work of unknown authorship entered under
title – 21.1C1(a) and 21.5A.

J. COCKERILL

Beatrix Potter's House

Hilltop, Sawrey, Near Hawkshead

This was Beatrix Potter's first home in the Lake District.
She moved here from London in 1904. Here she produced
some of her best loved works.

The house was built in 1602 and is little changed from the
days when Beatrix Potter lived here. It is now cared for by
the National Trust. In the cottage are items such as the
Welsh dresser, familiar from the illustrations in her books.
At the age of 47 Beatrix Potter married William Heelis and
moved to Castle Cottage. She continued to work at Hilltop.
In later years Beatrix Potter bought substantial amounts of
property with preservation in mind. She left some 4,000
acres to the National Trust.

Beatrix Potter died in 1943 at the age of 77. The cottage
was opened to the public three years later.

LOCAL HISTORY CARDS   No. 508   C Gatehouse Prints

SCREW JACK

Harry Davies - April 1948 - Birmingham   Scale 1 : 1

353

COCKERILL, J.
   Beatrix Potter's house : Hilltop, Sawrey,
near Hawkshead / [illustration by]
J. Cockerill. – [Robin Hood's Bay,
Yorkshire] : Gatehouse Prints, [197-?].
   1 study print : b&w ; 15 x 11 cm. –
(Local history cards ; no. 508).

   1.   Title

Description of study prints. (A study print is not
defined in AACR 2. It may be defined as: a
picture with accompanying text which makes
the print significant for study purposes).

Item is work of collaboration between artist and
writer. Normally, entry is under heading for
one named first, unless other is given greater
prominence. In this instance, only one is
named – 21.24A.

354

DAVIES, Harry
   Screw jack / Harry Davies. – Birmingham, 1948.
   1 technical drawing ; 43 x 30 cm.
   Scale 1:1.

   1.   Title

Description of technical drawings. Title
transcribed exactly as it appears on item –
8.1B1 and 1.1B1. Title statement followed by
statement of responsibility – 8.1F1 and 1.1F1.
Publication area contains place (8.4C1 and
1.4C1) and date (8.4F1 and 1.4F1); place of
publication and publisher not recorded for
unpublished graphic item – 8.4C2 and 8.4D2.
Number of physical units and an appropriate
term from a supplied list given as the specific
material designation – 8.5B1.

Dimensions (height x width) given – 8.5D1 and 8.5D6. Scale given as note – 8.7B10. (For cartographic materials, the scale is given in the mathematical data area, but no such area exists for graphic materials.)

Entry under heading for personal author, i.e. the person responsible for the intellectual and artistic content of the drawing – 21.1A1. Name is identical to that in example no. 293 . However, neither dates nor distinguishing terms are available, so same heading is used for both persons – 22.20A.

355

DISPLAY. – [1977].
    1 flip chart (22 sheets) : some col. ; 90 x 58 cm.
    Examples of posters, other publicity materials, lettering, etc.
    Prepared by Eric J. Hunter.
    Not generally available.

    1.   Hunter, Eric J.

Description of flip charts. Physical description – 8.5B1, 8.5B3, 8.5C2 and 8.5D1. Note on the nature and scope of the item – 8.7B1 and 1.7B1. Note on statement of responsibility – 8.7B6 and 1.7B6. Note on availability (optional) – 8.8D1 and 1.8D1.

Item treated as a collection of independent works by different persons or bodies and entered under title – 21.7A1(a) and 21.7B1.

356

FOSTER, C.R.
    1907 Napier [from] National Motor Museum, Beaulieu / C.R. Foster. – Alresford, Hants. : Etchmaster Originals, [197-?].
    1 art print : copper engraving ; 21 x 28 cm.
    Size when framed: 25 x 32 cm.

    1.   Title

Description of art prints. Word added to title enclosed in square brackets – 1.1A2. Name of county added to place of publication if

considered necessary for identification – 1.4C3. (If 'Hants' had not appeared on item, it would have been enclosed in square brackets and spelled out in full as no abbreviations are prescribed for counties in United Kingdom – B.14A). Printing process recorded – 8.5C1(b). Dimensions exclude frame – 8.5D4. Size when framed given as note on physical description – 8.7B10.

357

FREDDIE Mercury (Queen) / by London Features International. – London : Big O Posters, c1977.
    1 poster : col. ; 85 x 61 cm.
    B205.

    1.   London Features International

Description of posters. Copyright date given – 1.4F6. Physical description – 8.5B1, 8.5C2 and 8.5D1.

Work emanating from corporate body which does not fall within categories listed at 21.1B2 and is therefore entered under title – 21.1C1(c).

358

GOYA, Francisco
    Goya. – London : Visual Publications, [1969].
    1 filmstrip (38 fr.) : col. ; 35 mm. – (History of western art. Master painters ; no. 15).
    Cine mode.
    With teachers' notes (28 p.).

    1.   Series   2.   Master painters

Description of filmstrips. Number of frames added to designation – 8.5B2. No rules for distinguishing between cine mode (i.e. read top to bottom) and comic mode (i.e. read left to right or right to left); details are therefore given in note on physical description – 8.7B10 (see also example no. 366). Details of accompanying material recorded in note – 1.5E1(c), 8.7B11 and 1.7B11.

Work consisting of reproductions of the works of an artist without accompanying text is entered under heading for the artist – 21.17A1.

GRANT, Alexander
 The Union Jack / Alexander Grant. –
[1975].
 1 transparency (2 attached overlays) :
col. ; 14 x 20 cm.
 Illustrates how the Union Jack is made
up from the Crosses of St. George,
St. Andrew and St. Patrick.
 Size when framed: 32 x 32 cm.

 1. Title

Description of overhead transparencies. Number
of overlays added to designation and indication
given of whether they are attached – 8.5B4.
Dimensions exclude frame or mount – 8.5D4.
Note on nature of item – 8.7B1. Size when
framed given as note on physical description –
8.7B10.

HART, Tony
 [Meetings, bloody meetings. Selections]
 Planning – pre-notification – prepar-
ation – processing – putting it on
record – : drawings / by Tony Hart. –
London : Video Arts, c1976.
 5 pictures on 1 sheet : b&w ; 30 x
22 cm.
 ''From the film ''Meetings, bloody
meetings''.''

 1. Title
 2. Planning – pre-notification –
    preparation – processing –
    putting it on record

– replaces ... when the latter punctuation
mark appears in title proper – 1.1B1. Noun
occurring in conjunction with a statement of
responsibility which is indicative of the nature of
the work is treated as other title information –
1.1F12. Copyright date given – 1.4F6. This
item, which is considered to be a graphic, is
difficult to describe using Ch. 8. 'Picture' seems
to be the most relevant specific material
designation but

    1 picture : b&w ; 30 x 22 cm.
or 5 pictures : b&w ; 30 x 22 cm.

provide misleading information. The above
interpretation has therefore been formulated by
analogy with 3.5B2. An alternative interpretation
would be to treat the item as a printed sheet
according to Ch. 2, i.e.

    1 sheet : ill. ; 30 x 22 cm.

Entry is under the person responsible for the
artistic content – 21.1A1, 21.1A2 and 21.4A1.
When an item consists of a collection of three
or more unnumbered extracts from a work, the
uniform title for the whole work is used
followed by 'Selections' – 25.6B3.

HISTORICAL reconstructions of
   Pompeii. – Chicago : Encyclopaedia
Britannica Educational, 1965.
   4 study prints (1 attached overlay each) ;
33 x 46 cm. + 1 teacher's study guide
card. – (History series ; no. 5680).
   Each print shows part of ruins of
Pompeii. Addition of transparent overlay
depicts original building. Verso of each
print has historical details, photo.,
diagrams and questions for students.
   "Suggested uses: World history, Latin,
art".
   Produced in collaboration with John
W. Eadie.
   In plastic wallet.

   1.   Series

Description of study prints. Overlays for study
prints have been recorded by analogy with rules
for transparencies – 8.5B4 and 8.5B5. Detail
relating to accompanying material given at end
of physical description – 8.5E1 and 1.5E1(d).
Series statement recorded – 8.6B1 and 1.6.

INSECTS harmful to man / produced by
   Encyclopaedia Britannica Films in
collaboration with John A. Wagner. –
Chicago : E.B. Films, 1966.
   8 study prints : col. ; 44 x 28 cm. folded
to 22 x 28 cm. + 1 introductory card + 1
teacher's guide and answer card. – (Basic
life science program) (Study print series ;
no. 5650).
   Each card has holes at corners for
pinning to wall.
   Contents: Aphids – Boll weevils –
Earwigs – Cockroaches – Houseflies.

   1.   Encyclopaedia Britannica Films
   2.   Wagner, John A.   3.   Series

Description of study prints. Accompanying
material recorded in physical description area –
1.5E1(d). More than one series statement –
1.6J1.

See also example no. 378.

HOLOGRAPHIC portrait of Professor
   Gabor / produced by McDonnel Douglas
Electronics Company. – St Charles, Mo. :
The Co., [197-].
   1 hologram : col. ; on photographic
plate, 44 x 59 cm.
   "Taken with a 30 nanosecond, 10 Joules
pulsed laser of a coherent length of about 5
metres".

   1.   McDonnel Douglas Electronics
         Company

There are no specific rules in AACR 2 for
describing a hologram (a record of three-
dimensional images on a photographic plate).
Although the image projected from it is three-
dimensional, the hologram itself is two-
dimensional. It is therefore treated here as a
graphic, except that, as none of the listed
designations in rule 8.5B1 is appropriate, the
specific name is given by analogy with Ch.10.

JOHNSON, Jeanette
   Mother Earth : in the bosom of Mother
Earth radiates the life energy of the sun /
Jeanette Johnson. – [19--].
   1 art original : sand on board, col. ;
33 x 18 cm.
   Indian sand painting originating from
New Mexico.
   Size when framed: 35 x 20 cm.

   1.   Title

Description of art originals. Place of publication
and publisher not recorded for unpublished
graphic item – 8.4C2 and 8.4D2. Date of
creation given – 8.4F2. Combined note on
artistic form and history of item – 8.7B1 and
8.7B7. Size when framed recorded as note –
8.7B10.

Entry under person responsible for artistic
content – 21.1A1, 21.1A2 and 21.4A1.

LADYBIRD flash cards. – Lough-
borough : Ladybird Books, 1977.
2 sets.

Set 2: 128 word cards for school and
home use including spare blanks.
128 flash cards : b&w ; 9 x 24 cm. in
box 24 x 18 x 2 cm.
"For use with books 5a, 5b, 6a, 6b
of the Ladybird key words reading
scheme" – Box.
ISBN 0-7214-3018-X.

Description of flash cards. Optionally, in
describing a single part of a multimedia item, a
multilevel description may be used – 1.10D1
and 13.6. If item is in container, the container
may be named and its dimensions given –
1.5D2. Note consisting of quotation is given,
followed by an indication of its source if this is
not the chief source – 1.7A3.

The LAMBETH apocalypse. –
[Wakefield] : Micro Methods, 1963.
1 filmstrip (ca. 100 fr.) : col. ;
35 mm. + teacher's notes (31 p.).
Also known as: De Quincy apocalypse.
Original: "Ms 209, Lambeth Palace
Library late 13th century. Reproduced ...
by permission of His Grace the Lord
Archbishop of Canterbury and the Trustees
of the Lambeth Palace Library".
Cine mode, with title fr. and 1st fr. in
comic.

Description of filmstrips. Location and other
information about original given in note by
analogy with 8.7B22 and see also 4.7B1. Re.
note 'Cine mode' see also example no. 358.

LANGUAGE for learning. – Rev. and
expanded ed. – London : Heinemann
Educational : Inner London Education
Authority, Media Resources Centre, 1976.
5 units.
Devised by Eve Boyd ... [et al.] ;
editor: Sandy Mahon ; designer: Melvin
Raymond.
First published: ILEA, Media Resources
Centre, 1973.

Unit 1: Classification.
124 lesson cards : col. ; 8 x 11 cm. in
box 16 x 23 x 2 cm. + 1 teacher's guide
(19 p. ; 21 cm.).
Picture cards for various activities
involving classifying into sets.
ISBN 0-435-01920-1 (Heinemann).

Unit 2: Story telling.
74 lesson cards : col. ; 15 x 11 cm. in
box, 22 x 31 x 2 cm. + 1 board (col. ;
21 x 30 cm.) + 1 teacher's guide (23 p. ;
21 cm.).
Picture cards for arranging into
sequences to make stories.
ISBN 0-435-01921-X (Heinemann).

Multilevel description to identify both part and
comprehensive whole in single record – 13.6.
Second publishing agency included because it is
given prominence by typography; the two
names are separated by a colon – 1.4D5(c). A
third publishing agency, the Centre for Urban
Educational Studies is, however, omitted.
Specific name of item (i.e. 'lesson cards') given
as specific material designation by analogy with
rule 10.5B1. (See also example no. 381).

Item has no personal author and does not
emanate from corporate body, so entry is under
title – 21.1C1(a).

LETRASET UK
  Letratone / Letraset UK Ltd. –
London : Letraset, [197-].
  1 wallchart : b&w ; 102 x 76 cm. folded
to 34 x 38 cm.
  Shows all 236 Letratone patterns
(screens, grids, perspectives, etc.) with
three reductions from full size (¾, ½, ¼)
to illustrate which patterns reduce well.

  1. Title

Description of wallcharts. Height and width
when extended and (when appropriate) folded
given – 8.5D6. Note on nature of item – 8.7B1
and 1.7B1.

In the context of rule 21.1B2, this item most
certainly emanates from a corporate body and it
appears to fall within category (a) of that rule in
that it deals with the body itself and illustrates
its products. The question that is crucial,
however, seems to be whether the item is, in
the words of rule 21.1B2(a), 'of an administrative
nature'. The examples included in rule 21.4B are
not of any great assistance. The interpretation
that the above entry is based upon is that the
item *is* of an administrative nature because it
serves as an advertisement for the company.

MOMENTS in history. – [Birmingham] :
  Chad Valley, [19--].
  1 filmslip (7 fr.) : col. ; 45 mm. –
(Colour slide ; 87).
  Mounted in rigid format for use with
Chad Valley Give-a-show projector.

Description of filmslips in rigid format. Number
of frames included after specific material
designation – 8.5B2. Colour and size (i.e. width)
recorded – 8.5C2 and 8.5D2. (Dimensions of
filmslips and filmstrips, unlike those of other
graphic materials, are given in millimetres.)
Important physical details not included in
physical description area are given in note –
8.7B10. Both a filmstrip and a filmslip are
designed to be viewed frame by frame. They
differ in that a filmstrip is usually in the form of
a roll and a filmslip is a short length of film,
sometimes in rigid format.

MOON landing 1969 : NASA's Apollo
  project. – New York : GAF, 1969.
  3 stereograph reels (21 pairs of fr.) :
col. + 1 booklet.
  "Actual moon trip photographs July 21
1969".
  Reels in pocket at back of booklet.

Description of stereographs. (Stereographs are
slides presented in pairs, designed to produce a
three-dimensional effect when used with a
stereoscopic viewer or projector.) 'Reel' added
to specific material designation – 8.5B1.
Number of pairs of frames added – 8.5B2.
Indication of colour – 8.5C2. No dimensions
given for stereograph – 8.5D1.

PAINTINGS at Chatsworth : colour
  postcards of paintings in the Devonshire
Collection. – Derby : English Life
Publications, [196-?].
  8 postcards : col. ; 15 x 11 cm. in folder
16 x 12 cm.
  Contents: Trial by jury / Landseer –
The holy family / Murillo – Georgiano,
Duchess of Devonshire, with her daughter
Georgiano / Reynolds – The flight into
Egypt / Ricci – The Acheson sisters /
Sargent – Portrait of an oriental (King
Uzzich?) / Van Rijn – Arthur Goodwin,
M.P. / Van Dyck – The adoration of the
Kings / Veronese.

  1. Devonshire Collection †

Description of postcards. Optionally, if an item is
in a container, the container is named at the
end of the physical description area and its
dimensions given – 1.5D2. Contents note –
1.7B18 and 8.7B18.

Collection of independent works by different
persons entered under its collective title –
21.7A1(a) and 21.7B1. Added entry for the name
of the collection from which reproductions of art
works have been taken – 21.30H1.

[PLATED tibia and broken fibula]. –
[197-].
1 radiograph ; 29 x 24 cm.
Shows front view and side view.
Title supplied by cataloguer.
Photographed at Victoria General
Hospital, Wallasey, England.

Description of radiographs. Supplied title
enclosed in square brackets – 1.1B7 and 8.1B2.
Source of title given in note – 8.7B3. Place of
publication and publisher not recorded for
unpublished graphic item – 8.4C2 and 8.4D2.
Patient's name has been omitted for reasons of
confidentiality but it is recognized that this
would be of prime importance to certain
collections. In such cases entry might best be
made in the form:

OTHER, A.N. : plated tibia and broken fibula

Alternatively, patient might be identified by
number. Note on body connected with item –
8.7B6.

SPINK, Michael
The 1-2-3 frieze / Michael Spink. –
London : Cape, 1969.
2 pictures : col. ; 21 x 152 cm. folded to
21 x 16 cm.
One frieze has individual pictures
numbered 1 to 10, each showing the
appropriate number of a particular animal
or tree. Second frieze shows them
integrated into single country scene.
ISBN 0-224-61746-X.

1.   Title

Using the nearest related term in Ch. 8, 'picture',
as the specific material designation is not
particularly helpful. It might be better, by
analogy with Ch. 10, to use the specific name of
the item, i.e. 2 friezes.

The SUNDAY Telegraph chart of freshwater fish : angler's guide. – London :
Sunday Telegraph, [1966?].
1 chart : col. ; 27 cm. diam.
Circular chart with apertured rotating
overlay; by pointing arrow to figure
relating to a numbered illustration, the
name of the fish illustrated, together with
its general haunts, classification, average
length and record weight, will appear in
the apertures.
On verso: British freshwater fish : a
description classified by family.

Description of charts. Word added to indicate
which dimension is being given by analogy with
10.5D1. Note on nature of item – 8.7B1. Note
on partial contents – 8.7B18.

SUTCLIFFE, Frank Meadow
Boats in Whitby Harbour / Frank
Meadow Sutcliffe. – London : Camden
Graphics, 1977.
1 photograph : sepia ; 23 x 31 cm.
Reproduction of original taken: ca.1875.

1.   Title †

Description of photographs. Publication details
of reproduction given in publication area, details
of original given in note – 1.4B5.

Reproduction of art work (including photographs) entered under heading for original
work – 21.16B.

TURNER, J.M.W.
The fighting Temeraire / J.M.W.
Turner. – [London] : Athena, [196-?].
1 art reproduction : col. ; 55 x 75 cm.
Shows the Temeraire being towed to the
breaker's yard.

1.   Title

Description of art reproductions. Method of
reproduction should be included in physical
description area – 8.5C1(c). However, method
could not be ascertained from item itself and
publishers were not prepared to divulge it. Note
on the nature of the item – 8.7B1.

Entry under person responsible for artistic content – 21.1A1, 21.1A2 and 21.4A1. Rule 21.16B is also relevant: reproduction of art work is entered under heading for original work.

377

TWO stroke cycle. – Huddersfield : C.W. Engineering, [197-?].
1 transparency (3 attached overlays) : col. ; 26 x 22 cm. – (Viewpack o.h.p.).
Overlays can be moved up and down to demonstrate action of cycle.
On solid plastic base with rubber feet.

1. Series

Description of transparencies. Number of overlays added to specific material designation; if they are attached, this is indicated – 8.5B4. Colour and dimensions given – 8.5C2 and 8.5D4. No provision for describing transparencies mounted on solid base in physical description area, so details recorded in note – 8.7B10.

378

USING the encyclopedia / Encyclopaedia Britannica Films, in collaboration with Jean Lowrie ; producer, Jean E. Thomson, with the collaboration of the American Association of School Librarians. – Toronto : E.B.F., 1963.
1 filmstrip (42 fr.) : col. ; 35 mm. – (Using the library).
Summary: Designed to show children what encyclopedias are, why they are needed and how to use them.

1. Encyclopaedia Britannica Films
2. Lowrie, Jean
3. Thomson, Jean E.
4. American Association of School Librarians
5. Series

Description of filmstrips. Single statement of responsibility recorded as such whether persons or bodies named in it perform the same function or not. Producer named in statement of responsibility area by analogy with 7.1F1. Brief summary given – 8.7B17.

This item appears to be the result of collaboration between a person and a corporate body and should therefore, according to rules

21.6A1(f) and 21.6C1, be entered under the one named first. This appears to indicate that, in this instance, entry should be under the heading for the body. However, the work does not fall within any of the categories listed at 21.1B2 and is therefore entered under title.

379

VALLEY Forge, Pa. – Longport, N.J. : Jack Freeman, [19--].
10 pictures : col. ; 8 x 11 cm.
On single piece of card 74 x 11 cm. folded to 8 x 11 cm.
Contents: Fort Washington – Major General Anthony Wayne Statue – National Memorial Arch – Continental army huts – Interior, Washington Memorial Chapel – New Jersey Monument at dogwood blossom time – Washington's headquarters – Reception room, Washington's headquarters – Office and dining room, Washington's headquarters – Washington's bedroom, Washington's headquarters.

Description of pictures. Additional physical details recorded in note – 8.7B10. Individually named parts listed in note – 8.7B18.

380

WALTERS, Samuel
New Brighton packet / Samuel Walters. – 1835.
1 art original : oil on canvas ; 47 x 68 cm.
Shows the New Brighton with a storm damaged sailing ship in tow.

1. Title

Description of art originals. For art originals, only the date of creation is given in the publication area – 8.4C2, 8.4D2 and 8.4F2. Medium and base given – 8.5C1(a). Note on the nature of the item – 8.7B1.

Entry under person responsible for artistic content – 21.1A1, 21.1A2 and 21.4A1.

WHY-BECAUSE cards. – Wisbech,
Cambridgeshire : Learning Development
Aids, 1976.

30 lesson cards : col. ; 11 x 7 cm. in
box 13 x 8 x 2 cm. + 1 leaflet.

Fifteen pairs of picture cards. 1 card in
each pair has question on verso, the other
has answer.

Item must be treated as graphic material.
Strictly speaking, the term 'lesson cards' should
not be used as it does not appear in the list of
specific material designations for graphics –
8.5B1 – and there is no authority for using an
additional term. However, the nearest related
term – 'picture' – is inappropriate. This item
has therefore been catalogued by analogy with
Ch. 10 and the specific name of the item given.
The example given in rule 1.10C2(a) should also
be examined. Optionally, if an item is in a
container, the container is named at the end of
the physical description area and its dimensions
given – 1.5D2.

WILCOCK, H.
Aircraft / by H. Wilcock. – Wakefield,
Yorkshire : Educational Productions, 1973.
1 filmstrip (34 fr., 5 title fr.) : col. ; 35
mm. + 1 booklet ([18] p. ; 16 cm.).
"Produced in collaboration with The
Hamlyn Group".
Based on: Aircraft / by John W.R.
Taylor ; illustrated by Gerry Palmer. 1971.
(Hamlyn all-colour paperback series).
EP: C6870.

1. Title   2. Taylor, John W.R.
Aircraft

Description of filmstrips. Name and optionally
the physical description of accompanying
material recorded at the end of the physical
description – 8.5E1 and 1.5E1(d). Statement of
responsibility not recorded in title and statement
of responsibility area given in note – 8.7B6.
Note relating to history of item – 8.7B7.
Important number borne by item recorded in
note – 8.7B19.

Name-title added entry under heading for
related work – 21.30G1.

WILLARD, Archibald M.
"Spirit of '76" / Archibald M.
Willard. – Hackettstown, N.J. : Scheller,
1973.
1 postcard : col. ; 14 x 9 cm.
Reproduction of original painting:
Selectman's Room, Abbot Hall,
Marblehead, Mass.
Exact copy, painted by Robert B.
Williams: Memorial Building, Washington
Crossing State Park, Pa.

1. Title

Description of postcards. Postcard is also
reproduction of painting; details of original given
in note as though for ordinary reproduction –
8.7B22.

Reproduction of art work entered under heading
for original work – 21.16B.

YOUNG, J.B.
Reprographic principles made easy /
J.B. Young. – Godmanchester, Huntingdon : Transart in conjunction with the
National Committee for Audio Visual Aids
in Education and the Educational
Foundation for Visual Aids, 1970.
20 transparencies : b&w ; 22 x 28 cm.
in binder 28 x 25 cm. + 1 booklet (84 p. ;
ill. ; 21 cm.). – (Transart flipatrans).
Instructions for using with multiple-
shutter viewer and standard viewer on
inside cover.
With: Classified list of suppliers.

1. Title   2. Series

Description of transparencies. These transparencies are in the form of a flipatran (i.e. a book
designed to contain transparencies in looseleaf
format; it may be used as an entity on a
multiple-shutter viewer or the transparencies
can be taken out and used separately on a
standard viewer). Indication of colour – 8.5C2.
Dimensions (height x width) given – 8.5D1.
Optionally, if an item is in a container, the
container is named at the end of the physical

description area and its dimensions given — 1.5D2. Series statement presented in various forms. It also appears as "Flipatran visual aid". The series title chosen is that given first in the prescribed source of information which, for a graphic, is the whole item — 1.6B2. The other form could be given in a note if of value in identifying the item. Note on partial contents — 8.7B18. 'With' note — 8.7B21.

Chapter One and Chapter Nine

For computer files as accompanying material see example no. 98.

For computer files as part of a multimedia item see example no. 5.

For serials in the form of computer files see example no. 446.

385

BAKEWELL, K.G.B.
    BARL. – [1985-1986 ed.]. –
Computer data (1 file : 249 records). –
[1985].
    1 computer disk ; 5¼ in.
    Bibliographic data from which hard copy
reading lists are produced for B.A. Hons.
Librarianship students at Liverpool
Polytechnic.
    System requirements: Apple II; 48K;
DOS 3.3; Pfs and Pfs:Report; 2 disk
drives.
    Compiled by K.G.B. Bakewell.

    1.   Title

Description of a file of computer data. Title
statement is transcribed from the chief source
of information – 9.1B1 and 1.1B. Chief source
of information for a computer file is the title
screen – 9.0B1. No statement of responsibility
is available internally nor is one given on the
disk, its label, or its container. The file lacks an
edition statement but is known to contain
significant changes from previous editions; and,
optionally, therefore, an edition statement is
supplied and enclosed in square brackets –
9.2B3. Type of file indicated when this
information is readily available – 9.3B1,
followed, in parentheses, by the number of files
and the number of records, statements, etc.,
again if this information is readily available –
9.3B2 and 9.3B2(a). Place of publication,
distribution, etc. and publisher, distributor, etc. is

not recorded for an unpublished computer
file – 9.4C2 and 9.4D2. Date of creation of an
unpublished computer file given – 9.4F2.
Number of physical units and a term from a
supplied list given as the specific material
designation – 9.5B1 (optionally, if general
material designations (see page 39) are used,
the word 'computer' is omitted). Dimension, in
this case the diameter of the disk, given in
inches to the next ¼ inch up – 9.5D1(a). Note
on nature of file – 9.7B1(a). Note on system
requirements, i.e.: the make and model of
computer; the amount of immediate access
memory; the name of the operating system; the
software; and the peripherals – 9.7B1(b).
Statement of responsibility not recorded in the
title and statement of responsibility area given
in a note – 9.7B6.

Entry under the single person responsible for
the content – 21.1A1, 21.1A2 and 21.4A1.

386

BLOK, Alex
    AMX pagemaker / designed, conceived
and early development done by Alex
Blok ; ROMS and all machine code
routines written by Neil Lee. – Computer
program. – Warrington : Advanced
Memory Systems, 1985.
    2 computer EPROM chips : sd., col. ;
4 x 2 cm. + 2 computer disks (5¼ in.) +
1 user manual (93 p. : ill. ; 21 cm.) in
box 23 x 24 x 3 cm.
    Desktop publisher.
    System requirements: BBC Master; 80
track disk drive; EPROMS must be fitted
into ROM board within machine;
compatible with AMX mouse but can be
used with an analogue joystick or with the
cursor keys.
    Copyright Tecnation Graphics and
Advanced Memory Systems.
    Disks comprise System disk and Font
disk.

    1.   Title   2.   Lee, Neil
    3.   Tecnation Graphics
    4.   Advanced Memory Systems

Rule 9.0A1 states that "programs residing in the
permanent memory of a computer (ROM) or
firmware are considered to be part of the device
and should be described in conjunction with the
device". However, it may be necessary to

catalogue items such as this which is supplied as a package of ROMs, disks and manual. Where the chief source of information is concerned, if the information required is not available from internal sources, it is taken from, in order of preference: the physical carrier or its labels; information issued by the publisher; information printed on the container – 9.0B1. Type of file indicated when information is readily available – 9.3B1. None of the terms listed in 9.5B1 is appropriate, so specific name of physical carrier is given qualified by 'computer' and preceded by the number of physical units. File is encoded to produce sound and to display in two or more colours so this is indicated – 9.5C1. Dimensions given – 9.5D1(e). Accompanying material recorded at end of physical description area 9.5E1 and 1.5E1(d), with, optionally, a physical description of this material – 1.5E1(d). Optionally, container is named and its dimensions given – 1.5D2. Note on nature of item – 9.7B1(a). Note on system requirements – 9.7B1(b). Note on statement of responsibility not recorded in title and statement of responsibility area – 9.7B6. Note on physical description – 9.7B10.

Work of mixed responsibility, one to which different persons have made contributions by performing different kinds of activity. The relevant rules for entry of such a work are 21.24 – 21.27 but these rules do not cater for this particular type of item. The interpretation used here is that principal responsibility belongs to the person who designed, conceived and developed the item rather than the programmer. If there is considered to be no principal responsibility, then entry would be under the heading for the first named – 21.6C1.

387

BUSINESS and household utilities. –
    Computer programs. – [Cambridge] : Sinclair Research, 1981.
    1 computer cassette + 1 information sheet.
    System requirements: Sinclair ZX 81 or ZX 80 with 8K ROM; 16K.
    Contents: Side A. Telephone. Notepad – Side B. Bank account.

Item consists of two or more separate computer files and the container is therefore treated as

the chief source of information as it furnishes a collective title and the formally presented information in, or the labels on, the files themselves do not – by analogy with 9.0B1 (this rule refers to separate *physical* parts which is not the case in this instance as the separate files are all on one cassette). Separate files listed in contents note – 9.7B18 and 1.7B18.

Work of unknown authorship entered under title – 21.1C1(a).

388

CAMBASE database / Camsoft. –
    Computer program (12 files : 240K bytes). – Blaenau Ffestiniog, Gwynedd : Cambrian Software Works, 1986.
    1 computer disk ; 5¼ in. + 1 user guide ([71] leaves ; 32 cm.). – (Camsoft software products for micros).
    System requirements: IBM PC or IBM PC compatible.
    Issued also for Amstrad PCW 8256 and PCW 8512.
    Licence no.: 10011485.

    1.   Title   2.   Camsoft

Type of file indicated when information is readily available – 9.3B1, followed, in parentheses, by number of files and number of statements and/or bytes, again if information is readily available – 9.3B2 and 9.3B2(b). Note on other formats – 9.7B16. Note of important number borne by item – 9.7B19.

Item emanates from corporate body but does not fall within any of the categories listed in 21.1B2 and is therefore entered under title – 21.1C1(c).

EDUCATION materials in libraries,
pre-1800 to mid-1987 : a subset of the
OCLC online union catalog / OCLC
Reference Services. – Computer data. –
Dublin, Ohio : Online Computer Library
Center, 1987.
1 computer laser optical disk : col. ; 4¾
in. – (Search CD450).
System requirements: IBM PC XT/AT
or IBM PC XT/AT compatible; 512K
RAM and hard disk; OCLC Search
CD450 software (3 computer disks ; 5¼
in. + system and user guides); Philips,
Hitachi, Sony or Andek CD-ROM drive.
Also known as: EMIL 87-.

1. OCLC Reference Services
2. EMIL 87-

Description of digital optical disks. Type of file
indicated if information is readily available –
9.3B1. Number of physical units and, if the
information is readily available and if desired,
indication given of the specific type of physical
medium (rather than a selected term from the
supplied list) – 9.5B1. Series statement
recorded – 9.6B1 and 1.6. Note on system
requirements – 9.7B1(b). Note on variation of
title – 9.7B4.

Item emanates from a corporate body but does
not fall within any of the categories listed in
21.1B2 and is therefore entered under title –
21.1C1(c).

EVERYMAN'S encyclopaedia. – 6th
ed. – Computer data (50522
records). – Oxford : Dent, [198-].
Online access via Dialog Information
Services.

Description of a computer file that is available
only by remote access. Chief source of
information is the title screen(s) but, if the
information required is not available from
internal sources, it may be taken from
information issued by the publisher, creator, etc.
– 9.0B1. Type of file indicated when
information is readily available – 9.3B1,
followed, in parentheses, by number or
approximate number of records again if
information is readily available – 9.3B2(a).
Physical description is not given for a computer

file that is available only by remote access –
9.5(f.n.3). Mode of access specified if file is
available only by remote access – 9.7B1(c).

Work of unknown authorship is entered under
title – 21.1C1(a).

FACTS on file / Facts On File. –
Computer data. – New York : Facts
On File, [1988].
A weekly record of contemporary history
compiled from world wide news sources;
coverage 1982 to date.
Online access via Dialog Information
Services.
Corresponds to the printed Facts On File
world news digest.
File size: 25372 records in January 1988;
updated weekly.

Description of a computer file that is available
only by remote access. Type of file indicated
when information is readily available – 9.3B1.
Physical description is not given for a computer
file that is available only by remote access –
9.5(f.n.3). Mode of access specified if file is
available only by remote access – 9.7B1(c).
Other work for which the item depends for its
content is cited – 9.7B7. Note on file
characteristics that have not been included in
the file characteristics area – 9.7B8.

Item emanates from a corporate body but does
not fall within any of the categories listed in
21.1B2 and is therefore entered under title –
21.1C1(c).

FELLOWS, Paul
Database / Paul Fellows. – Computer
program. – Cambridge : Acornsoft, 1984.
1 computer disk : col. ; 5¼ in. + 1
user manual (44 p. ; 20 cm.). –
(Acornsoft business).
System requirements: BBC B; 40 or 80
track disk drive.

1. Title   2. Series

Series statement recorded – 9.6B1 and 1.6.

Entry under the single person responsible for
the intellectual content – 21.1A1, 21.1A2 and
21.4A1.

HUNTER, Eric J.

Subject index / Eric J. Hunter and John Willitts. – Computer program (4 files : 24, 151, 107, 50 statements). – 1986.

1 computer disk ; 5¼ in.

Enables the setting up of an online index.

System requirements: Apple II; Applesoft BASIC.

For use in teaching at Liverpool Polytechnic School of Information Science and Technology.

1. Title   2. Willitts, John

Description of unpublished computer files. Type of file indicated when information is readily available – 9.3B1, followed, in parentheses, by number of files and, for a program, the number of statements, again if information is readily available – 9.3B2 and 9.3B2(b). Place of publication, distribution, etc. and name of publisher, distributor, etc. of an unpublished computer file are not recorded – 9.4C2 and 9.4D2. Note on nature of item – 9.7B1(a). Note on system requirements, including programming language – 9.7B1(b). Note on publication, distribution, etc. – 9.7B9.

Work of shared responsibility between two persons with principal responsibility not indicated is entered under the heading for the one named first – 21.6C1.

INFORMATION skills / Akersoft. –

Computer programs (8 files). – Nottingham : Akersoft, [198-].

1 computer cassette : col. ; 3⅞ x 2½ in. + 1 operating instructions (2 leaves), 14 worksheets, 1 map.

System requirements: BBC B; cassette recorder.

Contents: Hello – ABC – Quiz – World – Safari – News1 – News2 – Index.

For use in a school library with classes of up to 32 students.

Issued also on disk.

1. Akersoft

Type of file indicated when this information is readily available – 9.3B1, followed, in parentheses, by the number of files, again if this information is readily available – 9.3B2. Number of physical units and term from a supplied list given as specific material designation – 9.5B1. Dimensions of cassette given – 9.5D1(c). Accompanying material recorded at end of physical description area – 9.5E1 and 1.5E1(d). Note on system requirements – 9.7B1(b). Contents note, in this case the names of the individual files – 9.7B18. Note on target audience – 9.7B14. Note on other formats – 9.7B16.

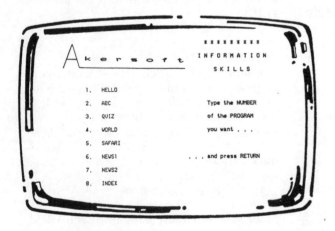

395

MONEYMARKET / program designed and developed by Halifax Building Society, Business Information Systems Division. – Computer program. – Halifax : Halifax B.S., c1985.

1 computer disk : sd., col. ; 5¼ in. + teaching guidelines and instructions (13 p. : ill. ; 16 cm.). – (The Halifax project).

Educational building society simulation game.

System requirements: BBC B or B + ; disk drive.

Also available as part of the kit: An introduction to building societies.

Disk in pocket of teaching guidelines. Issued also for BBC Master series 128. Free; copying for sale prohibited.

1. Halifax Building Society.
    Business Information Systems
    Division

Separate entry for accompanying material – 1.5E1(a).

Chief source of information is the title screen and, in this case, the title and statement of responsibility have been transcribed from this source – 9.1B1. If the information had been taken from the label on the physical carrier (the disk), 'a building society simulation game' would have been given as other title information but, in this interpretation, this information is merged into a note on the nature of the item – 9.7B1(a).

See also example no. 5.

396

The NEW electronic encyclopedia. – Computer data. – Danbury, Conn. : Grolier Electronic Publishing, c1988.

1 computer laser optical disk : col. ; 4¾ in. + 1 computer disk (5¼ in.) + 1 users guide (76 p. ; 25 cm.) in container 26 x 23 x 4 cm.

System requirements: IBM PC XT/AT, PS/2 or suitable IBM PC XT/AT compatible; DOS 3.0 or later; 512K RAM.

Disk title: The electronic encyclopedia; users guide title: The new Grolier electronic encyclopedia.

CD-ROM version of: Academic American encyclopedia. Rev. ed. Grolier, 1985? 21 v.

1. The Electronic encyclopedia
2. The New Grolier encyclopedia
3. Academic American encyclopedia

Description of digital optical disks. Title transcribed from chief source of information, i.e. the title screen – 9.1B1 and 9.0B1. Note on variant titles – 9.7B4 and 1.7B4. Note on edition and history – 9.7B7 and 1.7B7.

Entry under title as authorship is unknown or diffuse – 21.1C1(a). If considered necessary for access, added entries could be made under the variant titles – 21.30J1. An added entry is also required under the related work – 21.30G1. Some cataloguing agencies may prefer references for the variant titles.

397

OPEN access II / Software Products International, Inc. – Version 2.0. – Computer program. – San Diego, Ca. : SPI, 1986.

8 computer disks : col. ; 5¼ in. + manuals (6 v. ; 24 cm. in box 25 x 19 x 11 cm.).

Integrated package with word processing, spreadsheet, graphics, database, programming language and communication facilities.

System requirements: IBM PC or IBM PC compatible; 256K RAM; twin disk drives or hard disk.

1. Software Products International

Statement relating to edition or version – 9.2B1. Number of physical units and term from a supplied list given as specific material designation – 9.5B1. File encoded to display in two or more colours – 9.5C1. Accompanying material recorded at end of physical description area – 9.5E1 and 1.5E1(d), with, optionally, a physical description of this material – 1.5E1(d). Optionally, container is named and its dimensions given – 1.5D2 (in this instance the container holds the accompanying material only – compare with example no. 386). Note on nature of item – 9.7B1(a) and on system requirements – 9.7B1(b).

398

TMS : thesaurus development / Pyramid Software. – Computer program (14 files). – Reading : Pyramid, 1986.

2 computer disks ; col. ; 5¼ in. + 1 operating guide (28 leaves ; 30 cm.).

System requirements: IBM PC XT/AT or IBM PC XT/AT compatible with disk drive and hard disk; program disk must be copied to hard disk; second disk is a license disk which must be placed in the A drive.

Title on disk: TMS; title on operating guide: Thesaurus construction system; title on delivery note: Thesaurus management system.

1. Pyramid Software
2. Thesaurus construction system
3. Thesaurus management system

Title transcribed as it appears on chief source of information – 9.1B1 and 1.1B (chief source of information is the title screen – 9.0B1, which has been used in this case). Note on variant titles – 9.7B4. If the information is not available from internal sources, for example the cataloguer may not have access to equipment to mount or read the file, it is taken from, in order of preference: the physical carrier or its labels; information issued by the publisher; information printed on the container. In case of variation in fullness, the source with the most complete information is to be preferred. Added entries should be made from variant titles that might reasonably be sought – 21.30J1. Some cataloguing agencies might prefer references – 26.1B1.

399

UNIVERSAL decimal classification = Classification decimale universelle = Dezimalklassifikation / British Standards Institution. – International medium ed. English text. – Computer data. – London : BSI.

2 computer reels. – (BS 1000M) (FID publication ; no. 571).

Part 1: Systematic tables. – Computer data (7 files). – 1985.

1 computer reel.

9 track; odd parity; 1600 bpi; phase-encoded; EBCDIC character set; fixed block size of 1024 characters.

Distributed by Hutton and Rostron Data Processing Ltd.

Available in other formats, on tape or disk, to customer's precise requirement, and in hard copy.

1. British Standards Institution
2. Series
3. FID publication

Multilevel description for identification of both part and whole in a single record – 13.6A. Description of a computer reel. Number of units and a term from a supplied list given as the specific material designation – 9.5B1. Dimensions not given for computer reels – 9.5D1(d). Note on important file characteristics and on physical description – 9.7B8 and 9.7B10. Certain of the additional physical characteristics given here in a note, e.g. the bpi, could be recorded in the physical description area if desired – 9.5C2.

WILLIAMS, K.M.
  The starmaze / K.M. Williams. –
Computer program. – London : Software
Invasion, 1984.
  1 computer cassette : sd., col. ;
3⅞ x 2½ in.
  Game.
  System requirements: BBC B; cassette
recorder.
  Duplicate copy on side B.

  1.   Title

Number of physical units and term from a
supplied list given as specific material
designation – 9.5B1. Dimensions of cassette
given – 9.5D1(c). Note on the nature of the file,
i.e. 'Game' – 9.7B1(a). Note on physical
description – 9.7B10.

XTREE (TM) : the new standard for file
  and directory management / Executive
Systems, Inc. – 2nd ed. – Computer
program. – Sherman Oaks, Ca. :
Executive Systems, 1985.
  1 computer disk : col. ; 5¼ in. + 1
user guide (50 p. ; 13 x 14 cm.) in case
16 x 17 x 2 cm.
  System requirements: IBM PC XT/AT
or IBM PC XT/AT compatible; MS-DOS
or PC-DOS 2.0 or greater; 192K RAM.

  1.   Executive Systems

Title transcribed as it appears on chief source
of information – 9.1B1 and 1.1B. Other title
information recorded – 9.1E1 and 1.1E.
Statement of edition – 9.2B1 and 1.2B.
Accompanying material recorded at end of
physical description area – 9.5E1 and 1.5E1(d),
with, optionally, a physical description of this
material – 1.5E1(d). Optionally, container is
named and its dimensions given – 1.5D2.

Chapter One and Chapter Ten

For three-dimensional artefacts as accompanying material see example no. 79.

1914-1918 : [war medal awarded to]
   147780 Gunner S.W.W. Heaver,
R.A. – [1919 (London : Royal Mint)]
   1 medal : silver ; 4 cm. diameter.
   Recipient's name engraved on rim.

Description of three-dimensional artefacts (in
this case a medal). Title transcribed as it
appears on item – 1.1B1. Brief explanation
added to title – 1.1E6. Artefact not intended
primarily for communication has date of
manufacture as first element of publication, etc.
area – 10.4F2 – followed, as name of
publisher is not applicable, by place and name
of manufacturer in parentheses – 10.4G1 and
1.4G1. None of listed specific material
designation terms is appropriate, so specific
name of item is given as concisely as possible
with number of physical units – 10.5B1.
Material recorded – 10.5C1. Word added to
measurement to indicate which dimension is
given – 10.5D1. No authority to give
measurement less than 10 cm. in millimetres, as
is the case with printed monographs, although
this would seem more appropriate, i.e. 37 mm.
Note on important physical detail – 10.7B10.

Item could be said to emanate from a corporate
body, i.e. the Royal Mint, but it does not fall
within any of the categories listed in 21.1B2 and
is therefore entered under title – 21.1C1(c).

[ALARM clock]. – [197-] (Dumbarton :
   Columbia).
   1 clock ; 10 x 10 x 5 cm.
   Title supplied by cataloguer.

Title devised for item lacking one and enclosed
in square brackets – 1.1B7. Exact date of
publication, distribution, etc. unknown, but
decade known and enclosed in square
brackets – 1.4F7. Name of publisher not
applicable; place and name of manufacturer
recorded – 10.4G1 and 1.4G1. None of listed
specific material designation terms is
appropriate, so specific name of item is given as
concisely as possible – 10.5B1. When multiple
dimensions are given, the order is height x
width x depth – 10.5D1. Source of title, if other
than chief source of information, given in
note – 10.7B3 and 1.7B3. (Chief source of
information is object itself together with any
accompanying material and container –
10.0B1).

An AUTHENTIC replica of the Liberty
   Bell. – [United States] : Historical
Souvenir Co., 1975.
   1 bell : metal, bronze col. ; 7 cm. high
in box 7 x 6 x 6 cm.
   Brief history and other facts on box.

Chief source of information the object itself and
container – 10.0B1. If the first word of the title
of a work entered under its title proper is an
article, the next word is capitalized – A.4D1.
Exact place of distribution cannot readily be
established, so name of country is given –
1.4C6. Abbreviation (i.e. U.S.) not used because
it is not an addition to name – B.14. None of
specific material designation terms listed at
10.5B1 is appropriate, so specific name of item
given as concisely as possible. Material (10.5C1),
colour (10.5C2) and dimensions (10.5D1)
recorded. Name of container and dimensions
given – 10.5D2. Note on partial contents –
10.7B18.

BODY exerciser : the portable fitness
   gym / American Consumer. –
Philadelphia : American Consumer, [197-].
   1 exerciser : nylon rope and plastic + 1
pamphlet (15 p.).
   "Designed to permit almost everyone of
any age to exercise effectively at a time
and place convenient".

   1.   American Consumer

Chief source of information is the item itself
together with accompanying textual material –
10.0B1. Specific name used as material
designation as none of terms listed is
appropriate – 10.5B1. Material of which item is
made recorded – 10.5C1. Dimensions not
recorded as not appropriate in this instance –
10.5D1. Accompanying material given in
physical description area – 10.5E1 and 1.5E1(d).
Note on nature of item – 10.7B1; given as a
quotation – 1.7A3.

COLDSTREAM Guards drummer,
   1832. – [19 – ?] (Potschappell :
C. Thieme).
   1 figure : porcelain, col. ; 28 cm. high.
   Manufacturer deduced from factory
mark on base.

Artefact not intended primarily for communication has date of manufacture as first
element of publication, etc. area – 10.4F2 –
followed, as name of publisher is not applicable,
by place and name of manufacturer in
parentheses – 10.4G1 and 1.4G1. Material and
colour added to designation – 10.5C1 and
10.5C2. Word added to measurement to indicate
which dimension is being given – 10.5D1. Note
on source of detail relating to manufacturer –
1.7A5. (See also example no. 417).

FASCIOLA hepatica = The liver fluke /
   [mounted by] Liverpool School of
Tropical Medicine. – Liverpool : The
School, 1975.
   1 microscope slide : glass, stained ;
3 x 8 cm.

   1.   The liver fluke

Description of microscope slides. Parallel titles
recorded in order indicated by chief source of
information – 10.1D1 and 1.1D1. Body
responsible for display of item recorded –
10.1F1. Words added to statement of
responsibility to indicate relationship to title –
10.1F2. Place of publication, distribution, etc.
and publisher etc. recorded if naturally occurring
object is mounted for viewing – 10.4C2 and
10.4D2. Material of which object is made is
given – 10.5C1. If a microscope slide is stained
(i.e. chemically treated so that the specimen
turns a reddish brown colour and it becomes
possible to see an outline of its interior
structure), this is stated – 10.5C2.

Entry under title because item does not fall into
one of the categories listed at 21.1B2 –
21.1C1(c).

FLAX : from flax to linen. – Dundee :
   Flax Spinners' and Manufacturers'
Association, [196-?].
   1 display unit (various pieces) ; in box
22 x 29 x 2 cm.
   Contents include various types of flax,
drawing of plant from which linen is made,
2 pamphlets and map on lid.

If pieces of item cannot be named concisely, the term 'various pieces' is used – 10.5B2. Details may then optionally be given in a note – 10.7B10. Container named and its dimensions given – 10.5D2.

409

KENT State University, Ohio, 1910. –
  [197-] (East Liverpool, Ohio : W.C. Bunting).
  1 miniature souvenir tankard : pottery, black and gold ; 6 cm. high.

Title proper consists solely of the body responsible for the item – 1.1B3. Approximate date of manufacture – 1.4F7. Place and name of manufacture given – 10.4G1. Name of state added to place of manufacture if considered necessary – 1.4C3. Name of state is not abbreviated as it does not appear in list in B.14A. None of listed terms appropriate so specific name of item is given as concisely as possible – 10.5B1. Material recorded – 10.5C1, colours given – 10.5C2. Dimension given with word added to indicate which dimension – 10.5D1.

410

MAPS and man / The British Cartographic Society and the Science Museum. – London, [197-].
  1 exhibit (2 stereographs, 9 photos., 16 maps, microfilm map, Racal-zonal calculus) : col. – (Making maps : the science of cartography ; 8).
  Air photos. of Big Bend, Swaziland and the country around Stravrovouni Monastery, Cypress.

  1.   British Cartographic Society
  2.   Science Museum

Description of exhibits. Specific material designation chosen from list of terms – 10.5B1. Number and names of pieces added to designation – 10.5B2. Colour indicated – 10.5C2. Dimensions not appropriate in this instance, so omitted – 10.5D1. Summary given in note – 10.7B17.

Work emanating from corporate bodies but not falling within any of the categories listed at 21.1B2 is entered under title – 21.1C1(c). In

added entries initial articles omitted from headings for corporate bodies – 24.5A1. (When given as statements of responsibility, however, the names are recorded as they appear on the item – 1.1F1.)

411

MILKWEED = Danaus plexippus, Linnaeus. – [Liverpool : City Museum, 19--].
  2 butterflies : col. ; 7 cm. wingspan.
  Prepared for display by the Museum.

  1.   Danaus plexippus, Linnaeus

Description of exhibits. Parallel titles recorded in order indicated on chief source of information – 10.1D1 and 1.1D1. Specific name of item given as concisely as possible in physical description area – 10.5B1. Alternatively, the term 'exhibit' could be selected from the list of specific material designations and a more explicit description given in a note – 10.7B1. Word added to measurement to indicate what dimension is being given – 10.5D1. No statement of responsibility appears on item and so it is given in note – 1.1F2, 1.7B6 and 10.7B6.

412

NUFFIELD '460 farm tractor. –
  [Oxford?] : Morris Motors, [197-?].
  1 mock-up : red.
  Sectionalised representation of tractor, powered by electricity to demonstrate operation.
  Actual size.

Item is treated as 'mock-up', which is defined in AACR 2 as: 'a representation of a device or process that may be modified for training or analysis to emphasize a particular part or function; it usually has movable parts that can be manipulated' (p. 619).

413

[POD razor = Ensis siliqua].
  1 shell ; 18 cm. long.
  Title supplied by cataloguer.

  1.   Ensis siliqua

Description of a naturally occurring object. Title devised for item lacking one and enclosed in square brackets – 1.1B7.

Place of publication, name of publisher and date of publication omitted, unless object is mounted for viewing or packaged for presentation (see example no. 421) – 10.4C2, 10.4D2 and 10.4F2. Specific name of item given as concisely as possible in physical description area – 10.5B1. Dimension given – 10.5D1. Note on source of title – 10.7B3.

414

A POLLUTED beach. – [Liverpool :
  City of Liverpool Museums, 197-].
  1 diorama (various pieces) : col. ; in
glass-fronted container 238 x 80 x 105 cm.
  Prepared for display by the Museum.
  Items picked up along a 100-yard stretch
of beach in March 1972: oil-polluted
guillemots (stuffed), rusty cans, plastic bag,
cartridge cases, tyres, etc., in front of b&w
photo. of wrecked 'Torrey Canyon''.

Description of a diorama. Pieces cannot be named concisely in physical description area – 10.5B2. Container named and its dimensions recorded – 10.5D2. Note relating to history of item and giving brief summary of content – 10.7B7 and 10.7B17.

415

POTTER, Beatrix
  A jig-saw puzzle of Jemima Puddle-
duck : Beatrix Potter's famous
character. – London : Warne, [197-?].
  1 jigsaw puzzle (43 pieces) : wood, col. ;
in box, 22 x 22 x 4 cm.

  1. Title

None of listed terms is appropriate as specific material designation, so specific name is given as concisely as possible – 10.5B1. Number of pieces added – 10.5B2.

Material and colour recorded – 10.5C1 and 10.5C2. If object is in container, container is named and its dimensions given, either after those of the object or as the only dimension – 10.5D2.

Reproduction of art work entered under heading for original work – 21.16B.

416

QUIN, Vera
  Quin's reading games. – Peppard
Common, Oxfordshire : Cressrelles, 1976.
  1 game (various pieces).
  Lotto-type game.
  Contains 36 9-word cards, 324 single-
word cards, 4 boards, 6 counters, 2 dice
and explanatory leaflet.
  Exercises in pairing words to discrim-
inate between sounds, and games to
familiarize users with commonest printed
notices, forms and posters.

  1. Title

Description of games. If pieces cannot be named concisely, term 'various pieces' is added to specific material designation – 10.5B2. If more detailed description is considered useful, this is given in a note – 10.7B10.

417

[SHOE-HORN]. – 1912 (Birmingham :
  H.V.P. & Co.).
  1 shoe horn : silver ; 28 cm.
  Title supplied by cataloguer.
  Blade is silver plated.
  Date and place of manufacture derived
from hall-mark on handle.

Artefact not intended primarily for communi-
cation has date of manufacture as first element of publication, etc. area – 10.4F2 – followed, as name of publisher is not applicable, by place and name of manufacturer in parentheses – 10.4G1 and 1.4G1. Note on source of title – 10.7B3. No specific rule for making note on source of details of manufacture. However, this seems important and so has been included as 'useful descriptive information that cannot be fitted into other areas of the description' – 1.7A5.

418

SOUVENIR playing cards [of] Montreal
    and Quebec. – Montreal : Canadian
Playing Card Co., [192-?].
  1 game (54 cards) ; 9 x 7 cm. in case
10 x 8 x 3 cm.
  Faces of cards contain various b&w
views of Montreal, Quebec and Ottawa +
ill. of Caughnawaga Indian and map: The
principal highways of the Province of
Quebec.

Description of games. Number of pieces given after specific material designation – 10.5B2. Dimensions of objects and container given – 10.5D1 and 10.5D2. Important physical details not included in physical description area given in note – 10.7B10.

419

[TEA towel]. – Ireland : Irish Cabin
   Linens, [197-].
   1 tea towel : linen, col. ; 78 x 49 cm.
   Reproduction of map: The Countie
Pallatine of Lancaster, 1610.
   Title supplied by cataloguer.
   Probable cartographer: John Speed.

   1.   Speed, John

Item which is a reproduction in one material of a work originally presented in another material is described in terms of the former – 1.1C3. (See also section 0.24). In this instance, a map reproduced on a tea towel is described as a tea towel, i.e. an object of realia. British usage has been followed in the devised title and in the choice of specific material designation. In North America, 'Dish towel' or 'Dish cloth' would be more appropriate.

420

TRIVIAL pursuit : TM : master game. –
   Genus ed. – Leicester, England :
Pallitoy [distributor], c1983.
   1 game (board, one dice, 1,000
question-and-answer cards, 2 card boxes, 6
player tokens, 36 scoring wedges) + rules
of play (1 sheet) in box 27 x 27 x 9 cm. –
(Parker family game ; ref. 931325).
   Questions copyright: Horn Abbot
International Ltd.
   For 2 to 36 players, age 15 to adult.

Description of games. Distributor named in publication area – 1.4D1. Optionally, a statement of function is added – 1.4E1. Number of physical units and a term from a supplied list given as specific material designation – 10.5B1. Number and names of pieces added in parentheses – 10.5B2. Accompanying material named at end of physical description – 10.5E1 and 1.5E1(d). Container named and dimensions given – 10.5D2. Series recorded – 10.6B1 and 1.6. Numbering of series given in the terms used in the item – 1.6G1. Note on responsibility – 10.7B6. Note on target audience – 10.7B14.

421

UNITED States bicentennial silver
   proof set. – [Philadelphia] : U.S. Mint,
1976.
   3 coins ; in case 10 x 10 x 1 cm.
   Dollar, half-dollar, quarter, 40% silver,
dated 1776-1976.

Coins are not usually intended for communication and therefore the date would normally be given first in the publication, etc. area according to rule 10.4F2. However, in this instance, they are packaged and issued as a commemorative set. Physical description – 10.5B1 and 10.5D2. Material named in note – 10.5C1 and 10.7B10. Note on nature of the item – 10.7B1.

422

VEN, A.J. van der
   Eve / A.J. van der Ven. – Rome,
1841.
   1 sculpture : marble, white ; 107 cm.
high on base 144 x 80 x 73 cm.
   Presented to Bootle Library and
Museum by D.M. Glynn-Morris Nov.
1952.

   1.   Title

The term 'art original' is defined (see Appendix D) as 'a original two- or three-dimensional work of art ... e.g. a painting, a drawing, or sculpture'. 'Art original' is also included as a specific material designation in 10.5B1. However, it would seem more appropriate to use the term 'sculpture' in this case and, indeed, '1 sculpture' is used as an example in 10.5D1. Material added to specific material designation – 10.5C1. Colour added – 10.5C2. Dimensions, with explanatory word if necessary, given – 10.5D1. The dimensions of the base are given by analogy with the rule for recording the dimensions of a container – 10.5D2.

Dutch name containing prefix entered under part following prefix unless prefix is 'ver' – 22.5D1.

The WATERLOO cannons / Bassett-
Lowke Ltd. – Northampton : Bassett-
Lowke, [197-].
2 models : hardwood and metal ;
approx. 23 x 21 cm. long.
Replicas of the 9 pdr and 6 pdr field
guns used by the British at the Battle of
Waterloo.

1. Bassett-Lowke Ltd.

Description of models. Manufacturer is cited in
the chief source of information, i.e. the textual
material accompanying the items – 10.0B1 and
can therefore be given in the statement of
responsibility area – 1.1F1. Manufacturer is also
distributor and should be shown as such in
publication, distribution area – 1.4B2. Physical
description – 10.5B1, 10.5C1 and 10.5D1.

Items emanate from a corporate body but they
do not fit into any of the categories indicated in
21.1B2; they are therefore treated as if no
corporate body were involved and entered
under title – 21.1C1(c). In added entry heading,
'Ltd' is needed to make clear that name is that
of a corporate body – 24.5C1.

WOODCHUCK puzzle. – Wallop,
Hants. : Pentangle, [19--].
1 game (24 pieces) : wood ; in box
8 x 9 cm. diam.
Over 20 shapes can be constructed.
Selected for the Design Centre, London.
Registered design no.: 949574.

Description of games. Number of pieces –
10.5B2. Box is cylindrical, so explanatory word
is added to indicate which dimension is being
given – 10.5D1. Important physical details
not included in physical description area are
given as note – 10.7B10. Important number
recorded – 10.7B19.

Microforms

Chapter One and Chapter Eleven

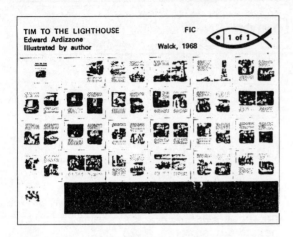

than 16x 'low reduction' is given – 11.7B10. Note relating to original – 11.7B22.

Entry under the single person responsible for the intellectual content – 21.1A1, 21.1A2 and 21.4A1.

426

DRAPER, Andrew S.
    American education / by Andrew S. Draper ; with an introduction by Nicholas Murray Butler. – Chicago : Library Resources, 1970.
    1 microfiche (399 fr.) ; 8 x 13 cm. – (Microbook [library series. Library of American civilization, beginnings to 1914] ; LAC 10589).
    Reproduction of: Boston : Houghton Mifflin, 1909. x, 383 p.
    Very high reduction.

1. Title   2. Series
3. Library of American civilization

Description of a microfiche. Series statement as it appears in chief source of information is: 'Microbook LAC 10589'. Additional series statement found in publicity material and so enclosed in square brackets within the parentheses enclosing the series statement – 1.6A2. Name of subseries follows that of series – 1.6H1. Note relating to original – 11.7B22. Reduction is 90x. 'Very high reduction' is term used – 11.7B10. Introductory wording of note separated from main content by colon and space – 1.7A1.

425

ARDIZZONE, Edward
    Tim to the lighthouse / by Edward Ardizzone. – [Ann Arbor, Mich. : University Microfilms, 1971?].
    1 microfiche (25 fr.) : ill. – (Xerox micromedia classroom libraries = Xedia).
    Low reduction.
    Reproduction of: New York : Walck, 1968. [48] p. ; 26 cm.

1. Title   2. Series

Description of microforms (in this case a microfiche). Title and statement of responsibility are recorded as they appear in chief source of information – 11.1B1, 1.1B, 11.1F1 and 1.1F (chief source of information for microfiche is the title frame or frames; the eye-readable data printed at the top of the fiche is used only if the title frames provide insufficient information – 11.0B1). Publication details of the microform and not of the original recorded – 11.4C1, 1.4C, 11.4D1, 1.4D, 11.4F1 and 1.4F. These details do not appear on the item but have been obtained from publicity material so they are enclosed in square brackets. Number of physical units and an appropriate term from a supplied list is given as the specific material designation – 11.5B1. Number of frames is added in parentheses if this can be readily ascertained – 11.5B2. Inclusion of illustrations indicated – 11.5C2 and 2.5C1. Standard dimensions (10.5 x 14.8 cm.) of microfiche are not recorded – 11.5D3. Series statement recorded – 11.6B1 and 1.6. Parallel title of series recorded – 1.6C1 and 1.1D. Reduction is outside 16x-30x range; as it is less details are, however, those relating to the microform itself as given on the rest of the item – 11.0B2 and 11.4. No instructions are given for recording the number of frames on a microopaque but, as this seems useful information, the rule for microfiche has been followed – 11.5B2. Dimensions (height and width) recorded – 11.5D5. Series statement recorded – 11.6B1 and 1.6. Variant title noted – 11.7B4. Reduction is between 16x and 30x so this need not be recorded – 11.7B10. Note relating to original – 11.7B22. The examples given in rule 11.7B22 include the dimensions of the original but clearly the cataloguer may not have access to this information.

Greene, Robert – Friar Bacon & Friar Bungay. London. 1594. 63p. complete on 1 card.

Courtesy of Henry E. Huntington Library

Three Centuries of Drama: English   1500 – 1641   Readex Microprint * New York 1965

427

GREENE, Robert
    The honourable historie of Frier Bacon and Frier Bongay : as it was plaid by Her Majesties servants / Robert Greene. – New York : Readex Microprint, 1965.
    1 microopaque (64 fr.) ; 23 x 16 cm. – (Three centuries of drama. English, 1500-1641).
    Title at head of opaque: Friar Bacon & Friar Bungay.
    Reproduction of: London : Printed for Edward White, 1594. 63 p.

1.   Title   2.   Series

Title recorded as it appears on chief source of information, i.e. the title frame, which is, in this case, a reproduction of the title page of the original work – 11.1B1 and 1.1B. Publication

428

LIBRARY OF CONGRESS. Subject Cataloguing Division. Processing Department
    Library of Congress subject headings / Subject Cataloguing Division, Processing Department. – 8th ed. in microfiche. – Washington, D.C. : The Library, 1975.
    22 microfiches : negative.
    ISBN 0-8444-0156-0.

1.   Title

Description of microfiches. Edition statement transcribed as given on item – 1.2B1. Number of frames added to specific material designation only if it can be easily ascertained – 11.5B2. Microfiche is negative (i.e. white lettering on black), so this is stated – 11.5C1. Dimensions (10.5 x 14.8 cm.) not recorded – 11.5D3.

Work emanating from corporate body which is of an administrative nature and which deals with the procedures and operations of the body is entered under the heading for the body – 21.1B2(a). Intervening element in the hierarchy of the heading is retained as the name of the subordinate body could be used by another body entered under the same higher body – 24.14A.

Currently (1989), this item is issued quarterly on a subscription basis and it could now be described not as a monograph but as a serial, i.e.:

LIBRARY OF CONGRESS
Library of Congress subject headings / Library of Congress. – [198-?]- . – Washington, D.C. : The Library, [198-?]- .
microfiches : negative.
Quarterly.
Description based on: June 1988.

Designation and date of publication of first issue are not known and cannot be determined so approximate chronological designation and approximate date of publication of first issue are supplied enclosed in square brackets – 12.3D1 (by analogy) and 1.4F7. Thus far an ISSN has not been assigned.

The Subject Cataloguing Division would not be used as main entry since it is neither on the header or on the first frame. Entry would therefore be under the name of the parent body – 21.1B4(b).

429

PHOTOGRAPH and slide classification for western art / Photograph and Slide Collection, Fine Arts Library, Fogg Art Museum. – Cambridge, Mass. : Harvard University Library, Microreproduction Dept., [1973?].
1 microfilm reel ; 35 mm.
Low reduction.
Comic mode.
Reproduction of: Rev. ed., 1973.

1. Fogg Art Museum. <u>Fine Arts Library. Photographic and Slide Collection</u>

Description of microfilms. Statement of responsibility recorded as it appears on item – 11.1F1 and 1.1F. There is no specific rule for recording the subordinate bodies of a higher body, but the example at rule 7.1F1 ('Flowering and fruiting of papaya / Department of Botany, Iowa State University') shows that two names in an hierarchy are separated by a comma. Microfilm is positive (i.e. black lettering on white), so this detail is not recorded – 11.5C1.

430

YOUNG, I.V.
An experimental investigation into children's comprehension of school atlas maps / I.V. Young. – Wakefield : Micro Methods, 1962.
1 microfilm reel ; 35 mm.
Low reduction.
Comic mode.
Thesis (M.A.) – London Institute of Education, 1952.

1. Title

Description of microfilms. 'Cartridge', 'cassette' or 'reel' added to specific material designation as appropriate – 11.5B1. Width of microfilm given in millimetres – 11.5D4. Reduction ratio is less than 16x, so 'Low reduction' is the term used – 11.7B10. If item is a dissertation, this is recorded in a note – 11.7B13, 2.7B13 and 1.7B13. If desired, this note could be combined with a note on the original (11.7B22) e.g.:

Reproduction of: Thesis (M.A.) – London Institute of Education, 1952.

Chapter One and Chapter Twelve

For indexes to serials published separately see example no. 75.

For a printed monograph also published as an issue of a serial see example no. 72.

For printed monographs published in parts see example no. 160.

For a special issue of a serial described as a printed monograph see example no. 59.

ACORN
USER

JULY/AUGUST 1982, NUMBER ONE

Editor
Jane Fransella
Sub-editors
Ann Nimmo
Tony Quinn
Production
Susie Home
Promotion Manager
Pat Bitton
Editorial Secretary
Jane Lake

431

ACORN user. – No. 1 (Jul./Aug. 1982)-   . – London : Addison-Wesley, 1982-   .

no. : ill. ; 30 cm.
Monthly.
Published: Newbury, Berks : Redwood, 1985-   .
ISSN 201-17002-7 [sic] (Addison-Wesley).
ISSN 0263-7456 (Redwood).

Description of incomplete serials. Title transcribed as it appears in chief source of information – 12.1B1 and 1.1B1 (chief source of information for a printed serial is the title page of the first issue – 12.0B1). Numeric designation of first issue recorded as given in that issue – 12.3B1. Chronological designation of first issue recorded in the terms used in that issue – 12.3C1. For both the numeric and chronological designation standard abbreviations are used – B.9 and B.15. As there is both a numeric and a chronological designation, the numbering is given first and the chronological designation is enclosed in parentheses – 12.3C4. Publication area includes: place of publication – 12.4C1 and 1.4C1; name of publisher – 12.4D1 and 1.4D1; and date – 1.4F1, followed by a hyphen and four spaces – 12.4F1. Date is recorded in the publication, etc. area even if it coincides wholly or in part with the date given in the chronological coverage – 12.4F1. Specific material designation for a printed serial is v., no. or pt. preceded by three

spaces – 12.5B1. Other physical details given – 12.5C1 and 2.5C1. Dimensions recorded – 12.5D1, 2.5D1 and 1.5D1. Frequency recorded in a note – 12.7B1. Note on change of publisher – 12.7B9 (chief source of information for the publication, distribution area is the title page, other preliminaries and colophon of the first issue – 12.0B1. Therefore the earlier publisher is recorded in the body of the entry). International Standard Serial Number recorded in a note – 12.8B1 and 1.8B1. If an item bears two numbers, *optionally* they can both be recorded and a qualification added – 1.8B2 and 1.8E1. Although this is an option, it would seem to be essential in a case such as this. The ISSN for Addison-Wesley appears to take the form of an ISBN; this possible inaccuracy is transcribed as it appears followed by [sic] – 1.0F1.

Entry under title because personal authorship is diffuse – 21.1C1(a) and 21.6C2. Editor is named on title page but is not recorded – 12.1F3.

THE

A L B U M.

VOL. I.

APRIL—JULY

LONDON:

PRINTED FOR J. ANDREWS,
NEW BOND STREET.

MDCCCXXII.

432

The ALBUM. – Vol. 1, no. 1 (Apr. 1822)-v. 4, no. 8 (Apr. 1825). – London : J. Andrews, 1822-1825.
   8 v. ; 21 cm.
   Two issues yearly.

Description of serial which has ceased publication and which is therefore complete. Title transcribed as it appears in chief source of information – 12.1B1; (chief source of information for a printed serial is the title page of the first issue – 12.0B1). If the first word of the title of a work entered under its title proper is an article, the next word also is capitalized – A.4D1. Numeric designation of first issue recorded – 12.3B1. Chronological designation recorded, using standard abbreviations (B.15), and enclosed in brackets – 12.3C1 and 12.3C4. Source of information for numeric and chronological designation is title page, other preliminaries and colophon (in this instance, title page and contents page have been used) – 12.0B1. Arabic numerals substituted for Roman – C.2B1. For completed serial, designation of first issue is followed by that of last – 12.3F1. (Note that, in this instance, both volumes and issues are numbered sequentially and the issues do not, as is more usual, form separate sequences within each volume.) Publication area includes: place of publication – 12.4C1; name of publisher – 12.4D1, and, for completed serial, date of publication of first and last issue, separated by hyphen – 12.4F2. Date is recorded in publication, etc. area even if it coincides wholly or in part with the date given in the chronological coverage – 12.4F1. Specific material designation for printed serial is v., no. or pt. – 12.5B1. Number of parts of completed serial given before specific material designation in Arabic numerals – 12.5B2. This should relate to the number of physical parts rather than the number of annual volumes. Dimensions of serial recorded – 12.5D1, 2.5D1 and 1.5D1. Frequency recorded in note – 12.7B1.

Entry under title because personal authorship is diffuse – 21.1C1(a).

AMERICAN libraries : bulletin of the
American Library Association. –
Vol. 1, no. 1 (Jan. 1970)-   . –
Chicago : ALA, 1970-   .
        v. : ill. (some col.), ports. ; 28 cm.
Monthly except bi-monthly Jul./Aug.
Continues: ALA bulletin.
Author-subject index normally in last
issue of vol., i.e. Dec., or Feb. issue of
next vol.; 1970-1977 vols. also have People
index.
ISSN 0002-9769.

1.   American Library Association

Note on indexes – 12.7B17.

Item emanates from a corporate body and is
the official journal of that body but material is
of general interest and authors' opinions are
usually regarded as their own. Item therefore
does not fall within any of the categories listed
in 21.1B2 and is entered under title – 21.1C1(c).

434

ANNUAL statement of the trade of the
United Kingdom with Commonwealth
countries and foreign countries. –
1853-1975. – London : H.M.S.O.,
1853-1975.
        344 v. ; 29-34 cm.
Title varies slightly: 1853-1870, Annual
statement of the trade and navigation . . .
Originally issued by Board of Trade;
subsequently by H.M. Customs and
Excise.
Continues figures previously published
in: Tables of the revenue . . .
Continued by: Overseas trade statistics
of the United Kingdom.
Shipping figures subsequently published
in: Annual statement of the navigation and
shipping . . .
Annual supplement to v. 2 (1940-1958)
superseded by: Protective duties . . .
Supplements to v. 4 published every
three years (1948-1960) and in 1962;
continued annually as v. 5 from 1963.
1900-1919 issued in 2 v. each year, with
annual supplementary v. 1904-1913.
1920-1962 issued in 4 v. each year. 1963-
issued in 5 v. each year.
1853-1920 published as Command
papers and also available bound up in
sessional set.

433

1.   Great Britain. Board of Trade
2.   Great Britain. Customs and Excise

Variation in title too slight to warrant new
entry – 21.2A1. Change recorded in note
area – 21.2A1, 1.7B4, 2.7B4 and 12.7B4. Note
on statement of responsibility – 1.7B6, 2.7B6
and 12.7B6. Notes on relationships with other
serials: continuation of previous serial –
12.7B7(b); continued by subsequently published
serials – 12.7B7(c). When an element ends with
the mark of omission and the subsequent
punctuation is or begins with a full stop, the full
stop is omitted – 1.0C1. Note on supplements – 12.7B7(j). Note on physical description – 12.7B10. Note that some issues are part
of a series – 1.7B12, 2.7B12 and 12.7B12.

Work emanating from corporate body but not
falling within any of the categories listed in
21.1B2 is entered under title – 21.1C1(c).
Added entries under the corporate bodies –
21.30E1.

435

BATH UNIVERSITY PROGRAMME
OF CATALOGUE RESEARCH
Newsletter / Bath University Programme
of Catalogue Research. – No. 1 (Jul.
1978)-no. 2 (Apr. 1979). – Bath : The
Programme, 1978-1979.
        2 no. ; 30 cm.
Continued by: Newsletter / Centre for
Catalogue Research to no. 14 (Apr. 1987);
Newsletter / Centre for Bibliographic
Management from no. 15 (Mar.
1988)-

1.   Title

Serial which emanates from a corporate body
and which is of an administrative nature dealing
with its internal policies, procedures and/or
operations entered under the heading for the
body – 21.1B2(a). The name of the body
changed in 1979 and 1988 and new entries are
made following these changes – 21.3B1(a) (see
examples no. 440 and 441).

BAUTATIGKEIT im Jahre. –
1952-1955. – Stuttgart : Kohlhammer,
1952-1955.
    4 v. ; 30 cm.
    Annual.
    Compiled by the German Federal
Republic Statistisches Bundesamt.
    Issued as: Bd. 93, 111, 140 and 160 of
Statistik der Bundesrepublik Deutschland.
    Continued by: Bauwirtschaft,
Bautätigkeit, Wohnungen ; Reihe 3.

    1.   Germany. (Federal Republic).
        Statistiches Bundesamt

Serial that has ceased publication; designations
and dates given for first and last issues –
12.3F1 and 12.4F2. Note on statement of
responsibility – 1.7B6, 2.7B6 and 12.7B6. Serial
is part of a larger serial but rules are not clear
as to treatment. The particular situation is not
specifically covered in the rule for relationships
with other serials, although this rule does state
that a note should be made about a relationship
with any simultaneously published serial –
12.7B7. An alternative solution would be to
record the larger serial in the series area –
12.6B1 and make a note that the numbering
within the series varies from issue to issue –
12.7B12.

Work emanating from corporate body but not
falling within any of the categories listed at
21.1B2 is entered under title – 21.1C1(c). The
form of heading for the added entry is chosen
in accordance with rules 23.2A1, 24.6A1 and
24.6C.

BRITISH LIBRARY. Bibliographic
   Services
    The British Library Bibliographic
Services newsletter. – No. 39 (Feb.
1986)-   . – London : BLBS, 1986-   .
    no. : ill., ports. ; 30 cm.
    Three to four issues yearly.
    Continues: The British Library
Bibliographic Services Division newsletter.
    Free to subscribers of Bibliographic
Services.
    ISSN 0268-9707 = British Library
Bibliographic Services newsletter.

As statement of responsibility appears as part
of the title proper a further statement is not

given – 12.1F2. Numbering, etc. of the first
issue under the new title recorded – 12.3B3.
When serial is continuation of one previously
published, name of latter is given in a note –
12.7B7(b). Key-title recorded if found on the
item or is otherwise readily available – 12.8C1.

Issue 39 contains a change in the first five
words of the title (other than the initial article)
and the title therefore must be considered to
have changed – 21.2A1 and a separate main
entry made for the new title – 21.2C1 (see next
example). (There is also a change in the name
of the corporate body under which the serial is
entered and a new entry would also be required
according to 21.3B1).

BRITISH LIBRARY. Bibliographic
   Services Division
    The British Library Bibliographic
Services Division newsletter. – No. 1
(May 1970)-no. 38 (Oct. 1985). –
London : BLBSD, 1976-1985.
    38 no. : ill., ports. ; 30 cm.
    Three to four issues yearly.
    Continued by: British Library
Bibliographic Services newsletter.
    ISSN 0308-230X = British Library
Bibliographic Services Division newsletter.
    ISSN 0265-1386 (No. 33 (Apr.
1984)-   ).
    Free to subscribers of BSD publications.

Note on relationship to another serial; when a
serial is continued by another serial, name of
latter is given in note – 12.7B7(c) (see also
previous example). Key-title recorded if found
on item or otherwise readily available even if it
is identical with title proper – 12.8C1. If an
item bears two numbers, optionally they can
both be recorded and a qualification added –
12.8B1, 1.8B2 and 1.8E1. (Any source may be
used for this information and it does not matter
therefore that it could not, as in this instance,
appear on first issue). Optional note on terms of
availability – 1.8D1 and 12.8D1.

Work emanating from corporate body which is
of an administrative nature dealing with the
operations and procedures of the body entered
under the heading for the body – 21.1B2(a).
No added entry under title as title proper is
essentially the same as the main entry heading – 21.30J1(a).

one previously published, name of latter given in note – 12.7B7(b) (see also example no. 444). Note that serial is a supplement to another serial – 12.7B7(j). Note on contents, a special item with a specific title – 12.7B18.

Work emanating from corporate body but not falling within any of the categories listed at 21.1B2 is entered under title – 21.1C1(c).

First Quarter **1965**

Bulletin of Labour Statistics

International Labour Office · Geneva

439

BULLETIN of labour statistics. – 1st
  quarter 1965-   . – Geneva :
International Labour Office, 1965-   .
    v. ; 27 cm.
  Quarterly. Kept up to date by a
supplement issued in intervening months to
1980 and four times a year from 1981.
  Text in English, French and Spanish.
  Continues: International labour review
statistical supplement.
  Supplement to: The year book of labour
statistics.
  October enquiry, a ILO world-wide
annual survey of occupational wages and
hours of work, initiated in 1924, included
in the second quarterly issue of each year
to 1984 and as a separate issue each year
from 1985.
  ISSN 0007-4950.

  1. International Labour Office

Chronological designation recorded in terms used in item – 12.3C1. Arabic numerals substituted for numbers expressed as words – 12.3C1 and C.3B1(b). Note on language – 12.7B2. When name of serial is continuation of

NEWSLETTER

Centre for
Bibliographic
Management

No. 15   March 1988

ISSN 0953-5144

We Change Our Name!

On 1st November 1987 the Centre for Catalogue Research became the Centre for Bibliographic Management. Mr Kenneth Cooper, Chief Executive of the British Library gave notice of the new name at a dinner held at the University of Bath on 14th September 1987 to mark the 10th anniversary of the establishment of the Centre.

Staff News

Many visitors to Bath have been surprised to find that despite the rather grand title of 'Centre' the team is in fact a very small one.

440

CENTRE FOR BIBLIOGRAPHIC
   MANAGEMENT
   Newsletter / Centre for Bibliographic
Management. – No. 15 (Mar.
1988)-   . – Bath : University of Bath.
Centre for Bibliographic Management,
1988-   .
      no. : ill. ; 30 cm.
   Irregular.
   Continues: Newsletter / Centre for
Catalogue Research.
   ISSN 0953-5144.

   1.   Title

New entry for serial when name of corporate body under which serial is entered changes – 21.3B1(a). (See also next example).

441

CENTRE FOR CATALOGUE
   RESEARCH
   Newsletter / Centre for Catalogue
Research. – No. 3 (Dec. 1979)-No. 14
(Apr. 1987). – Bath : University of Bath.
Centre for Catalogue Research, 1979-1987.
   12 no. ; 30 cm.
   Irregular.
   Continues: Newsletter / Bath University
Programme of Catalogue Research.
   Continued by: Newsletter / Centre for
Bibliographic Management.
   ISSN 0144-5073.

   1.   Title

New entry for serial when name of corporate body under which serial is entered changes – 21.3B1(a) (see example no. 435). The name of the body changed again in 1987 and a further new entry is therefore required (see previous example).

442

CLASSIFICATION RESEARCH
   GROUP
   Bulletin / Classification Research
Group. – No. 1 (1956)-   . – London :
CRG, 1956-   .
      no. ; 30 cm.
   Irregular.
   Nos. 1-3 duplicated.
   From no. 4 issued with: Journal of
documentation, starting v. 14, no. 3 (Sept.
1958)-   , one issue every four, five or
more years.

   1.   Title
   2.   Journal of documentation

Note on physical description – 12.7B10. "Issued with" note for separately titled part of another serial – 12.7B21.

Work emanating from corporate body which deals with the activities and operations of the body entered under the heading for the body – 21.1B2(a). Added entry under related work – 21.30G1.

HISTORICAL abstracts. Part B,
Twentieth century abstracts
(1914-   ). – Vol. 1, no. 1
(1955)-   . – Santa Barbara, Calif. :
American Bibliographic Center-Clio Press ;
Oxford : European Bibliographic Centre-
Clio Press, 1955-
v. ; 28 cm.
4 issues yearly.
Also available online as File 39 of Dialog
Information Services.
Indexes: Issue index in no. 1 and no. 2;
cumulative annual index published as
no. 4; five-year indexes are also available.
Description based on: Vol. 23, no. 1
(Spring 1977).
ISSN 0363-2725.

Serial is separately published section of another
serial and title proper consists of the title
common to all sections and the title of specific
section, these two parts being grammatically
independent of each other. Therefore the
common title is given followed by the section
title preceded by a full stop – 12.1B4. Title of
the section is preceded by an alphabetic
designation so latter is given before section title
which is preceded by a comma – 12.1B5.
Note on other formats – 12.7B16. Note on
indexes – 12.7B17. Description is not based
upon first issue so note made of issue upon
which it is based – 12.7B23. Details of
bibliographic history are included in the
preliminaries of this issue so no square brackets
are required for numeric and chronological
designations and publication date.

INTERNATIONAL labour review. –
Vol. 1 (1921)-   . – Geneva :
International Labour Office, 1921-   .
v. ; 25 cm.
Monthly (1921-1975), six issues yearly
(1976-   ).
Volumes renumbered every six months
to 1977 and annually from 1978.
Vol. 66 (Jul.-Dec. 1952)-v. 90 (Jul.-
Dec. 1964) includes: Statistical supplement,
which is continued from 1965 by: Bulletin
of labour statistics.
ISSN 0020-7780.

1. International Labour Office
2. International labour review
statistical supplement

Note on change of frequency – 12.7B1.
Note on numbering – 12.7B8. Note on
supplement – 12.7B18 (see also example
no. 439).

Work emanating from corporate body but not
falling within any of the categories listed at
21.1B2 is entered under title – 21.1C1(c). The
International Labour Office would have to be
linked by references to the related corporate
heading International Labour Organisation –
26.3B1.*

INTERNATIONAL studies quarterly /
International Studies Association. –
Vol. 11, no. 1 (Mar. 1967)-   . –
Detroit : Wayne State University,
1967-   .
v. ; 22 cm.
Continues: Background.
Published: Beverly Hills ; London :
Sage, 1971-1982. London : Butterworth,
1983-   .
ISSN 0020-8833.

1. International Studies Association †

Numeric and chronological designations of
the first issue under the new title recorded –
12.3B3. Serial continues a previous serial but
numbering is unchanged. Note of preceding
serial – 12.7B7(b). Note on change of
publisher – 12.7B9. Frequency is not recorded
in a note as it is apparent from the title –
12.7B1.

Work emanating from corporate body but not
falling within any of the categories listed at
21.1B2 is entered under title – 21.1C1(c).

An analytical entry for an article from this serial
is illustrated in Appendix 1.

JFI. – Issue 1 (1985)-   . – Computer
   data. – Mansfield : Wheel Publications,
1986-
      computer disks ; 5¼ in. +
explanatory notes and comments.
   1 issue (1985), 4 issues yearly
(1986-   ).
   Index to junior fiction reviews.
   System requirements: BBC B; 40 track
disk drive.
      ISSN 0268-8808.

Description of serials issued in the form of
computer files – Ch. 1, Ch. 9 and Ch. 12.
Instructions for sources of information taken
from relevant chapter for material, e.g. Ch. 9
for computer files – 12.0B2. Numeric and
chronological designation recorded as given
in the first issue – 12.3B1 and 12.3C1. Type of
file indicated when information is readily
available – 9.3B1. Relevant specific material
designation recorded, preceded by three
spaces – 12.5B1 and 9.5B1. Name of
accompanying material that is to be issued
regularly and is intended to be used in
conjunction with the serial recorded at end of
physical description – 12.5E1. Note on
frequency – 12.7B1. Note on nature of item –
1.7B1 and 9.7B1(a). Note on system
requirements – 9.7B1(b). ISSN recorded –
1.8B1, 9.8B1 and 12.8B1.

The JOURNAL of documentation :
   devoted to the recording, organization
and dissemination of specialized
knowledge. – Vol. 1, no. 1 (Jun.
1945)-   . – London : Aslib,
1945-   .
      v. ; 25 cm.
   Quarterly.
   From v. 14, no. 3 (Sept. 1958) includes:
Bulletin / Classification Research Group,
no. 4-   , an irregular publication which
appears at intervals of four, five or more
years.
      ISSN 0022-0418.

Other title information recorded – 1.1E1 and
12.1E1. Note on serial within a serial – 12.7B18.

Liverpool Polytechnic	No. 75/1	10 January 1975

LIVERPOOL POLYTECHNIC.
   The bulletin / Liverpool Polytechnic. –
No. 75/1 (10 Jan. 1975)-   . – Liver-
pool : The Polytechnic, 1975-   .
      no. ; 30 cm.
   Irregular in term time.
   Continues: Livepolybulletin.
   Occasional unnumbered special issues.

   1.   Title

See annotation following next example.

LivePOLYBULLetin

9th May 1974		Vol. 1 No. 1

LIVERPOOL POLYTECHNIC
   Livepolybulletin. – Vol. 1, no. 1
(9 May 1974)-v. 1, no. 15 (18 Dec.
1974). – Liverpool : The Polytechnic,
1974.
      15 no. ; 30 cm.
   Weekly in term time.
   Continued by: The bulletin / Liverpool
Polytechnic.

   1.   Title   2.   Polybull

Separate main entry made if title proper of
serial changes (see also previous example) –
21.2A1 and 21.2C1.

Work of administrative nature emanating from a
corporate body and dealing with the body itself
is entered under heading for body – 21.1B2(a).
Typography emphasizes 'Polybull' and therefore
added entry under this alternative title is
considered necessary for access – 21.30J1.

MEDIA, culture and society. – Vol. 1,
no. 1 [Jan. 1979]-   . – London :
New York : Academic Press, [1979]-   .
v. ; 22-25 cm.
Quarterly.
Published: Beverly Hills ; London :
Sage, v. 7, no. 1 (Jan. 1985)-   .
Library has v. 4, no. 3 (Jan. 1982)-   ,
and description based on that issue.
ISSN 0163-4437.

First issue not available to cataloguing agency;
chief source of information becomes first issue
that is available (i.e. v. 4, no. 3) – 12.0B1.
Chronological designation and date of first issue
obtained from reference source and enclosed in
square brackets because it has been taken from
outside the prescribed source – 12.0B1.
Dimensions of serial which has changed its size
recorded by analogy with 2.5D3 and see
example in rule 12.5D1. Note on change of
publisher – 12.7B9. Note on library's holdings if
required – 1.7B20, 12.7B20 and 2.7B20.
Description not based upon first issue so note
made of issue upon which it is based –
12.7B23. The ISSN is the same for both
publishers so no qualification is required.

| National Library of Canada | Bibliotheque nationale du Canada |

NATIONAL LIBRARY NEWS

NOUVELLES de la BIBLIOTHÈQUE NATIONALE

November-December 1977   Vol.9,No.6   Novembre-Décembre 1977   Vol.9,No6

NATIONAL LIBRARY ADVISORY BOARD MEETING

The ninth meeting of the National Library
Advisory Board was held on October 20-21,
1977, and was chaired by Professor René
de Chantal. In addition to hearing reports
on the DOBIS (Dortmunder Bibliothekssystem)
system, on changes in Canadiana and on a
number of other recent activities, the
Board discussed the Multilingual Biblioservice, the serious problem of the lack
of space in the National Library, and the
increased role that the Board itself might
play. After making a few amendments, the
Board approved the recommendations of the
Committee on Bibliographical Services for
Canada (see below). The Board appointed
Dr. Frances Halpenny to succeed Miss
Margaret Williams as Chairman of the
Committee. (Following her resignation as
Chairman, Miss Williams was reelected to
the Committee as a member.) The Board
also asked its Chairman to write to the
Secretary of State, requesting him to
expedite the construction of a new building
for the Public Archives. Finally, the
Board decided to devote its next meeting
to the study of the awaited report on the
role of the National Library.

RÉUNION DU CONSEIL CONSULTATIF DE LA
BIBLIOTHÈQUE NATIONALE

Le Conseil consultatif de la Bibliothèque
nationale a tenu sa neuvième réunion les
20 et 21 octobre 1977 sous la présidence
du professeur René de Chantal. En plus
d'être saisis de renseignements à jour
sur le système DOBIS, sur les modifications à Canadiana, et sur quelques autres
activités récentes, les membres discu-
tèrent surtout du Biblioservice multi-
lingue, du sérieux problème que pose le
manque d'espace, du rôle accru que pour-
rait jouer le Conseil consultatif; et il
approuva, avec quelques modifications,
les recommandations du Comité des services bibliographiques (voir ci-dessous).
Le Conseil nomma Mlle Frances Halpenny
présidente de ce comité pour succéder à
Mlle Margaret Williams démissionnaire
(cette dernière a été réélue membre du
comité). Le Conseil invita aussi son
président à écrire au Secrétaire d'État
pour lui demander d'activer la construction d'un nouvel édifice pour les Archives
publiques. Enfin, le Conseil décida de
consacrer sa prochaine réunion à l'étude
du rapport attendu sur le rôle de la Bibliothèque nationale.

NATIONAL LIBRARY OF CANADA
National Library news / National
Library of Canada = Nouvelles de la
Bibliothèque nationale / Bibliothèque
nationale du Canada. – Vol. 1, no. 1
(Jan./Feb. 1969)-   . – [Ottawa] :
National Library of Canada, 1969-   .
v. : ill., ports. ; 28 cm.
Six issues yearly (1969-1979), monthly
with occasional combined numbers
(1980-1982), ten issues a year (1983-   ).
Text in English and French.
Indexes: Vols. 10-14 (1978-1982)
published separately. Vols. 15-
in last issue of vol., i.e. Dec., or first
issue of next vol., i.e. Jan.
ISSN 0027-9633.
Available free upon request.

1. Title
2. Nouvelles de la Bibliothèque
    nationale

Parallel titles recorded – 1.1D1 and 12.1D1.
Statement of responsibility appears in
abbreviated form as part of the title proper, but
it is given as further statement of responsibility
as well, since it appears separately in chief
source of information – 12.1F2. When item has
parallel titles and statements of responsibility in
more than one language, each statement is
given after the parallel title to which it relates –
1.1F10. Chronological designation appears in
two languages, so designation appearing first is
recorded – 12.3C3. Note on changes of
frequency – 12.7B1. Note on languages –
12.7B2. Note on indexes – 12.7B17. Optional
note on availability – 12.8D1.

Work emanating from a corporate body which is
of an administrative nature dealing with the
operations and procedures of the body is
entered under the heading for the body –
21.1B2(a). Name appears in two languages, both
of which are official, so entry is under the
English form – 24.3A1.* See also example no.
75 for an index to this serial catalogued
separately as a printed monograph.

NEW statesman & society. – Vol. 1,
no. 1 (10 Jun. 1988)-   . – London :
Statesman & Nation, 1988-   .
v. : ill. (some col.) ; 30 cm.
Weekly.
Cover title: Newstatesman society.
Merger of: New statesman and New
society.
Absorbed: The nation, The Athenaeum
and The week-end review.
Issues also called: New statesman v. 115,
no. 2984-   ; New society v. 84, no.
1327-   .

Title proper transcribed exactly as to wording,
order and spelling – 1.1B1 and 12.1B1. Note of
serials that have been merged – 12.7B7(d).
Note of serials that have been absorbed –
12.7B7(f). Note on numbering – 12.7B8.

NOTIONS : your creative Options. –
June 1988-   . – London : Carlton
Magazines, 1988-   .
v. : col. ill. ; 30 cm.
Issued with: Options.

1.   Options

No indication of frequency on first issue and, as
it is unknown therefore, no frequency note is
made – 12.7B1. "Issued with" note for serial
issued with another – 12.7B21.

Added entry under related work – 21.30G1.

OLDIES UNLIMITED
Oldies Unlimited : the Albums B
Cassettes Compact discs of popular
recorded music. – Sale no. 1-   . –
Telford, Shropshire : Oldies Unlimited,
[1988]-   .
no. ; 21 cm.
Six issues a year.
A catalogue with the same title proper
which covers singles records is also
available in serial form from this publisher.

Catalogue in serial form. Other title information
transcribed exactly as to order, wording and
spelling – 1.1E1, 1.1B1 and 12.1E1. Numeric
designation of first issue recorded as given in
that issue – 12.3B1. Standard abbreviation

used – B.9. Chronological designation not given
as it is recorded only if first issue is identified
by such a designation – 12.3C1.

Work emanating from corporate body which is
of an administrative nature in that it is a
catalogue of items available from that body
entered under the heading for the body –
21.1B2(a). No title added entry as title proper is
the same as main entry heading – 21.30J1(a).

PC : personal computing with the
Amstrad. – Vol. 1, no. 1 (May
1987)-   . – Stockport, Cheshire :
Database Publications, 1987-   .
v. : col. ill. ; 30 cm.
Monthly.
Free computer disks with some issues.

Note on accompanying materials which are not
a regular feature – 12.7B11.

PLANNING outlook. – Vol. 1, no. 1
(July 1948)-v. 6, no. 2 (1964) ; Vol. 1
(Dec. 1966)-   . – London : Geoffrey
Cumberlege, Oxford University Press,
1948-   .
v. ; 24-30 cm.
Irregular (1948-1965), 2 issues yearly
(1966-   ).
Journal of the School of Town and
Country Planning, King's College,
University of Durham (later the
Department of Town and Country
Planning in the University of Newcastle
upon Tyne) and, from 1973 to 1976, of
the Department of Town Planning of
Oxford Polytechnic.
Imprint varies; new series 1966-
first published by Oriel Press and
subsequently by the University of
Newcastle.
ISSN 0032-0714.

1.   University of Durham. King's
College. School of Town and
Country Planning
2.   University of Newcastle upon Tyne.
Department of Town and
Country Planning
3.   Oxford Polytechnic. Department
of Town Planning

Serial which starts a new designation system without changing its title proper; designation of first and last issues of the old system given, followed by the designation of the first issue of the new system – 12.3G1. Serial which changes its size 12.5D1 and 2.5D3. Note on change of frequency – 12.7B1. Note on statement of responsibility – 12.7B6. Note on publication – 12.7B9.

PTB : personnel training bulletin. –
    Issue 1 (May 1983)-   . –
Huntingdon, Cambridgeshire : Didasko, 1983-   .
        sound cassettes : analog, 1⅞ ips, stereo., Dolby processed.
    Monthly.

    1.   Personnel training bulletin

Description of serials issued in the form of sound recordings – Ch. 1, Ch. 6 and Ch. 12. Instruction for sources of information taken from relevant chapter, e.g. Ch. 6 for sound recordings – 12.0B2. Numeric designation of first issue recorded as given on that issue – 12.3B1. Relevant specific material designation recorded, preceded by three spaces – 12.5B1. Other physical details appropriate to the item given – 12.5C1, 6.5C3, 6.5C7 and 6.5C8.

SUMMER jobs abroad ... – 16th ed.
    (1985)-   . – Oxford : Vacation Work, 1985-   .
        v. ; 21 cm.
    Annual.
    Continues: The directory of summer jobs abroad.
    Library has current issue only.
    ISSN 0308-7123.

Editor is named on title page but statements of responsibility relating to editors are not recorded – 12.1F3. Statement could be given in a note if considered necessary. Date or numbering that appears in title proper (see example no. 213) is omitted and replaced by the mark of omission – 12.1B7. (If such date or numbering occurs at the beginning of the title proper, the mark of omission is not included.) When an element ends with the mark of omission and the subsequent punctuation begins with a full-stop, the full-stop is omitted – 1.0C. Numeric and chronological designations are recorded as given in the first issue – 12.3B1 and 12.3C1 (see also 12.2B2, where the instruction that statements indicating volume numbering or designations are not to be treated as edition statements but are to be given in the numeric designation area). Note on library's holdings – 12.7B20. Note on standard number – 12.8B1 and 1.8B1.

Each volume of this item also carries an International Standard Book Number and some cataloguing agencies may prefer to catalogue the work as a printed monograph as illustrated in example no. 213.

459

TOYNE, Peter
 Rector's review / Peter Toyne. – No. 1 (10 Sep. 1986)- – [Liverpool : Liverpool Polytechnic], 1986-
  no. ; 30 cm.
 Irregular.
 Intended audience: Staff of the Polytechnic.

 1. Liverpool Polytechnic

Chronological designation recorded in terms used in the first issue – 12.3C1. Place of publication and publisher enclosed in square brackets as information has not been taken from prescribed source – 1.4A2. Note on intended audience – 1.7B14 and 12.7B14.

Serial entered under the heading for the person responsible for the intellectual content – 21.1A1 and 21.1A2.

It might be argued that this work emanates from a corporate body and, as it describes the operations and activities of that body, entry could be made under the heading for the body according to 21.1B2. However, the Rector's purpose in writing it is simply to keep in touch with the staff and the view taken here is that the work is a personal rather than a corporate statement.

460

UNITED STATES. President
 Economic report of the President transmitted to the Congress. – 1950- . – Washington, D.C. : G.P.O., 1950-
  v. ; 24 cm.

 1. Title

Serial which is an official communication from Head of State entered under the corporate heading – 21.4D1(a). Head of state entered subordinately – 24.18A (Type 9). Heading consists of the jurisdiction followed by the title of the official in English – 24.20B1. Dates and names omitted from heading which applies to more than one incumbent – 24.20B1.

Appendix 1
Added entries

AACR 2 is based upon the proposition that one main entry is made for each item described and that this is supplemented by added entries. An added entry is defined as "an entry, additional to the main entry, by which an item is represented in a catalogue; a secondary entry." Although tracings have been given, no added entries as so defined have been included in the main sequences of this work. Such inclusion would have unnecessarily complicated matters, especially as methods of formulating added entries vary from library to library. However, the following notes on possible layouts and examples of added entries will serve to illustrate some of these methods and the form that added entries may take.

THE UNIT ENTRY METHOD

The full main entry, with the addition of appropriate headings, is used for all entries in the catalogue, e.g. from example no. 95.

Added entry (collaborator – 21.30B)

HAWK, Dick
GONZALES, Pancho
How to play and win at tennis / by Pancho Gonzales & Dick Hawk ; edited by Gladys Heldman. – 1st British ed. – London : Souvenir Press, 1963.
123 p. : 126 ill. ; 23 cm.
Originally published: New York : Fleet Publishing, 1962.

THE ALTERNATIVE HEADING METHOD

The description is used as a basis for entry and the various required headings are simply added above the title statement, e.g.

HAWK, Dick
How to play and win at tennis / by Pancho Gonzales & Dick Hawk ; edited by Gladys Heldman. – 1st British ed. – London : Souvenir Press, 1963.
123 p. : 126 ill. ; 23 cm.
Originally published: New York : Fleet Publishing, 1962.

With this method, filing is simplified. All access points are treated as equal; a full description is included under each heading and, if a tracing is given with each entry, the need to choose a particular heading for a main entry is eliminated.

AACR 2 recognises that many libraries have adopted the alternative heading method. These libraries are recommended to use Chapter 21 as guidance in determining all the entries required in particular instances (see p. 2 of AACR 2).

ABBREVIATED ADDED ENTRIES

The International Conference on Cataloguing Principles of 1961 defined an added entry somewhat differently from AACR 2 as: "any entry giving partial or full information about a particular bibliographical unit, other than the main entry." The word "partial" indicates that the detail given in added entries may be simplified and, from this point, all of the added entries in this appendix are in an abbreviated form. For each example two entries have been prepared. In one, the main entry heading is interposed, where necessary, between the added entry heading and the title statement (as with the unit entry) and, in the other, it is not (as with the alternative heading method), e.g.

HAWK, Dick
GONZALES, Pancho
How to play and win at tennis. – 1st British ed. – 1963.

or

HAWK, Dick
  How to play and win at tennis / by
Pancho Gonzales & Dick Hawk. – 1st
British ed. – 1963.

The amount of detail to be included in a
simplified added entry will depend upon the
policy of the individual library or cataloguing
agency. However, the minimum requirement
would seem to be: Title / statement of responsibility (if necessary). – Edition statement (if
applicable). – Date. – Specific material
designation (if necessary).

It should also be pointed out that, in certain
instances, references may be employed in lieu
of added entries (see Appendix 2).

In abbreviated added entries, the catalogue user
must be given enough information to enable
him or her to find the main entry so that full
details of an item can be traced if required. In
this connection, there is no great difficulty when
the main entry heading is given after the added
entry heading. When it is not, however, certain
problems are posed. These problems can be
solved, in part, in several ways:

(1) By indicating the main entry heading in a
note, e.g.

    Example no. 238 (added title entry)

A DIGEST of the results of the census of
    England and Wales in 1901 : arranged
in tabular form, together with an explanatory introduction / compiled by William
Sanders. – 1903.
    Full details are entered under:
    United Kingdom. General Register
Office

(2) By the use of capitalization, e.g.

    Example no. 258 (added title entry)

    The SIDE of the angels / by John
Rowan WILSON. – 1968

(3) Another procedure used in some libraries,
either alone or as a supplement to other
methods, is to indicate the main entry heading

following the class number, which is included in
every entry, e.g.

    823.91/WILSON or 823.91/WIL

The last two of these methods are problematic
in that their intention may not be clear to the
catalogue user. There must be an adequate
explanation in the guide to the use of the
catalogue. But do catalogue users bother to
read such guides? The best solution, therefore,
seems to be the first method but, even here,
care must be taken. A note such as "Main entry
is at: United Kingdom. General Register Office"
could have the user asking two questions:
"What is a main entry?" and "Why do I have to
go to London to find out more about this item?"

ADDED ENTRY EXAMPLES

The following examples are given in the order
of the sections of rule 21.30.

Designations of function are omitted from
headings, although it should be noted that
AACR 2 *optionally* allows certain designations
such as *comp., ed., ill., tr.,* and *arr.* to be given in
added entry headings for persons (see rules
21.0D1 and 21.18B1). It must be appreciated
that such omission may necessitate more detail
being supplied in the body of the entry to
clarify the relationship to the publication of the
person or body under which added entry is
made. If the reason for an added entry is not
apparent from the body of the description, then
a note must be provided (see rule 21.29F).

Rules 21.30A and 21.30B

Two or more persons or bodies involved –
Collaborators

From example no. 318

  FLYE, James Harold
AGEE, James
  James Agee : a portrait / James Agee
reading [from his work ; Father Flye reads
from Agee's work and reminisces about the
author]. – 1971.
  2 sound discs.

or

FLYE, James Harold
  James Agee : a portrait / James Agee
reading [from his work ; Father Flye reads
from Agee's work and reminisces about the
author]. – 1971.
  2 sound discs.

From example no. 51

METHODIST CHURCH
CHURCH OF ENGLAND
  Conversations between the Church of
England and the Methodist Church : an
interim statement. – 1958.

or

METHODIST CHURCH
  Conversations between the Church of
England and the Methodist Church : an
interim statement. – 1958.

From example no. 16

AMERICAN LIBRARY
ASSOCIATION
ANGLO-American cataloguing rules. –
  2nd ed., 1988 revision / prepared under
the direction of the Joint Steering
Committee for AACR, a committee of the
American Library Association [et al.]. –
1988

or

AMERICAN LIBRARY ASSOCIATION
  Anglo-American cataloguing rules. –
2nd ed., 1988 revision / prepared under
the direction of the Joint Steering
Committee for AACR, a committee of the
American Library Association [et al.]. –
1988.

Rule 21.30C

Writers

From example no. 161

  MELVILLE, Robert
NOLAN, Sidney
  Ned Kelly : 27 paintings / by Sidney
Nolan ; [text by] Robert Melville. – 1964.

or

MELVILLE, Robert
  Ned Kelly : 27 paintings / by Sidney
Nolan ; [text by] Robert Melville. – 1964.

Rule 21.30D

Editors and compilers

From example no. 77

  SHUGRUE, Michael
FARQUHAR, George
  The recruiting officer / edited by
Michael Shugrue. – 1966.

or

SHUGRUE, Michael
  The recruiting officer / by George
Farquhar ; edited by Michael Shugrue. –
1966.

Rule 21.30E

Prominently named corporate bodies

From example no. 12

  BRITISH COUNCIL OF
  CHURCHES.
  Education Department
ALVES, Colin
  Religion and the secondary school : a
report undertaken on behalf of the British
Council of Churches. – 1968.

or

BRITISH COUNCIL OF CHURCHES.
  Education Department
  Religion and the secondary school : a
report undertaken on behalf of the British
Council of Churches / by Colin Alves. –
1968.

From example no. 445

  INTERNATIONAL STUDIES
  ASSOCIATION
INTERNATIONAL studies quarterly. –
  Vol. 11, no. 1 (Mar. 1967)-   . –
1967-   .
    v.

or

INTERNATIONAL STUDIES
 ASSOCIATION
 International studies quarterly. – Vol.
11, no. 1 (Mar. 1967)-   . – 1967-
  v.

Rule 21.30F

Other related persons or bodies

From example no. 178

 HAYEK, Friedrich A. von
ROADS to freedom : essays in honour of
 Friedrich A. von Hayek. – 1969.

or

HAYEK, Friedrich A. von
 Roads to freedom : essays in honour of
Friedrich A. von Hayek. – 1969.

From example no. 326

 ISAAC, Anthony
KHACHATURIAN, Aram
 The "Onedin Line" theme ; Sabre
dance / Khachaturian. – 1971
 1 sound disc.
 First item consists of "Music from
"Spartacus" as adapted for the BBC-TV
series by Anthony Isaac".

or

ISAAC, Anthony
 The "Onedin Line" theme ; Sabre
dance / Khachaturian. – 1971
 1 sound disc.
 First item consists of "Music from
"Spartacus" as adpated for the BBC-TV
series by Anthony Isaac".

From example no. 13

 JOECKEL, Carleton Bruns
AMERICAN LIBRARY ASSOCIATION.
 Committee on Post-War Planning
 Post-war standards for public libraries /
Carleton Bruns Joeckel, Chairman. –
1943.

or

JOECKEL, Carleton Bruns
 Post-war standards for public libraries /
prepared by The Committee on Post-War
Planning of the American Library
Association ; Carleton Bruns Joeckel,
Chairman. – 1943.

Rule 21.30G

Related works

From example no. 92 (Name-title added entry)

JOYCE, James
 Ulysses
GILBERT, Stuart
 James Joyce's Ulysses : a study. –
1930.

or

JOYCE, James
 Ulysses
 James Joyce's Ulysses : a study / by
Stuart Gilbert. – 1930.

From example no. 30

 RADIO Times
BBC
 Talking points, third series : B.B.C.
comments on questions that viewers and
listeners ask. – 1969.

or

RADIO times
 Talking points, third series : B.B.C.
comments on questions that viewers and
listeners ask. – 1969.

Rule 21.30H

Other relationships

From example no. 371

 DEVONSHIRE COLLECTION
PAINTINGS at Chatsworth. – [196-?].
 8 postcards.

or

DEVONSHIRE COLLECTION
 Paintings at Chatsworth. – [196-?].
 8 postcards.

Rule 21.30J

Titles

From example no. 375

    BOATS in Whitby Harbour
SUTCLIFFE, Frank Meadow
    Boats in Whitby Harbour. – 1977.
    1 photograph.

or

BOATS in Whitby Harbour / Frank
    Meadow Sutcliffe. – 1977.
    1 photograph.

From example no. 305

    El SOMBRERO de tres picos
FALLA, Manuel de
    El sombrero de tres picos = Le
tricorne = The three-cornered hat :
ballet. – c1921.
    1 miniature score.

or

El SOMBRERO de tres picos = Le
    tricorne = The three-cornered hat :
ballet / [music by] Manuel de Falla. –
c1921.
    1 miniature score.

Title proper of second item in collection without collective title

From example no. 63

    RUTH
CUNDALL, Arthur E.
    Judges / [Arthur E. Cundall]. Ruth /
[Leon Morris]. – 1968.

or

RUTH / [Leon Morris]. – 1968.
    Full details are entered under:
    Cundall, Arthur E.
    Judges / [Arthur E. Cundall]. Ruth /
[Leon Morris]

A name-title added entry under the heading for Morris would also be necessary – see rule 21.7B1 and 21.7C1.

Title proper of an item entered under uniform title – rule 25.2E1.

From example no. 202

    The TALE of the armament of Igor,
    A.D. 1185
[SLOVO o polku Igoreve. English]
    The tale of the armament of Igor, A.D.
1185 : a Russian historical epic. – 1915.

or

The TALE of the armament of Igor,
    A.D. 1185 : a Russian historical epic. –
1915.
    Full details are entered under:
[Slovo o polku Igoreve. English]

Rule 21.30J

Uniform titles

From example no. 40

    [L'ADORATION. English]
BOREL, Jacques
    [L'adoration. English]
    The bond. – 1968.

or

[L'ADORATION. English]
    The bond / by Jacques Borel. – 1968.

An added entry under the title proper (see below) and a name-title reference (see Appendix 2) would also be required.

Rule 25.2E2 directs that an added entry be made under the title proper of a work, entered under a personal heading when a uniform title has been used:

    The BOND
BOREL, Jacques
    [L'adoration. English]
    The bond. – 1968.

or

The BOND
  [L'adoration. English]
  The bond / by Jacques Borel. – 1968.

Different versions of a title (cover title, caption title, running title, etc.), if considered necessary for access.

Parallel title

From example no. 305

  The THREE-CORNERED hat
FALLA, Manuel de
  El sombrero de tres picos = Le tricorne = The three-cornered hat : ballet. – c1921.
  1 miniature score.

or

The THREE-CORNERED hat : ballet. – c1921.
  1 miniature score.
  Full details are entered under:
  Falla, Manuel de
    El sombrero de tres picos

Container title

From example no. 333

  GREGORIAN chants from Hungary
SCHOLA HUNGARICA ENSEMBLE
  Magyar Gregorianum : a karácsonyi ünnepkör dallamai. – [1976].
  1 sound disc.

or

GREGORIAN chants from Hungary. – [1976].
  1 sound disc.
  Full details are entered under:
  Schola Hungarica Ensemble
    Magyar Gregorianum

Variant title

From example no. 310

226

REFORMATION [symphony]
MENDELSSOHN-BARTHOLDY, Felix
  [Symphonies, no. 5, op. 107, D minor]
  Symphony no. 5, D minor (Reformation), op. 107. – [1960?].

or

REFORMATION [symphony]. – [1960?].
  1 miniature score.
  Full details are entered under:
  Mendelssohn-Bartholdy, Felix
    [Symphonies, no. 5, op. 107,
D minor]

Some cataloguing agencies might prefer references rather than added entries from titles other than the title proper – see p. 229.

Rule 21.30K1

Translators

From example no. 138

  CAMPBELL, Roy
JOHN, of the Cross, Saint
  Poems / with a translation by Roy Campbell. – 1968.

or

CAMPBELL, Roy
  Poems / by Saint John of the Cross ; with a translation by Roy Campbell. – 1968.

Rule 21.30K2

Illustrators

From example no. 87

  SCOTT, Peter
GALLICO, Paul
  The snow goose / illustrations by Peter Scott. – [New] illustrated ed. – 1946.

or

SCOTT, Peter
  The snow goose / by Paul Gallico ; illustrations by Peter Scott. – [New] illustrated ed. – 1946.

Rule 21.30L

Series

From example no. 155

ENGLISH linguistics 1500-1800 : a
collection of facsimile reprints.
MONBODDO, James Burnet, <u>Lord</u>
Of the origin and progress of
language. – 1967.
6 v.

or

ENGLISH linguistics 1500-1800 : a
collection of facsimile reprints.
Of the origin and progress of language /
by James Burnet. – 1967.
6 v.

Optionally, the numeric or other designation of
each work in the series can be added.

The above format would be used if
arrangement under the series heading was to be
alphabetical by the authors of the parts of the
series. An alternative arrangement could be
numerical by the number of the part of the
series, e.g.

ENGLISH linguistics 1500-1800 : a
collection of facsimile reprints.
No. 48: Of the origin and progress of
language / by James Burnet. – 1967.
6 v.

Rule 21.30M

Analytical entries

From example no. 58 (Name-title added entry)

MAXCY, George
The motor industry
COOK, P. Lesley
Effects of mergers : six studies. – 1958.

or

MAXCY, George
The motor industry
Effects of mergers : six studies /
P. Lesley Cook with the collaboration of
Ruth Cohen. – 1958.

The above method is appropriate when direct
access to the part is wanted without creating an
additional bibliographic record for the part –
see rule 13.4. Alternatively, the "In" analytic
entry may be considered – see rule 13.5, e.g.

MAXCY, George
The motor industry / George Maxcy. –
p. 351-393 ; 23 cm.

In Cook, P. Lesley. Effects of mergers :
six studies. – London : Allen & Unwin,
1958.

or, if an "In" analytic entry is required under the
title:

The MOTOR industry / George
Maxcy. – p. 351-393 ; 23 cm.

In Cook, P. Lesley. Effects of mergers :
six studies. – London : Allen & Unwin,
1958.

Further examples of "In" analytic entries are:

From example no. 445

WALKER, R.B.J.
Realism, change and international
political theory / R.B.J. Walker. –
p. 65 – 86 ; 22 cm.
In International studies quarterly. –
Vol. 31, no. 1 (March 1987).

From example no. 339 (with uniform title used
for part)

BEETHOVEN, Ludwig van
[Sonatas, piano, no. 14, op. 27, no. 2,
C# minor]
Moonlight sonata / Ludwig van
Beethoven. – on side B of 1 sound disc
(ca. 6 min.) : analog, 33⅓ rpm, stereo. ;
12 in.

In The world of your hundred best
tunes : the top ten. – London : Decca,
1970.

ANALYSIS

Apart from analytical added entries and "in" analytics, there are three other ways in which AACR 2 indicates that analysis may be achieved. These are described in Ch. 13 of AACR 2, viz:

(i)   A complete bibliographic description may be prepared for the part (rule 13.3). This is illustrated in examples no. 13, 57, 89, 131, 139, 221

(ii)   A contents note may be made in a detailed entry for the larger work (rule 13.4). This is illustrated in examples no. 59, 167, 222, 224, 231, 318, 339, 341, 363, 371, 379

(iii)   A multi-level description may be used (rule 13.6). This is illustrated in examples no. 20, 82, 83, 132, 299, 365, 367

Appendix 2
References

The function of a *see* reference is to direct the user of a catalogue from a form of heading or title that might be sought, but which has not been chosen specifically by the indexer as an access point, to the heading, title or uniform title that has actually been used.

The function of a *see also* reference is to link headings or uniform titles which are related to each other.

When adequate direction cannot be given by a simple *see* or *see also* reference, a more detailed reference, the *explanatory* reference, is made.

See and *see also* references may be made in the form of *name-title* references which refer from or to the person or corporate heading followed by the title concerned.

AACR 2 summarizes the requirements for references in Chapter 26. The rules in Chapters 21 to 25 also indicate particular types of references that are commonly needed in specific situations.

The following are examples of some of the various occasions when references are required. The number of the example in the main entry sequences to which the reference is related is indicated.

SEE REFERENCES

Rule 26.1   Basic rule

This rule states that a *see* reference should be made from a form of the name of a person or corporate body or title of a work that might reasonably be sought to the form that has been chosen as a name or uniform title heading. However, examples of references from one form of title to another are not included in Ch. 26 and rule 21.30J instructs that, when considered

necessary for access, an *added entry* should be made for different versions of the title (see p. 224). For those cataloguing agencies that may prefer references, a few examples are given below, but it should be remembered that AACR 2 does not specifically advocate references of this nature.

Example no.

Alternative title   **154**

A BIT of a book
   see MILLIGAN, Spike
      A book of bits

Parallel title   **305**

The THREE-CORNERED hat
   see FALLA, Manuel de
      El sombrero de tres picos

Variant title   **310**

REFORMATION [symphony]
   see MENDELSSOHN-BARTHOLDY,
      Felix
      [Symphonies, no. 5, op. 107,
   D minor]

A further example of an occasion when a reference would be required is when a title begins with a number and a reference is made necessary by the filing system (see also rule 26.3A5).

                        402

ONE thousand, nine hundred and
   fourteen-one thousand, nine hundred
   and eighteen
   see 1914-1918

Rule 26.2   Names of persons

Rule 26.2A1   Different names

Rule 26.2A2   Different forms of name

Rule 26.2A3   Different entry elements

Rule 26.3   Names of corporate bodies and geographic names

Rule 26.3A1   Different names

(Not strictly anonymous but often taken to be for cataloguing purposes, although some cataloguing agencies may require a more exact interpretation (see also the explanatory reference in rule 26.3C1(c)(ii).

Rule 26.3A2   General and specific names of conferences

Rule 26.3A3   Different forms of name

Rule 26.3A4   Initials (when made necessary by filing system)

Rule 26.3A7   Different forms of heading
Subordinate heading and its variants to name entered directly

UNITED KINGDOM. Department **148**
of Education and Science. Library
Advisory Council (England)
see LIBRARY ADVISORY COUNCIL
(England)

UNITED KINGDOM. Law **146**
Commission
see LAW COMMISSION

UNITED KINGDOM. Library **148**
Advisory Council (England)
see LIBRARY ADVISORY COUNCIL
(England)

WORLD HEALTH ORGAN- **139**
ISATION. Joint F.A.O./W.H.O.
Expert Committee on African
Trypanosamiasis
see JOINT F.A.O./W.H.O.
EXPERT COMMITTEE ON
AFRICAN TRYPANOSAMIASIS

(and a similar reference under Food and
Agricultural Organisation. References would also
be required from the initials of the two
organisations).

Name and its variants in the form of
subheadings under the immediately superior
body when the name has been entered under a
body higher than the immediately superior
body.

UNITED KINGDOM. Board of **237**
Trade. Committee of Inquiry into
Trawler Safety
see UNITED KINGDOM. Committee
of Inquiry into Trawler Safety

UNITED STATES. Department of **246**
Commerce. Patent Office
see UNITED STATES. Patent Office

For bodies entered subordinately, the name and
its variants in the form of independent headings
whenever the name does not necessarily
suggest subordinate entry

GENERAL REGISTER OFFICE **238**
see UNITED KINGDOM. General
Register Office

Rule 26.4   Uniform titles

The square brackets could be left out of the
examples given below as in the examples
provided in AACR 2.

Rule 26.4A1   Different titles or variants of the
title

THOUSAND and one nights **17**
see [ARABIAN nights]

Rule 26.4A3   Titles of parts catalogued under
the title of the whole work

NEW TESTAMENT **36**
see [BIBLE. N.T.]

LUKE (Book of the Bible) **107**
see [BIBLE. N.T. Luke]

SEE REFERENCES – NAME-TITLE REFERENCES

Rule 26.2B1   Works of a person entered under
two or more different headings

HARRIS, John **115**
The Lion at sea
see HENNESSY, Max

(The cover of this work reads;

JOHN HARRIS
writing as Max Hennessy

although John Harris is not mentioned on the
title page.)

Rule 26.2B2   Initials

B., E.R.P. **71**
Nursery rhymes of Gloucestershire
see E.R.P.B.

Rule 26.4   Uniform titles

Rule 26.4B1   Different titles or variants of the title

DICKENS, Charles   66
   The story of David Copperfield
      see DICKENS, Charles
         [David Copperfield]

        Translated titles

BOREL, Jacques   40
   The bond
      see BOREL, Jacques
         [L'adoration. English]

Rule 26.4B2   Titles of parts of a work catalogued separately

JACOB, Naomi   131
   The Gollantz saga. 4, Four generations
      see JACOB, Naomi
         Four generations

SEE ALSO REFERENCES

Rule 26.2   Names of persons

Rule 26.2C1   Works of one person entered under two different headings

DODGSON, Charles Lutwidge   11
   see also CARROLL, Lewis

Rule 26.3   Names of corporate bodies and geographic names

Rule 26.3B1   Related corporate headings

INTERNATIONAL LABOUR   444
   ORGANISATION
   see also INTERNATIONAL LABOUR
         OFFICE

EXPLANATORY REFERENCES

Rule 26.2   Names of persons

Rule 26.2D1   General rule

HARRIS, John   108, 114–5
   For works of this author written under
     pseudonyms, see
   HEBDEN, Mark
   HENNESSY, Max

HENNESSY, Max
   For works of this author written under
     other names, see
   HARRIS, John
   HEBDEN, Mark

BLOOM, Ursula   175
   For works of this author written in
   collaboration with Charles Eade, see
   PROLE, Lozania

(and a similar reference under Eade)

PROLE, Lozania
   The joint pseudonym of Ursula Bloom
   and Charles Eade. For works written by
   Bloom under her own name, see
   BLOOM, Ursula

Rule 26.2D2   Separately written prefixes (Optional)

VON   178
   Names beginning with this prefix are
   entered under the part following the prefix
   when the person's language is Dutch,
   Flemish, German or Scandinavian. In
   other cases entry is under the prefix

Rule 26.3   Names of corporate bodies and geographic names

Rule 26.3C1   General rule

Scope of heading

CATHOLIC CHURCH. Pope   135
   (1958-1963 : John XXIII)
   Here are entered works of the Pope
   acting in his official capacity. For other
   works, see
   JOHN XXIII, Pope

(assuming headings are established for the Pope both as person and religious official)

References applicable to several headings (when appropriate in a catalogue where verbal subject and name-title entries are interfiled)

EXHIBITIONS   127
Works reporting the collective activity of an exhibition are entered under the name of the exhibition or the title of the publication if the exhibition lacks a name

Earlier and later headings

Simple situations

SOUTHPORT HIGH SCHOOL   102
FOR GIRLS see also the later heading
GREENBANK HIGH SCHOOL FOR
GIRLS (Sefton)

Complex situations

SEFTON LIBRARIES AND   61
ARTS SERVICES
This heading is used for publications from 1974 onwards. The County Boroughs of Bootle and Southport, the Municipal Borough of Crosby, and parts of the County of Lancashire, i.e. the Urban Districts of Formby and Litherland and parts of West Lancs Rural District, were merged in the local government reorganisation of that year to form the Metropolitan District of Sefton. Works of the previously existing library authorities are entered under the names used at the time of publication

Rule 26.3C2   Acronyms – when the filing system used distinguishes between initials with full stops and initials without full stops

C.A.S.   89
see CENTRE FOR ADMINIS-
TRATIVE STUDIES
When these initials occur in a title or other heading without spaces or full stops, they are filed as a single word

CENTRE FOR ADMINISTRATIVE
STUDIES
Identified in some publications as CAS.

When these initials occur in the form of an acronym at the beginning of titles and other entries, they are filed as a single word

26.4   Uniform titles

26.4D2   Titles of parts catalogued independently (optional)

JACOB, Naomi   131
The Gollantz saga
For the separately published parts of this work, see
JACOB, Naomi
Four generations

See also p. 232   (rule 26.4B2)

REFERENCES INSTEAD OF ADDED ENTRIES

Rule 26.6A   If a number of added entries are required under the same heading, they may be replaced by appropriate references

HAMLET   334
For editions of this work, see
SHAKESPEARE, William
Hamlet

Rule 26.6B   Alternative format

HAMLET
SHAKESPEARE, William
Hamlet. – c1964.
1 sound disc.
For other editions, see
SHAKESPEARE, William. Hamlet

AUTHORITY FILES

As references do not appear in tracings, a separate authority file is necessary. This shows, in alphabetical order, the headings used and the references made, and is used to control the provision of references in the catalogue. Examples of entries in the authority file follow.

Barber, Margaret Fairless
see FAIRLESS, Michael

BIBLE
ref. from Holy Bible

CAMPBELL, Patrick
    ref. from Glenavy, Patrick Campbell, Baron

CARROLL, Lewis
    see also DODGSON, Charles Lutwidge

CATHOLIC CHURCH
    ref. from Roman Catholic Church

DODGSON, Charles Lutwidge
    see also CARROLL, Lewis

FAIRLESS, Michael
    ref. from Barber, Margaret Fairless

General Register Office
    see UNITED KINGDOM. General Register Office

Glenavy, Patrick Campbell, Baron
    see CAMPBELL, Patrick

GREENBANK HIGH SCHOOL FOR GIRLS (Sefton)
    see also the earlier heading
    SOUTHPORT HIGH SCHOOL FOR GIRLS

Holy Bible
    see BIBLE

A Lady of Richmond
    see PUTNAM, Sallie

LAW COMMISSION
    ref. from United Kingdom. Law Commission

PUTNAM, Sallie
    ref. from A Lady of Richmond

Roman Catholic Church
    see CATHOLIC CHURCH

SOUTHPORT HIGH SCHOOL FOR GIRLS
    see also the later heading
    GREENBANK HIGH SCHOOL FOR GIRLS (Sefton)

UNITED KINGDOM. General Register Office
    ref. from General Register Office

United Kingdom. Law Commission
    see LAW COMMISSION

The information in the authority file may, of course, be presented in a different way to that shown above. For instance, the abbreviations sa, x and xx could be used, as in the *Library of Congress subject headings*.[1] This would give entries such as

FAIRLESS, Michael
    x Barber, Margaret Fairless

which would mean that a *see* reference is to be made from Barber to Fairless, and

CARROLL, Lewis
    sa DODGSON, Charles Lutwidge
    xx DODGSON, Charles Lutwidge

which would indicate that a *see also* reference is to be made from Carroll to Dodgson and a reverse *see also* reference from Dodgson to Carroll.

[1] It is appreciated that the latest edition of *Library of Congress subject headings* uses more standard abbreviations: BT for Broader Term, NT for Narrower Term, etc.

Appendix 3
Examples of entry layout when paragraphing is not employed

ABRAHAMS, Gerald
　　Trade unions & the law / by Gerald
Abrahams. - London : Cassell, 1968. - xix,
254 p. ; 22 cm. - ISBN 0-304-91599-8.

The ALBUM. - Vol. 1 , no. 1 (Apr.
　　1822)-v. 4, no. 8 (Apr. 1825). -
London : J. Andrews, 1822-1825. - 8 v. ;
21 cm. - Two issues yearly.

BEE GEES
　　How deep is your love / Bee Gees. -
[London] : RSO Records, 1977. - on 1 side
of 1 sound disc (ca. 3 min.) : analog, 45 rpm,
stereo. ; 7 in. - "From the Paramount/Robert
Stigwood motion picture: Saturday night
fever". - RSO: 2090 259. - With: Night
fever.

CARTER, Craig J.M.
　　Ships of the Mersey / Craig J.M. Carter. -
London : Record Books, 1966. - 79 p., 1 leaf
of plates : ill. ; 20 cm. + 2 sound discs
(analog, 33⅓ rpm, mono. ; 7 in.) - (Sound
picture series). - Discs, which are recordings
of ship's sounds, in pocket.

LAST, James
　　Love must be the reason / James Last
[and his orchestra] ; produced and arranged by
James Last. - [London] : Polydor, 1972. - 1
sound disc (ca. 40 min.) : analog, 33⅓ rpm,
stereo. ; 12 in. - Issued also as stereo cassette
and 8-track stereo cartridge. - Partial
contents: Wedding song / Stookey - Heart of
gold / Young - I don't know how to love him
/ Lloyd Webber - Love must be the
reason / Schuman. - Polydor: 2371-281.

PAINTINGS at Chatsworth : colour
　　postcards of paintings in the Devonshire
Collection. - Derby : English Life
Publications, [196-?]. - 8 postcards : col. ;
15 x 11 cm. in folder 16 x 12 cm. -
Contents: Trial by jury / Landseer - The
holy family / Murillo - Georgiano, Duchess of
Devonshire, with her daughter Georgiano /
Reynolds - The flight into Egypt / Ricci -
The Acheson sisters / Sargent - Portrait of an
oriental (King Uzzich?) / Van Rijn - Arthur
Goodwin, M.P. / Van Dyck - The adoration
of the Kings / Veronese.

PHOTOGRAPH and slide classification
　　for western art / Photograph and Slide
Collection, Fine Arts Library, Fogg Art
Museum. - Cambridge, Mass. : Harvard
University Library, Microreproduction Dept.,
[1973?]. - 1 microfilm reel ; 35 mm. - Low
reduction. - Comic mode. - Microreproduction of: Rev. ed., 1973.

RASMUS, Carolyn J.
　　Agility / Carolyn J. Rasmus. - Cambridge,
Mass. : Ealing, 1969. - 1 film loop (3 min.,
35 sec.) : si., col. ; super 8 mm. -
(Functional fitness). - Consultants: The
American Association for Health, Physical
Education and Recreation. - "Licensed only
for direct optical projection before a viewing
audience" - Box. - Notes on box.

XTREE (TM) : the new standard for file
　　and directory management / Executive
Systems, Inc. - 2nd ed. - Computer
program. - Sherman Oaks, Ca. : Executive
Systems, 1985. - 1 computer disk : col. ; 5¼
in. + 1 user guide (50 p. ; 13 x 14 cm.) in
case 16 x 17 x 2 cm. - System requirements:
IBM PC XT/AT or IBM PC XT/AT
compatible; MS-DOS or PC-DOS 2.0 or
greater; 192K RAM.